A People, A Place:
The Story of Abilene
Volume 1
The Future Great City
1881–1940

A People, A Place: The Story of Abilene
Volume 1
The Future Great City
1881–1940

Robert W. Sledge

Library of Congress Cataloging-in-Publication Data

Sledge, Robert W.
    A people, a place: the story of Abilene / Robert W. Sledge.
    v. cm.
    Includes bibliographical references and index.
    Contents: v. 1. The future great city, 1881-1940 –
    ISBN 978-1-933337-31-9 (v. 1)
1. Abilene (Tex.)–History. I. Title.

F394.A15S58 2009
976.4'727–dc22

2008050767

Copyright © 2008, State House Press
All Rights Reserved

State House Press
P.O. Box 818
Buffalo Gap, TX 79508
(325) 572-3974
www.mcwhiney.org/press

Distributed by Texas A&M University Press Consortium
(800) 826-8911
www.tamu.edu/upress

Printed in the United States of America

ISBN 978-1-933337-31-9

Book designed by Rosenbohm Graphic Design

Dedicated to Ryan (AHS, 2003) and Eric (AHS, 2008)

Table of Contents

Preface 9

Preliminary. **Abilene 1881** 13

Chapter 1. **Prairie** 17
    The Place 17
    Flora and Fauna 24
    The First People 27
  ■ *Portrait—Prairie Dogs: Pests or Pets?* 33

Chapter 2. **Pioneers 1540–1875** 35
    T47he End of the Frontier 35
    Settlement 47
  ■ *Portrait—How Lost Was Coronado? How Lost Was*
    Judge Wagstaff? 53

Chapter 3. **Planners 1875–1881** 55
    The Railroad 55
    The Future Great 65
    The Founders 67
  ■ *Portrait—How John and Clabe Got Clabe Out of Trouble* 68

Chapter 4. **Priority 1881–1885** 69
    The Kentucky Connection 69
    The Raw Place 70
    The Rough Place 75
  ■ *Portrait—The San Jacinto Day Shootout* 82

Chapter 5. **Propriety 1881–1891** 83
    Political Infrastructure 83
    Physical Infrastructure 89
    Cultural Infrastructure 93
    Economic Infrastructure 101
  ■ *Portrait—The Secret of the Chinese Laundry* 111

Chapter 6. **Promoters 1892–1906** 113
    Political 115
    Facilities 119
    New Institutions 123
    Business 128
    Culture 134
    Education 137
  ■ *Portrait—The Galloping Goose Gets Loose* 143

Chapter 7. Progress 1907–1919 145
   Politics 145
   Schools 149
   Construction 152
   Economic Development 157
  ■ *Portrait—Captain Eddie Gets Stumped* 164

Chapter 8. Peril 1911–1919 165
   Destruction 165
   Danger 169
   End of An Era 179
  ■ *Portrait—Losing the Normal School* 181

Chapter 9. Prosperity 1920–1929 183
   The Great Expansion 184
   Modernization 193
   Education 201
  ■ *Portrait—The Man Who Built Abilene* 207

Chapter 10. Positioning 1920–1929 209
   Pursuit of The Past 210
   Pursuit of Pleasure 218
  ■ *Portrait—The Goo-Goo Eyes Ordinance* 223

Chapter 11. Poverty 1930–1939 225
   The Ordeal of Depression 226
   The Crisis of Agriculture 241
  ■ *Portrait—Around the World Backwards* 246

Chapter 12. Possibility 1933–1940 249
   Abilene and the New Deal 249
   Another Side of the Depression 260
   A New Day Dawning 263
  ■ *Portrait—Stuck in the Mud* 267

Notes 269

Select Bibliograhy 293

Appendixes 300

Index 305

Preface

The town was invented. Railroad investors determined that there would be a major community right about . . . there. They called it "the Future Great City of Texas." Working with local ranchers who sought the benefits of the railroad running near or on their land, the railroad entrepreneurs designated the spot where a city should develop. After its birth, it grew in fits and starts, not so much by natural advantage as by sheer determination.

The Place had always been there, but the People made it a city. Most major communities developed on choke points of transportation—a pass, a port, a river confluence, a rapid, a lakeside, a portage. Geography dictated where they would form. At first glance, Abilene, Texas, was only marginally one of those sites. Most likely, the city should have grown along the banks of the Clear Fork of the Brazos a few miles north, or perhaps in the pass of Buffalo Gap a few miles south. The middle of the rolling prairie *seemed* to have few features to recommend it.

So—why there?

Americans completed their first transcontinental railroad in 1869, tying into the existing railroad net at Chicago, then building westward through Omaha to South Pass in Wyoming and thence across Utah to the Sierra Nevada mountains of California, ending finally in San Francisco. This proved an immense financial boon to every place along the route.

Southerners wished in the following years to have a similar line benefiting their section, from perhaps Memphis or New Orleans or Vicksburg and connecting with San Diego or Los Angeles. But the projected "Texas and Pacific Railroad" ended at Fort Worth, Texas. Funding and the political will to extend it any further seemed to have dried up. Famous entrepreneurs tried and failed. The political establishment, dominated by Northern Republicans, had no particular incentive to accommodate the development of the Southern dream. But the presidential election of 1876 was so closely contested that it was finally decided by a compromise. The Republican candidate, Rutherford B. Hayes, would be declared the winner, provided (among other things) that he and his allies would undertake to support the southern transcontinental railroad. It was not until near the end of Hayes's term that the support was forthcoming, but the T&P finally commenced construction westward in 1880.

Though construction had begun, it was not yet clear precisely what the path of the line would be. Surveyors and land lawyers began to scout the way west. There were several possibilities as the projected path crossed between the 99th and 100th meridians. The most likely possibility funneled the route along the existing cattle trail passage through the Callahan Divide at Buffalo Gap, a three-year-old village in the newly organized Taylor County. Unfortunately for the railroad men, speculators sensed this logical path of construction and bought up most of the land along the likely locus of the line. Besides, Buffalo Gap was not quite as appealing as its citizens thought.

At this point, ranchers from northern Callahan and Taylor counties persuaded the planners to run the route through their lands, offering clearer titles, lower prices, and a better terrain than were available in Buffalo Gap. The railroad men agreed to run the line that way, and reciprocated by designating a spot near Cedar Creek as the site of the "Future Great City." Lots would be surveyed, platted, and sold at auction. The result in March of 1881 was a community that sprang instantly to life, from zero population to over a thousand in a month's time. Abilene was born when and where it was because the Texas and Pacific decreed it so, but also because it was the best spot for miles around.

Over the next century and beyond, the town grew and prospered because of its own desire as much as because of the few natural advantages it might have had. It kept reinventing itself. In its search for an identity, Abilene has had several nicknames, none of which has stuck very well—"The Future Great City of West Texas," "The Wind City," "The Capital of West Texas," "The Queen City of the West," and "The Key City." It is the urban center of a region, which is itself amorphous and ambiguous—"West Central Texas," "The Texas Midwest," "The Big Country," "The Friendly Frontier." There may be more to come.

A town is, on the one hand, a specific location on the face of the earth, complete with physical infrastructure and architectural artifacts. It is a Place. On the other hand, a town is a collection of human beings who hold a common sense of identity with each other and with the location. It is a People. Both these facets characterize Abilene, and neither can be discounted. Abilene is a People and a Place, inseparably linked. Together, they can be home, what A.C. Greene called "the village of my heart." Not a bad place to be...

Abilene owes a debt of gratitude to those who have chronicled its story over the years. Most notable among these are Katharyn Duff, longtime columnist for the *Abilene Reporter News* and Rupert N. Richardson, whose master's degree students at Hardin-Simmons have uncovered a treasure trove of facts about Abilene's past. Nor could one ignore Richardson's own major contributions to the history of the area.

There are others—Tommie Clack, Mollie Clack, Juanita Zachry, Hugh Cosby, Vernon Gladden Spence, Larry Abrigg, Emmett Landers, Naomi Kincaid Hatton, Jewell Pritchett, Alfred Menn, Fane Downs,

B.W. Aston, Richard Dillard, Sylvia Ferris, Kenneth Jacobs, Kenneth Jones, Paul D. Lack, Gerald McDaniel, Claudia Wilson, Donald Frazier, Robert Pace, Tracy Shilcutt, David Coffey—these and more paved the way for this and future histories.

In the preparation of this work, special help was given by Carisse Berryhill, special collections librarian, ACU; Dixie Hoover, special collections librarian, HSU; Gary Lindsey, History Center Supervisor, HSU; Alice Specht, Dean of Libraries at HSU; Joe Specht, Head Librarian, McMurry, and later collections manager, McWhiney Foundation; Terry Young, reference/interlibrary loan librarian, McMurry University; Janice Test, Abilene Public Library; Dan Carpenter and Judy Deaton at the Grace Museum; Ann McGuffin Barton and staff at Texas Woman's University, Denton; Christine Paterson; and Larry Abrigg and Ben Bryner of the city of Abilene, among others.

Glenn Dromgoole served as copy editor and made numerous suggestions for titles, concept, and design. Carly Kahl was the overall editor for most of the preparation of the book. Robert F. Pace and Amy Smith of the McWhiney Foundation facilitated the later part of the process. Dr. Pace prepared the maps, and the incomparable Henry Rosenbohm made it all fit together. Philip Miculka was the invaluable research assistant and compiler of bibliography and appendixes. The author expresses his gratitude to each.

Preliminary
Abilene 1881

Birth of the Town

It was a raw winter morning in West Texas—March 15, 1881. A norther the previous day brought freezing temperatures, lowering clouds, high winds, and rain turning to sleet—altogether miserable conditions for the tent city huddled beside the railroad line. One hastily erected frame building stood next to the shiny new tracks, and a lonely freight car sat on a siding. Otherwise, tents of all shapes and sizes dominated the scene, interspersed here and there with tented wagons. Altogether, as many as 800 people huddled in their shelters on the prairie. Over the past few days, an occasional locomotive passed along the tracks, pulling a supply train heading for the construction sites near Sweetwater as the Texas and Pacific Railway construction raced west.

At four o'clock in the morning, a Texas and Pacific train of five cars rattled to a stop at the siding. The passengers, mostly land speculators from the Fort Worth area, stayed aboard until daylight, then disembarked to inspect the site before returning to the train or to one of the tent saloons to seek refuge from the cold. Sleepy faces emerged from the tents and wagons as the sun rose. The good news was that the day would be sunny and still for a change; the sun would chase the chill and moderate the mud. But most people did not much mind the weather. They were there for a town lot auction that would shape the "Future Great City of West Texas"—Abilene.

The crowd could already see the outlines of the city-to-be. Over the preceding month, surveyors had laid out a grid of streets and lots on both sides of the track for a dozen or more blocks parallel to the rails and eight blocks deep on each side. Stakes on the grassy plain indicated the sites to be auctioned. Since the right-of-way angled slightly to the northwest, the streets parallel to the line also angled slightly off plumb. These streets were numbered away from the railroad in both directions, starting from South First and North First. The streets vertical to the line also ran just slightly off true north and south. These streets had the names of trees, in no particular sequence. Unlike the case in most railroad towns, the north-south streets did not meet exactly at the tracks; they were offset everywhere by half a block. Thus the railroad designated no grade crossings, and no street name would be used on both sides of the tracks.

At the appointed time, the crowd, now perhaps 2,000 strong, gathered around the frame building and its loading dock. "For a frontier town," one witness observed, "the day was remarkably quiet."[1] The building belonged to Theo Heyck, a German by birth, who had made a good life for himself in Texas before moving to Buffalo Gap on the frontier. Now he was ready to move one last time to become a commission merchant in the new town. The auctioneer, Captain J.H. Hasack of Jefferson, Texas, mounted the loading dock platform and opened the bidding.[2]

The plat for the settlement laid out lots in such manner as to suggest that the surveyors expected the business district to be both north and south of the rails. Deep, narrow lots on both North and South First Streets faced the railroad. There was provision for a courthouse on the south side and a schoolhouse on the north side. Apparently, one side was not preferred over the other. There was no "wrong side of the tracks" planned for Abilene. This balance continues in law. Abilene elects a city council, three of whose members must live north of the tracks and three who must reside south of the tracks.

Sociologically, the balance was not always so clear. At the dawn of the twentieth century, it looked as if the upper class was in the west (on both sides of the tracks) and the lower classes to the east (also on both sides of the tracks).[3] A.C. Greene recalled that, in his youth (1930s), there was discernable a distinct pattern. The south side was considered "country" and several notches lower.[4] But thirty years later, when the school district divided the high school and built Cooper on the south side, many believed it was for the upper class. This perception has flip-flopped several times since school boundaries have been changed to cross the tracks.

Nevertheless, bidders at the town lot auction kept a wary eye on the pattern of sales, looking for a trend as to where the main business district would likely develop. Two prospective buyers, lawyers G.A. Kirkland and K.K. Legett of Buffalo Gap, waited in front of the auctioneer, seeking to ascertain a pattern for the purchases. J.T. Berry, one of the founders of the town, won the first two lots at North Second and Pine. William Cameron, a major Texas lumber dealer, took the next two adjacent to the tracks on the north side. For Kirkland, that was the straw in the wind that tipped the scales in favor of the northside. When the next purchases also fell north of the rails, Legett began to bid on bargain lots on that side. But many business lots on the southside also sold the first day, and both sides of the tracks had commercial enterprises from the start.[5]

The train from Fort Worth returned east late in the afternoon, but the auction continued for another day. Altogether, the two-day sale netted $51,360 and sold 317 lots. The T&P and the original landowners divided the proceeds equally between them. The unsold lots later went to buyers in private sales.[6]

The first frame buildings went up almost at once. Trains from East Texas hauled in lumber as fast as they could, and the several lumberyards along the tracks sold out almost before they could unload the arriving flatcars. Within a couple of months, the tent city began to give way to frame buildings lining the streets on both sides of town. Abilene was underway. The People had come to The Place.

Chapter One
Prairie

The Place

In the beginning, there was only the grass. From horizon to horizon, The Place was part of an endless ocean of tall grass waving gracefully in the prairie breezes in such way as to remind later travelers of ocean billows. This spot on the face of the earth, 32°27'N, 99°45'W, was the southeastern corner of the great North American grassland that stretched from Canada to Mexico. It was ideal country for large herds of grazing animals, in this case mammoth, bison, and antelope. It constituted the southern end of the great North American "buffalo" range, and the teeming herds grazed the land, passing south through "Buffalo Gap" to additional fertile plains ending at the Colorado River.

This was the fringe of what came to be called "the Great Plains," that vastness of land that historian Walter Prescott Webb defined as being flat, treeless, and subhumid.[1] Webb argued that the character of the Plains was so different from the familiar, well-watered timberlands farther east that new methods of survival had to be found. Spanish settlement from the south failed because it could not adapt to the Plains environment. American settlement from the east stalled for two decades until new techniques (barbed wire, windmills, six-shooters, sod- and plank-houses, dry-land farming) could be worked out to allow the newcomers to thrive.

The Place was not, however, entirely treeless. In the well-watered creek beds that veined the area were oaks, elm, hackberry, chinaberry. Mesquites dotted the open prairies, and there were some dense mesquite forests a few miles to the north and to the east. The hills to the south and east sported cedar and other hardy timber.

The Place was not entirely flat; it is called today the "Rolling Plains" to distinguish it from the High Plains tablelands farther west. Elevations ranged between 1,600 and 2,000 feet on the prairies and over 2,400 on the mesas of the Callahan Divide.

The Place was not entirely subhumid—with an average annual rainfall of just under twenty-four inches, it almost but not quite met Webb's definition of "subhumid"—twenty inches or less a year.

The Place was on the cusp—the boundary between the Great North American Steppe and the Gulf Coast.

The Terrain

A major (for Texas) river runs through the region—the Clear Fork of the Brazos. Its most significant tributary, Elm Creek, passes through Abilene to join the Clear Fork north of town.

Elm Creek rises southwest of town in the range of low hills called the "Callahan Divide." It drains from west to east through southern Nolan and Taylor counties, then turns abruptly north through Buffalo Gap on the way to its confluence with the Clear Fork. Elm Creek has the unusual but not unique characteristic of having banks that are higher than the surrounding terrain. This feature is called a "natural levee" and is in evidence all along its passage through Abilene. When Elm Creek floods, its waters, having crested the natural levee, spread for some distance across the adjacent lower-lying areas.

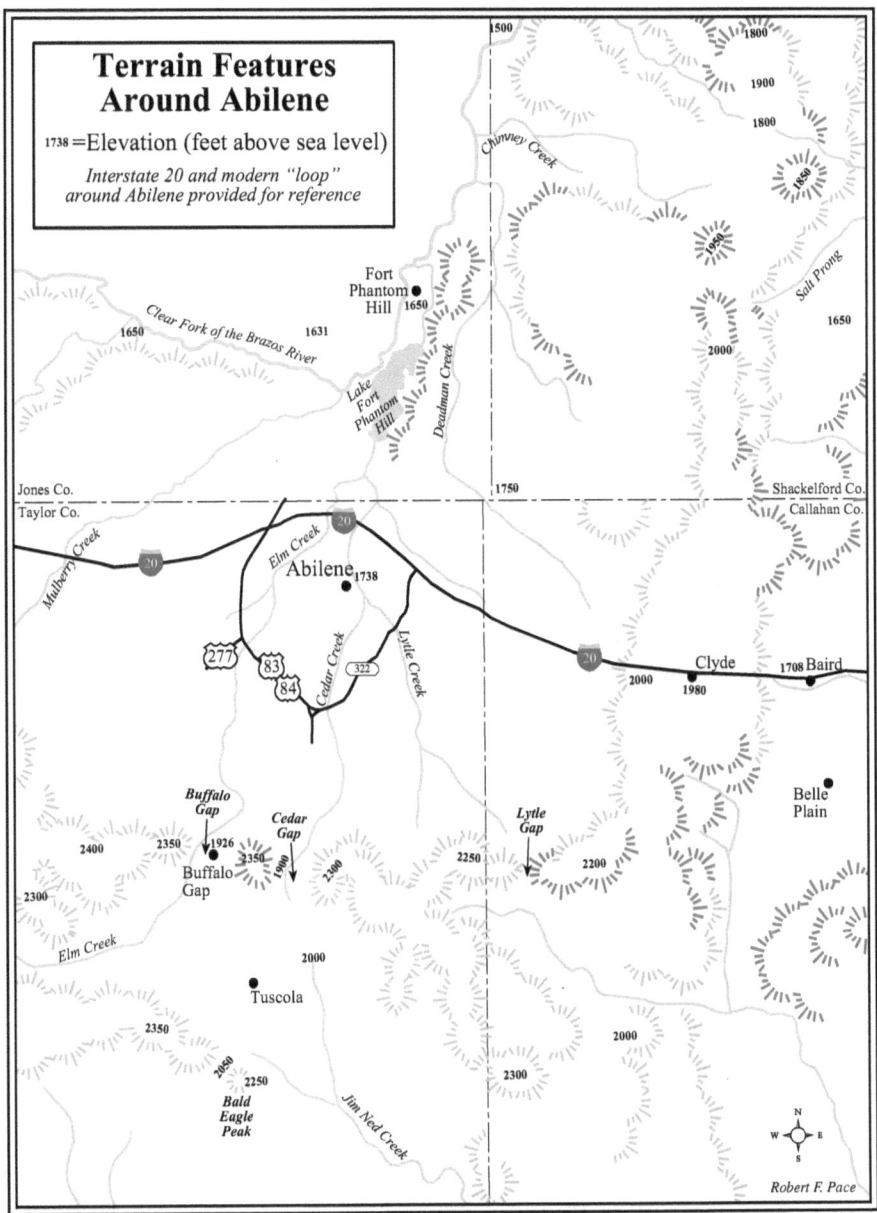

The Elm Creek watershed is unusual in that it drains to the north, rising on the slopes of the Callahan Divide and flowing northward into the Clear Fork of the Brazos.

Several tributaries of Elm Creek converge through The Place—Catclaw Creek, Buttonwillow Creek, Lytle Creek,[2] Little Elm, Rainy Creek, Cedar Creek. Their collective drainage basins funnel the rains falling north and west of the Divide into Elm Creek. Heavy rainfalls between Abilene and "the mountains" lead to brief flash floods on occasion, but the time interval between rainfall and flood is brief. Elm Creek is the exception. Hard rains high on its watershed in Nolan County may take a day to reach the city.

All of these except the Clear Fork are now intermittent streams—they channel torrents downstream after a rain but are otherwise mostly dry. Before the settlers came, however, several of the creeks flowed year-round. The grass allowed precipitation to remain long enough to sink into the soil. Further, underground pumping had not yet lowered the water tables. The creeks often held populations of fish, sustained even in the intermittent watercourses by basins that never went dry, such as "Blue Hole" on Lytle Creek.

The Callahan Divide marks the end of the Rolling Plains. To the east lie wooded hills and valleys called the Cross Timbers. The mesa-like top of the Divide is the northernmost extension of the Texas Hill Country, featuring limestone soils and numerous cedar trees. It reaches elevations surpassing 2,400 feet above sea level. South of Abilene, the Divide is punctuated by several passes. From east to west, they are called Lytle Gap, Cedar Gap, Buffalo Gap, and Mountain Pass. Lytle Gap penetrates the crook of the Callahan Divide, where the ridge turns a right angle. Though the Callahan Divide is not a formidable barrier, rising only about four hundred feet above the surrounding terrain, the passes were attractive alternatives to crossing the Callahan heights. The dramatic west-east escarpment in southern Nolan and Taylor counties shifts due north near Dudley to form a gentler but definable ridge east of Abilene. The rise stretches northward through eastern Callahan and central Shackelford counties, forcing the Clear Fork of the Brazos into a sweeping northerly detour on its way east. Clyde sits atop the ridge, Baird and Albany on its eastern foot.

Within the city of Abilene, the land rises slowly toward the south, interspersed by a central ridge that represents the watershed between the Elm-Catclaw drainage and the Cedar-Lytle-Buttonwillow drainage systems. Sayles Boulevard and Buffalo Gap Road follow roughly the crest of the central ridge south of the railroad. North of the tracks, the ridge, in much gentler form, follows near Grape Street and over to the Hardin-Simmons campus. The highest points inside the Winters Freeway are near South Eleventh between Sayles and Highland and Buffalo Gap Road at Winters Freeway—both 1,784 feet above sea level. The northeast corner of the city sits on a hill overlooking Cedar Creek. Abilenians often call it "Holy Hill" because Abilene Christian University occupies a prominent place on its crest. Nevertheless, this bulge peaks at about 1,735 feet and is lower than the central ridge.

The overall elevation of Abilene makes it, on average, higher than Mason and Kerrville and about the same as Fredericksburg and Junction, all in the Texas Hill Country. The Callahan Divide also surpasses the Hill Country heights in elevation. On the other hand, Texas in general rises toward the northwest, so Sweetwater and Snyder are substantially higher than Abilene.

Underlying the terrain is the geology of The Place. The mesas of the Callahan Divide are a remnant of the Edwards Plateau. The Colorado River to the south and the Brazos River to the north eroded the beds of hard Edwards Plateau limestone laid down in the Cretaceous period and uncovered the underlying softer sandstones and shales of the Permian era. Over the years, this erosion narrowed the remaining limestone crust so that here and there, passes (or gaps) appeared.

No major aquifer sits under Abilene. While other dry areas can depend upon subsurface water for their needs (San Antonio and Lubbock come to mind), Abilene cannot. The modest subsurface water that is present is often so laden with natural chemicals as to be undrinkable. That means that the Abilene area must depend for its water supply on the impoundment of surface water. As noted before, perennial streams in the area no longer exist due to the removal of the grass.

No good aquifer, no gold or silver, no iron or copper or coal, no caverns or majestic forests or spectacular mountain scenery—Abilene seemed bereft of natural attractions.

The Climate

The area sat, and still sits, in the transition zone overlapping what geographers call "humid subtropical" climate to the south and east and "steppe" climate to the north and west.[3] In the spring and summer, the region comes under the maritime influence of the Gulf of Mexico, as earth-girdling belts of prevailing easterlies (the trade winds) shift northward; the wind direction in that season is largely from the south and southeast. The winds bring Gulf humidity northward and westward and make spring and summer the wet season, with average rainfall totals exceeding two inches per month. In the spring, those wet Gulf winds collide with the dry continental air masses of central North America, creating weather fronts laden with squall lines, hailstorms, and tornadoes. The temperatures become warm, often even hot. The maximum temperature ever recorded at Abilene was 109 degrees. There have been summers where the temperature exceeded 100 for forty days and more, and only five (the most recent, 2007) when the thermometer never quite reached triple digits. Convectional cumulus clouds dump rain on the region throughout the summer season. At the end of summer, the area sometimes shares the monsoonal moisture sweeping northeastward from the Pacific, a pattern more typical of New Mexico and Arizona. On rare occasions, hurricane systems from the Gulf of Mexico and/or the Pacific may dump torrential amounts of rain in a short period.

In fall and winter, weather patterns migrate south again, returning the region to the influence of the mid-latitude westerlies and bringing continental weather patterns—dry north winds and wide temperature ranges. In this season (November to March), monthly rainfall totals run around one inch. When a weather front comes through, it often announces itself in the form of a dark rim lining the northern horizon, signifying the rapid approach of a "blue norther." Sometimes these storms bring snow and high winds. The creeks could freeze, and so could unprotected animals.

Although Abilene's rainfall averages just under twenty-four inches per year, the annual totals can vary from under ten to over forty in no particular pattern. When successive years of below-average rainfall occur, inhabitants speak of a drought. Crops wither, creeks dry up, rivers run low, grass fires race across the landscape, animals die off, water rationing is imposed, humans pray for rain. Because the normal rainfall totals provide only marginally sufficient moisture for crops, a prolonged drought can be devastating in ways that are not so apparent in areas of either greater or lesser average rain.

Abilenians have a drought mentality and are ever sensitive to the danger of a "dry spell." One wet March a few years ago, a local television weatherman admonished his listeners to make special note that the city had received above-average rainfall so far that year. "Remember this time," he said. "It only happens once in a great while." Of course, by definition, you get above-average rainfall half the time, so this was not strictly true. But it illustrated the drought mentality. Fear of drought is so prevalent that the city fathers retained water rationing, even after the rains of 2007 completely filled the main local water sources.[4]

Drought also fostered dust storms. The extensive farming of the high plains farther west in the early twentieth century stripped away the protective grass cover and made the land particularly vulnerable to wind erosion. This was seen most vividly in the decade of the 1930s when a protracted dry spell affected most of the central United States. Farther north, this came to be known as "the Dust Bowl." Abilene suffered the same drought but was not as severely hurt, save that the dust from the plains often ended up here. In the twenty-first century, a springtime westerly wind still heralds the approach of dust, first smudging the horizon to the northwest and eventually enveloping everything.

The Flora and Fauna
The Plant Life

Prairie vegetation consisted mainly of grasses, but trees sprang up along the watercourses. Likewise, timbered areas could be found nearby, atop the Callahan Divide to the east and the south, with several types of oaks and the juniper trees that inhabitants of the area call "cedar." Buffalo Gap, one of the passes through the Divide, allows a stream, Elm Creek, through the mountain wall. In this pass could be found a real forest—pecan, tall oaks, elms, and more. One large, hospitable elm tree in the western part of the county was a favorite campground and was known to early cowhands as "the Elm Hotel."[5]

Sam Chalk, one of the first surveyors of Taylor County, encountered three distinct types of mesquites. Large ones, as much as two feet in diameter, were all dead, victims of some long-past ecological crisis. "In Jones and Haskell counties, [there were] vast forests of them with no living timber at all." All seemed to have died at the same time.[6] Chalk noted that the mesquites took forever to rot. A second variety of mesquite appeared "mostly in the creek valleys" where they could draw moisture from the soil. These were thriving but had not yet reached the size of the giants to the north. Finally, small scrub mesquite appeared here and there at random across the prairies.[7]

The grass that Chalk saw was "short thick curly mesquite grass which seems to be always waving, even without a breeze. And this grass carpet is profusely decorated with blue bonnets (buffalo clover), wild marigold, blue bells, poppies, wild hollyhock."[8]

The prairie, the hills, and the gaps each provided habitat for large varieties of animals. The "shinnery" (scrub oak) belt north of Abilene remains remote and underdeveloped, the habitat of coyotes and other ominous creatures. One of these was a fabled beast dubbed "the Hawley Him," apparently a cousin of the Sasquatch of the Pacific Northwest and the Yeti of the Himalayas, which was allegedly sighted in 1977.[9]

Animal Life

On the plains, the largest, most dramatic animal in historic times was the North American bison—the buffalo. The bison roamed and grazed at large throughout the region in enormous herds. Estimates of the total population of the plains bison herds run as high as ten million, spread out across the vastness of the Canadian and American prairies. The bison provided almost all the needs of the plains Indians —food, shelter, clothing, fuel, and additional implements of survival. Later, they attracted hunters seeking hides, meat, and even bones. While Buffalo Gap earned its name by providing passage to herds moving to the Colorado basin, the last major herd in the county, 800 cows and calves, was seen in Mulberry Canyon in 1877. Later that year, these were all hunted out, and the creatures were seldom seen in the county after that.[10]

Other grass eaters flourished on the prairies. Antelope herds were prolific. Mollie Clack told of antelopes tame enough to come into her dooryard in 1879. A herd of several hundred lived in her vicinity, and when the men sought antelope meat, they made sure to hunt among the herds farther away. The local antelopes were viewed as friendly neighbors. When wild horses, descendants of Spanish importations, made their appearance, they too proliferated on the plains. Any place that provided a roost hosted flocks of wild turkeys.

The hills supported predatory creatures such as bears and cougars. The latter, which also went by the names panther, jaguar, Mexican lion, or mountain lion, found sufficient prey and sufficient cover on the wooded slopes and plateaus to survive without having to venture very often onto the plains.[11] Early settlers encountered the occasional bear sharing the same habitat. Deer were present in adequate numbers to support high concentrations of predators. In the modern world, with the bears and cougars gone, the deer population is held in check by a more sophisticated predator; deer provide a source of revenue for landowners who lease their property for hunting.

The plains harbored numbers of lesser hunters such as coyotes and bobcats. Though they are fewer in number in recent years, the occasional stray bobcat may even today wander along the creeks into the city to frighten the people and menace their pets. Coyotes can still be seen and heard on the edges of populated areas.

The Place was near a flyway for migratory birds. Accordingly, seasonal visitations of waterfowl could be seen resting in the creeks—geese, cranes, mudhens.[12]

The region hosted mockingbirds, kildee, snipe, plover, cardinals, blackbirds, shrikes, wrens. Owls and hawks preyed on rodents and other small game. Buzzards were sometimes sighted circling high in the sky. Once in a while a whippoorwill could be heard. Small clumps of trees hosted wild turkeys. Turkeys were numerous in the hills to the south. In the first years after Abilene sprang up, displaced turkeys moved a couple of miles north to make their home in the scrub trees near the present site of Hardin-Simmons University.[13]

More recent avian infestations are the grackles that congregate around the Mall of Abilene, befouling cars and annoying the citizenry with their raucous commotion.

The First People
Prehistoric Indians

They were nomads, those first humans to pass through The Place. They descended from the immigrants who crossed the Bering Strait from Siberia many forgotten generations before. The first ones did not stay; they simply followed the herds of bison into the region. Probably they did not even camp in The Place very often; safer campsites beckoned only a few miles farther south in the shadow of the Callahan Divide, where there was abundant water and wood. From there they could mount hunting forays onto the plains, using the serrated skyline of the Divide to guide them back to camp. They could lie in wait for the herds passing through Buffalo Gap. They could scout the surrounding landscape from the heights of the Divide.

There is considerable debate among archeologists about the earliest humans in North America. The current consensus is that they arrived about 14,000 years ago and spread quickly over the continent. The earliest certain evidence was found in the 1920s near Clovis, New Mexico in the form of distinctive spear points associated with mammoth bones. These points were Paleolithic (Old Stone Age) artifacts. Searchers have excavated other "Clovis" points across North America. The Clovis site itself dates to about 11,500 B.C. This hunting technology is used to define what is called the Paleoindian era. These points were roughly attached to throwing or thrusting spears used in hunting large game animals, notably the mammoths and bison that roamed the Great Plains at the time. A slightly later type of artifact was first found near Folsom, New Mexico. "Folsom" points are longer and feature fluting on either side of the base, making the point easier to fix firmly on a spear shaft.

Typically, the first nomads were few in number, hardly more than an extended family. Their men hunted the bison and other game while their women searched the surroundings for edible plants, berries,

COURTESY OF THE BUFFALO GAP HISTORIC VILLAGE

nuts, and roots to fill out their diet. They lived hand to mouth, with no substantial storage capacity. Starvation was always just around the corner, yet the abundance of the earth usually saw them through. Later generations referred to this lifestyle as the "hunter-gatherer culture" and considered it the most primitive possible. Although they were nomadic, they did not have the wheel or domestic beasts of burden. Their hunting implements were spears. Their shelters and their clothing came from the hides of animals. Stone and wood and bone provided their tools. Where wood was scarce, buffalo dung provided their fuel.

A second era, called Archaic, featured barbed dart points for smaller spears launched by an atl-atl. This spear-throwing device enabled the hunter to achieve higher velocities and much longer ranges than the hand-held spear. Populations on the plains were probably denser in this period, reducing the range of a given hunting group. Spears were effective devices for hunting big animals like mammoth and buffalo, though it is likely the mammoths were gone by this period. They were also effective for medium-sized prey such as antelope and deer. Still, this wrought few changes in the basic lifestyle.

There is evidence that "Clear Fork Man" occupied The Place during this period. An eccentric Abilene physician named Cyrus Ray scoured the region in the 1920s and 1930s looking for evidences of prehistoric occupation. His searches turned up numerous artifacts of what he called the "Clear Fork Culture," a pre-pottery society dating to about 1,000 B.C. Joined by fellow Abilenian Edwin B. "Ted" Sayles, he co-founded the Texas Archaeological and Paleontological Society in 1928. Sayles went on to a distinguished career as an archeologist across the southwest. Among many other items, Ray and Sayles found artifacts which they called "Clear Fork Darts," a "Nolan Beveled Stem," a "Baird Beveled Blade," and a "Taylor Thinned Base" as evidence of the Clear Fork Culture. Both men published articles on their finds in distinguished journals.[14]

The third era, also identified by its hunting technology, is the Late Prehistoric era. About A.D. 600-800, Texas Indians began to employ the bow and arrow. This opened up wider possibilities for game. By this time, some tribal groups on the edges of the plains were engaging in crude forms of agriculture and settling in established locations for longer periods. This allowed them to utilize less portable technologies such as pottery. Most plains tribes still followed the buffalo.[15]

While life remained much the same in many ways, much change also took place. The plains climate warmed with the receding of the sheet glaciers. The lush, tall grasses nourished by abundant rainfall began to recede as the plains became dryer. The large animals that grazed the tall grasses were unable to survive on the short grasses that remained. The mammoths and the large bison disappeared, their

Tepee Village at McMurry University is an annual celebration of the plains Indian culture that draws thousands of area schoolchildren.
COURTESY OF MCMURRY UNIVERSITY

place being taken by a smaller bison species migrating north from Mexico. So climatic and technological advances continued to fuel economic, political, social, and cultural change. Modern observers tend to think of Indian life as having been constant, stable, and static, but Native Americans were affected by the same forces of change that impacted more "advanced" cultures in Europe, Asia, and Africa.

Two Invasions

The advent of the Spanish in Mexico and the French in Canada began the greatest era of change for the plains tribes. The contacts were tragic for many Indians, as European diseases wiped out perhaps sixty to eighty percent of the native peoples. However, the "Columbian exchange" wrought a great forward leap for plains culture. Part of this advance was the access to iron tools and iron weapons, but more important was the advent of the horse. Escaped Spanish ponies found the plains an ideal stage for proliferation. Nomadic Indians who adapted to the horse now could travel in much wider circles seeking prey, could direct the movements of the bison herds, could carry larger loads farther and faster. This also meant that social-political structures would be greatly expanded, and family groups could coalesce into tribal associations. The plains Indians adapted so well to the horse that they came to be called "the finest light cavalry in the world" by their opponents.

At the time of Columbus, The Place was the hunting ground of Lipan Apaches and Wichitas. The first post-Columbian invasion began a century or so later. An obscure Shoshonean tribe called the Comanches moved south from the northern plains and made themselves the lords of the prairies. Their emergence came from their full adoption of a horse culture. Painter George Caitlin said of them that they were corpulent, ungraceful, "one of the most unattractive and slovenly looking races of Indians that I have ever seen; but the moment they mount their horses, they seem at once metamorphosed, and surprise the spectator with the ease and elegance of their movements."[16]

The Comanches quickly established a solid control over the south plains, raiding all the way to the Gulf and across the Rio Grande to the southwest. They were united by nothing but their taste for warfare, their lust for stealing horses, and weak loyalties to chieftains. Comanchería, as their domain came to be known by the Spanish and Americans, included The Place well within its bounds. While the Comanches were a single linguistic and cultural grouping, they were never united as a tribe. Instead, they were subdivided into several "bands."

When the next invasion came—the whites—this lack of Comanche cohesion became a problem. Treaties and agreements between whites and the Comanches were often fragile because the talks never included, and therefore never bound, all the bands. The southernmost of the bands, the Penateka,[17] were the ones who claimed sovereignty over The Place when the first English-speaking settlers began to impinge upon their range. Differing ambitions, differing standards of property, differing levels of wealth, differing population size—all made warfare between the two inevitable. Treaties were made and broken by both sides, sometimes as the result of misunderstandings, sometimes because a handful of men would not be bound by treaties. The result, from the 1830s on, was merciless border warfare punctuated by occasional truces. The Comanches continued sporadic raids into central Texas (once as far as Corpus Christi) into the 1870s. Isolated farmsteads, unattended livestock, and small traveling parties were all fair game for the Comanches. Raids perpetrated by a few braves provoked retaliations against any Indians who happened to be handy.

The Kwahadi band, which normally ranged farther west, supplanted the Penateka in the mid-nineteenth century and intensified the conflict. The last Kwahadi chief was Quanah Parker, the son of Chief Peta Nocona and the captive white woman Cynthia Ann Parker. The Kwahadis created turmoil and fear along the Texas frontier far out of proportion to their numbers, estimated at about 2,000 in 1867.[18] Eventually, the white technological and numerical supremacy forced the surviving Comanches onto reservations.

As increasing numbers of whites crowded westward, confrontations between the new settlers and the current inhabitants were inevitable.

Prairie Dogs: Pests or Pets?

Colonies of prairie dogs lived on the plains; their burrows proved a deadly trap for any large animal unlucky enough to drop a hoof into a hole. When settlers came, they might find that they had planted their gardens on or near a prairie dog town, in which case their produce was forfeit to the hunger of the rodents. Early settler Mollie Clack saw them as her wagon entered Taylor County. "There was . . . something about the appearance of the earth's surface that suggested gold digging; or was it more like ousting rats in a barn-yard? . . . I soon discovered that we had come upon a prairie-dog town. The little animals could be seen sitting on the rims of their cells, while others scudded across the plain at our approach. Yet they were not greatly frightened, it seemed."

Surveyor Sam Chalk saw them as pests. "The only blot on this picture," he said while rhapsodizing on the beauty of the prairie, "is the pesky prairie dog. He not only cuts great holes in this beautiful carpet, but is an all-round nuisance and he is numbered by the millions."

It took imagination to make a profit from those pesky prairie dogs, but someone did. The spring of 1882 saw the brief development of a thriving trade in the animals. A man named Bateman figured out how to capture them and also figured out how to sell them as pets in the north. "A party here," the paper announced, "had collected two hundred prairie dogs, which he shipped to St. Louis." The trick to catching them, it seemed, was to dig ditches that would channel water into their holes during a rainstorm, and then capture them when the rain flooded their nests.

After his first shipment, Bateman had a large pen built in the southeastern part of town, where he was gathering and taming them. A visitor found him in the pen with about sixty of the rodents. "They appeared very gentle, running into his lap, climbing over him, and as many as could gain position getting on top of his head and looking out on the prairie, as if they were not entirely satisfied with their new home." He expected to have over a hundred of "his prairie pets" after the next good rain. The next rain, however, was a little too heavy, and many of them drowned, along with hundreds of sheep. That was the end of the prairie dog business.

The critters ceased to be a factor on the local scene for over a century, when the town hosted a professional baseball team called the Abilene Prairie Dogs.

Sources: Clack, *Pioneer Days*, pp. 51, 92-93, 96-98; *ADR*, April 29, 1928, p. B18; Menn, "The Abilene Story," pp. 50-53, 56.

Chapter Two
Pioneers 1849–1879

The End of the Frontier
Abilene and the Frontier Hypothesis

Few places better exemplified the march of the American frontier than did the Abilene area. The classic discussion of the frontier experience appeared in 1893 when a young professor at the University of Wisconsin read a paper entitled "The Influence of the Frontier on American History" at the Columbian Exposition in Chicago. His name was Frederick Jackson Turner.

The occasion for Turner's essay was a declaration by the United States Census Bureau after the 1890 census that the American frontier was now gone. Every decade since the first census in 1790, the bureau had mapped the geographic boundary of the frontier. Its definition was that any area that had more than two inhabitants per square mile was on the civilized side of the frontier and anything with less was beyond it. While there were plenty of places in the west that still had less than the requisite population in 1890, the bureau declared that it was no longer useful to talk about a "line" because there were so many pockets of denser population scattered west of what would usually be considered the frontier. The frontier experience, the bureau decreed, was over.

In the decade between the 1880 and 1890 censuses, Taylor County gained enough population to qualify as being settled. So too did several counties to the west, where the railroad had established towns. In 1890, Abilene was only nine years removed from being "beyond" the frontier line, so the frontier experience could still be considered fresh in the community. In this light, the birth of Abilene perfectly exemplified the closing of the frontier.

From the Turner perspective, the community's experience was almost, but not quite, typical of the classic frontier sequence. Turner argued that the frontier was not a single westward-moving line, as the Census Bureau seemed to think. It was, rather, a series of lines, similar to the layers of an onion, so that one had to speak of several frontiers. The sequence went something like this: Indians, then explorers, then soldiers, hunters, herdsmen, subsistence farmers, commercial farmers, villages, towns, and finally cities, each type with its own style of frontier.

The settlement of Taylor County indeed began with Indians, followed by explorers, soldiers, hunters, stockmen and a few subsistence farmers, but then telescoped the farmer-village-town stages into a very brief span before completing the process in a more leisurely fashion.

Explorers and Soldiers

Occasional Spanish explorers may have wandered across the Place. Perhaps Coronado was the first, or perhaps not. Later Spanish parties moving between San Antonio and Santa Fe may also have passed through. In 1849, the United States Army dispatched a detachment of troops led by Capt. Randolph B. Marcy westward from Fort Smith, Arkansas. They headed for Santa Fe on a route along the Canadian River and across the plains, looking for a safe route through Comanchería to the California gold strikes. On the return trip, Marcy left

The first Taylor County Courthouse and Jail, erected at Buffalo Gap in 1880, still stands as the centerpiece of the Buffalo Gap Historic Village.
COURTESY OF THE BUFFALO GAP HISTORIC VILLAGE

the Rio Grande near El Paso and aimed for "the big spring" east of the Pecos on the south plains. From there, Marcy angled northeast, mapping and marking a route through Fisher and Jones counties, on the way to Fort Belknap (near Graham). Marcy's 1849 expedition also scouted locations for a line of forts that would protect the westward-moving Texas settlements. Based in part on Marcy's recommendations, Lt. Col. John J. Abercrombie set up a post near the confluence of Elm Creek and the Clear Fork of the Brazos in 1851. The actual proposed site was on Pecan Bayou in Coleman County, but Abercrombie chose instead to settle his men on what they called "Phantom Hill," overlooking Elm Creek. The small rise upon which they established the post looked like a good-sized hill from the east, but when Abercrombie and his men finally reached the place, the hill seemed to have disappeared—a "phantom" hill.[1]

It was not a particularly good location since it had no reliable water supply; timber for construction was even harder to come by. The soldiers erected several stone buildings and hauled in enough timber to provide rough barracks. The troops were infantry, a military type not well suited for controlling the well-mounted plains Indians, though a small troop of cavalry was eventually posted there. After less than three years of uneventful occupation, the army abandoned the "Post on the Clear Fork," as it was officially known, in 1854. The wooden portions of the post soon burned, an act usually blamed on the retiring soldiers. Rupert Richardson considered it more likely that the arsonists were Indians.[2]

In the late 1850s, the remains of Fort Phantom Hill became a relay station on the Butterfield stage line. During and after the Civil War, the fort was intermittently a base for frontier soldiers. By the time of the establishment of Abilene, the ruin was a picnic site for curious farm and ranch families from Taylor County . . . in other words, a tourist attraction even then.[3]

Not long after the closing of the "Post on the Clear Fork," military operations resumed in the area with the completion of Camp Cooper on the Clear Fork in Throckmorton County. Its task was to keep watch on the nearby Comanche reservation and generally protect the frontier. Camp Cooper continued operations until the outbreak of the Civil War, at which point it was abandoned and the frontier receded eastward. Texas state troops set up a chain of temporary camps that included Camp Breckinridge in Stephens County, Camp Salmon in northeastern Callahan County, and Camp Pecan in southeastern Callahan County. State troops, sometimes including Texas Rangers, occupied these posts from 1862 through 1864, offering protection from marauding Indians, Jayhawkers, Confederate deserters, and other frontier ne'er-do-wells. Patrols from these bases scouted the area to their west. A soldier on one such expedition recorded that a

"Norther blew up last night very cold ... At day light March and froze to Phantom Hill Commence snowing in the evening Slept under a green buffalo hide froze stiff in the Morning."[4]

After the Civil War ended, the frontier line began creeping westward again, necessitating an advanced military presence. In 1867, a new post went up on a bluff overlooking the Clear Fork of the Brazos a few miles southeast of the site of Camp Cooper. It was called Fort Griffin, and its remains are now the basis for a state park. Four troops of the U.S. Sixth Cavalry provided the first garrison, joined by infantry the following year. A rip-roaring frontier town grew up around Fort Griffin, especially in the 1870s when buffalo hunters began to use the location as a base for forays against the buffalo herds on the plains to the west.[5] But its usefulness vanished with the elimination of the Indian threat, and Fort Griffin closed in 1881, two months after the founding of Abilene.[6]

The Butterfield Trail

In 1858, the Southern Overland Mail Company refurbished the ruined structures of Fort Phantom Hill and turned the post into a stage stop for what was called the "Butterfield Mail." The spectral aspect of the ruins made some travelers think that Phantom Hill had been named for the whitened stone buildings and chimneys. The Overland Mail was a route set up for the purpose of providing stagecoach service from St. Louis to San Francisco via a route that swept through Texas, southern New Mexico and Arizona, on through Los Angeles and north to San Francisco. An enterprising New York stagecoach tycoon, John Butterfield, got the contract on the promise that he could deliver the mail, and passengers, to San Francisco in twenty-five days or less. For two years, the Butterfield Mail made good on that promise.

Butterfield built a chain of stations and roads across the west. The relay stations, featuring a place to sleep (occasionally), fresh mules,

The powder storehouse at the ruins of old Fort Phantom Hill.
COURTESY OF BETTY LOU GIDDENS

and a meal, dotted the route every twenty to thirty miles. West of Fort Belknap (near present-day Graham, Texas), the stages were drawn by mules rather than horses because mules were not such tempting targets for thieves, red or white. The mule-powered vehicles used on this part of the route were called "celerity wagons," light-weight four-wheelers with a roof, open sides, and a minimum of padding.[7]

Early passengers marveled at the courage of the Fort Phantom Hill station-keepers, a couple named Burlington, because of the station's exposed location on the main Comanche path leading south.[8] In the main, Indian problems were minimal for the Butterfield people in this section of the run. However, an Indian raid in 1859 stampeded most of the Phantom Hill mule herd just before the stage arrived.

Leaving the Fort Phantom Hill station, the stages followed a path southwest to the next station, located at Mountain Pass (Abercrombie Peak) in the Callahan Divide in western Taylor County. "The road," said one early traveler, "was across a smooth plain studded with the everlasting mesquite timber."[9] The station-keeper here was an Englishman named Lambshead. Lambshead's brother manned the next station south, at Valley Creek in southeastern Nolan County.[10] The next stop beyond Valley Creek was Fort Chadbourne.

The Butterfield stage plied its route for nearly three years before economic, political, and personal differences brought it to an end. The 1860 emergence of the Pony Express along the shorter Oregon Trail route contributed to the company's demise by winning the government transcontinental mail contract on promise of a ten-day delivery schedule. Certainly, the onset of the Civil War would have ended the experiment had not other issues done so first. The stage stations were abandoned, but the area was now fairly well known. When the clouds of war dissipated, there might be those who wished to settle in the region.

The Buffalo Hunters

Several events conspired to bring a brief but lucrative new industry into the Taylor County area after the Civil War. One such occurrence was the slaughter of the northern buffalo herds on the plains of Kansas and Nebraska between 1870 and 1873. With the growing scarcity of buffalo in those areas, hunters began to turn their eyes southward, to the Texas Panhandle, the South Plains, and the Rolling Plains of west central Texas. There, adventurous souls might hope to make money in buffalo meat and hides and, later, buffalo bones. Most of these men came south from the depleted hunting grounds of Kansas.

A second factor was the edging of the frontier line westward after the end of the war. A new line of forts, including Fort Griffin, brought a measure of security against the Comanche-Kiowa threat in north central Texas. U.S. census figures show that the most rapidly growing states between 1870 and 1880 were Kansas and Texas, with Nebraska trailing slightly and no other state anywhere near. These states (minus Oklahoma, which was still mainly Indian reserve) constituted the edge of the Great Plains. Most of the growth in that decade represented movement farther and farther onto the plains. Settlers were learning that the "Great American Desert" could be settled and farmed if one had the proper techniques and tools. In Texas, new towns sprang up and old ones revived as displaced Southerners sought a new start on the edge of the frontier. From those towns, such as Jacksboro, Weatherford, Brownwood, and Comanche, men made up expeditions to hunt the buffalo only a few dozen miles from home. The continuing demand for buffalo hides in the east and in Europe made it seem a likely enterprise.

A third factor followed from the first two. The Indians were being driven off their hunting grounds by a combination of aggressive hunters, veteran soldiers, and the diminution of the herds. Hunters, ranchers, frontier settlers, and the troops all suffered casualties in this confrontation between the encroaching whites and the natives who were defending their accustomed means of existence. Atrocities and massacres were abundant on both sides. It was a dangerous time on the frontier.

The first major base of operations for the assault on the south plains buffalo herds was Fort Griffin. The near-extinction of the North American bison began in earnest in the 1870s in Kansas. Major markets were developing for buffalo meat and buffalo hides. Adventurous young men like J. Wright Mooar and his brother John of Vermont reaped substantial profits from butchering the herds.[11]

The result was that the Kansas herds were nearly gone by 1873, so the hunters cast their eyes farther south, into the Texas Panhandle, and when that became too dangerous, further south still to the area known as the rolling plains. Hunters from Fort Griffin and a new temporary town called Rath City in southern Stonewall County engaged in a slaughter on the southern herds beginning in 1874 and continuing for the next three or four years, by which time the buffalo were nearly wiped out.

After the hide trade and the meat supply business were gone, there was still a residue of the buffalo that provided an opportunity for further financial gain. Scattered all over the prairies were myriads of bones, a minor windfall that could be exploited for profit. Some buffalo bones were ground up and used in the process of refining sugar, some were made into a very effective fertilizer, and some were used in the production of "bone china." Buffalo horns were prized as the raw material for combs, buttons, and knife handles.[12]

When the Texas and Pacific built its line west from Baird and onto the buffalo range in 1881, its stations became the collection points for tons and tons of bones. The bone trade was a principal industry for Abilene for its first couple of years. At first, bone collectors gathered near the line of westward-moving railroad construction, then ranged farther afield to collect the more remote remains in Haskell, Jones, and Shackelford counties.[13] In Abilene and other towns, gatherers hauled their wagonloads of bones into town, where there awaited bone buyers who would make bids on each lot. Once the sale was made, the sellers took the bones to a designated pile by the tracks. Bones were sold by the ton, and the sharp collector could add weight and gain extra money by soaking his "dry" bones in a creek before making the sale. "Ben Middleton, one of the gatherers who sold at Abilene, recalled that a huge pile of bones could usually be seen on North First Street, just east of Pine Street. There he generally received eight dollars a ton, which meant about three dollars a load. Later as the bones became scarce, the price rose to twenty-one . . . dollars a ton. All through the summer and fall of 1881, Abilene dealers were busy shipping the bleached remainders of the vanished buffaloes. They loaded and dispatched thirty-three carloads with 465 tons in July, thirty-seven carloads with 555 tons in August, and thirty-nine carloads with 585 tons in September."[14] Tommie Clack remembered seeing those same piles. "My brother, John, used to make some spending money, gathering and selling buffalo bones. I can recall making only one buffalo-bone hunting trip ... John hitched a team to the wagon and we drove over somewhere south of the [Buffalo] Gap and gathered bones all afternoon.... My bone-picking experience was very short-lived."[15] Abilene's bone enterprise was also brief, but it was an important impetus for the early days of the town's economy.

The Herdsmen

The buffalo massacre opened the way the next phase of the frontier—the herdsmen. Now there was no more buffalo meat to send east. Now the Indians who dominated the plains were reduced to quiescence on reservations. Now the buffalo were no longer in the way of other creatures that might thrive on the plains grasses. Gen. Phil Sheridan had it right in 1874. Praising the buffalo hunters for "destroying the Indians' commissary," he urged that, "for the sake of lasting peace, let them kill, skin and sell until they have exterminated the buffalo. Then your prairies will be covered with speckled cattle and the festive cowboy."[16]

The first phase of the herdsman's frontier penetrated into the Place in 1874, when a South Texas cattleman named John T. Lytle drove some 3,500 wild cattle north toward Nebraska. Trail driving began to thrive after the Civil War, with ranchers and veterans pushing herds of feral longhorns to railheads in Missouri and Kansas. The most famous of these, the Chisholm Trail, crossed central Texas and central Oklahoma in 1867 to a newly established railroad town called Abilene, Kansas. The success of the Chisholm Trail led to its undoing. The trail towns attracted settlers, including those who wished to farm and fence the land. The farmers' interests and those of the drovers conflicted, and the drovers' solution was to send the cattle north by a more westerly route. The railroad was extended across the Kansas prairie to Dodge City.

This new route, called the "Western Trail," assembled herds from all over southern Texas. From Brady, the path came north through Coleman, along the east edge of the Callahan Divide past the village of Belle Plain in Callahan County, near the present-day site of Baird, through the eastern edge of Albany, across the Clear Fork at Fort Griffin and north to Doan's Crossing on the Red River and finally to Dodge City in Kansas. It crossed perilously close to the Comanche reservation in Oklahoma, but that threat had mostly subsided during the heyday of the Western Trail. By 1879, the Western Trail was the main artery connecting supply in South Texas with demand on the railroad in Kansas. Even after railroad lines reached the trail in Texas in 1880, cattlemen continued to move their herds north to Dodge City for a few more years. The trail left its mark on the area, from the wide main street of Coleman to ephemeral trail towns like Belle Plain and Callahan City. The Belle Plain cemetery is still in use today, and the ruins of Belle Plain College may be seen rising above the mesquite. Other ruins are scattered throughout the area, including the home of a prominent cattleman, John Merchant. Merchant was one of a hardy breed of frontiersmen who sought to make a living by ranching on the newly opened western grasslands.

Cattlemen were not the only ones who saw possibilities in the virgin land. Much of West Texas looked like good sheep country, and there were those, especially Englishmen, who sought to exploit it. One of the aptly named Lambshead brothers who operated the Butterfield stage stations southwest of Abilene ran a herd of sheep in the 1850s. For several years, Abilene was a principal wool and mutton shipping point. Prominent early sheep raisers included Capt. John Trent near Dudley,[17] Sam Butman in Mulberry Canyon,[18] J.F. Fletcher in Lytle Cove[19] and Colonel R.K. Wylie.[20]

There were problems for sheep raisers that eventually became insurmountable. One was the substantial population of predatory animals resident in the brush and defiles of the Callahan Divide.[21] Another was weather. Flash floods could wipe out an entire flock, as happened to M.M. Clack's herd of 350 Angora goats on Lytle Creek.[22] The drought of 1886-87 may have killed thousands of sheep. Certain breeds of sheep did not fare well in the climate. Herders were sometimes ignorant of the special needs of sheep in this climate and lost thousands of head during severe winters.[23] A change in national tariff policy allowed cheap foreign wool into the United States, reducing the profit margin for Taylor County sheepmen into negative numbers. A few sheepmen blamed the Democrat Grover Cleveland for the problem and became "Sheep Republicans."[24]

There were also confrontations between sheepmen and cattlemen. Cattleman Doc Grounds, one of the earliest ranchers in the western part of the county, tried very hard, but unsuccessfully, to intimidate Sam Butman when Butman brought his sheep into the region. Butman considered himself a sheepman all his life, but he was flexible enough to raise cattle as well.[25] J.F. Fletcher raised both kinds of stock but eventually got out of the sheep business after his sheep did not do well. When cowman D.E. Coffman's herds were destroyed by cold weather, he supported his family by hiring out as a sheep shearer.[26] Confrontations between shepherds and cowboys may have taken place, but they were probably not as dramatic as legend holds.[27] Among other reasons, cattlemen and sheepmen made common cause against the introduction of wire fencing in the county in the 1880s, and that was a much more important issue.[28]

Sheep outnumbered cattle in Taylor County 5,837 to 1,214 in 1880, a margin of almost five to one. However, John Simpson claimed to have 14,000 cattle at the time. This discrepancy probably relates to Simpson's herds being on open range and not necessarily in the county, even though he himself might be.[29] Cattle and cattlemen had the publicity, but sheep raising was important to Taylor County from the beginning.

Settlement
The Farmers

The first farmers began drifting into the southeastern part of Taylor County in the late 1870s. Most people in Precinct 2 (eastern Taylor County north of the Callahan Divide) in 1880 were stockraisers, either cattle or sheep. A few began to clear and plow land, but their crops were for their own consumption, not for sale. In western Callahan County, this process was a little further advanced, and the area seemed more oriented toward Taylor County and to Buffalo Gap or Abilene than toward Belle Plain or Baird. The bulk of this population centered in the Potosi area, and almost none lived in the northeast. Precinct 3 (eastern Taylor County south of the Callahan Divide) also had modest farming, but again, mostly stockraising.

Precinct 4 (southwestern Taylor County) was dedicated exclusively to cattle, and Precinct 5 was the same. Both were sparsely settled. Precinct 1, which included the area in the center of the county around Buffalo Gap, had more agriculture. Lawyer S.C. Simmons reported that he had 120 acres under cultivation. Mostly, though, Precinct 1 was focused on town tasks—merchants, saloonkeepers, carpenters, masons, smiths, printers, hotelkeepers, surveyors, freighters, attorneys, law enforcement, and many housekeepers. A fair number of citizens in the precinct called themselves stockmen. Well over half the population of the county resided in Precinct 1.

When Abilene was born, Taylor County's agriculture consisted only of subsistence farming. All 107 farms reported in the county were operated by their owners, none by tenants. Commercial agriculture, especially cotton, would await the next decade, and when it came, tenant farming would begin to dominate the county's agricultural scene. But not yet.[30]

The Colonists

The American frontier was always an inviting place for people who wanted to start afresh, to make a new beginning, perhaps to build an ideal community from scratch, with no historical underbrush to clear away.

An individual would usually make that decision for himself and would band together with others as a temporary traveling community (wagon trains, for example) just until they could get to wherever they were going.[31] But sometimes entire groups organized to create their dream home as a community, bound together by mutually agreed-on presuppositions and goals. In the late 1870s, there were at least three attempts at building a utopian colony of like-minded souls in southeast Taylor County.

The most important was the Eagle Colony. Most of the settlers were recent German immigrants who worked in manufacturing in Dayton, Ohio. One of their number, a shoemaker named Karl Kaltwasser, conceived the notion of establishing a settlement on the Texas frontier. Kaltwasser, who anglicized his name to Charles Coldwater, incorporated with other investors the "Eagle Colonizing Association" in 1877. The association gathered a capital stock of $140,000 and dispatched a team to Texas to find a suitable site.

The first wave of colonists from Ohio arrived in Fort Worth in 1878 with their worldly possessions, including draft animals and a number of good Studebaker wagons. These were only partly paid for. Migrating west to their land in Taylor County, the colonists began their community on the banks of Lytle Creek, now the southeast edge of Abilene. They laid out streets and began houses.

But disaster struck before the town could get fairly under way. The agent of disaster was Charles Coldwater, who disappeared in the summer of 1878 with most of the invested money, leaving a cloudy title to the land and indebtedness on animals and equipment. Penniless, the shocked colonists were in dire straits. The houses could not be completed; the fields were left half-plowed; food supplies had to be improvised from whatever was at hand. Neighboring ranchers, sympathetic to the plight of the families, donated an occasional beef and hired a few of the men as ranch hands in the summer of 1878.

Most of the defeated Eagle Colonists returned east, but a few remained in the area, principally in Callahan County, working as ranch hands, stonemasons, and bakers. Some of those who stayed owed their survival to the largesse of neighboring ranchers. John Simpson of the Hash Knife Ranch was a special benefactor.[32] A year later, Anglo settlers in the area of Eagle Colony found but few traces of the failed attempt.

Next came a band of Methodists from North Texas, led by a preacher named McQuistian, who proposed to develop a moral community of farmers on the frontier. Since surveyor Sam Chalk's father was a Methodist minister in North Texas, the colonists prevailed on Rev. Chalk to enlist Sam in showing them around Taylor County. From fifty to a hundred of them came. They camped, they fished the creeks, they explored, they held a week-long revival, and then—they left. Apparently the site did not suit them.[33]

The Franco-Texan Land Company was chartered by the state in 1876. At one point, it owned 600,000 acres in West Central Texas.[34] In the attempt to gain some return on its investment, the company tried to settle a group of some two hundred Russian Mennonites in Taylor County. An advance party of twenty arrived, and Chalk conducted them on a survey of the area, but they too opted to return east and finally settled in Arkansas.[35]

The Villagers

People probably camped in Buffalo Gap for centuries—Indians, buffalo hunters, explorers, drovers. Buffalo Gap was a natural place for human habitation—wood, water, shade, sheltering hills, abundant game, grass. A party of buffalo hunters spent some time camped in the Gap in 1874, killing a few of their quarry and missing many others because of the hunters' inexperience.[36]

Seasonal occupation gave way to a more permanent settlement as stockmen and a few farmers came into the vicinity. Things began to move fast after the defeat of the Comanches in 1874. At first there were only a few tents, then dugouts, then a cabin or two, and perhaps a crude store to serve the surrounding meager population.[37] Since this was the best pass through the Callahan Divide for miles around, it was the route of occasional cattle drives. The gap's namesake bison had long since pioneered the best trails through the pass.

A few stockmen and hunters moved onto Elm Creek a bit north of the pass in 1876. By 1877, a permanent village had begun. Buffalo Gap was a depot for the last vestiges of the buffalo hide trade, and the huge stacks of hides made some early settlers think that they were buildings. There may have been an early dugout store run by Abe Hunter and another run by "Hog" Jackson soon after.[38] Two men named Wylie and Davis opened a general store where the town developed to serve the needs of travelers, hunters, and about a dozen nearby families. The stores carried the usual necessary stock and then added lumber for the upgrading of housing in the area. All their goods came by wagon from Fort Worth or Round Rock. Late in the year, the first regular (twice a week) U.S. mail run came to Buffalo Gap from Eastland via Belle Plain.[39] Other crude mercantile establishments followed, including a couple of saloons, one run by early ranchers J.W. Carter and Doc Grounds. The early years of the town featured gamblers, prostitutes, and gunmen, the kind of folk that were typical of a boomtown. Shooting up the streets became a nightly occurrence. The Gap gained a short-lived reputation for roughness, with rumors of shootings, hangings, and general frontier rowdiness.[40]

But solid, stable citizens also arrived to take up residence in Buffalo Gap. More businesses appeared in 1878, and the governor tentatively named it to be the first seat of the newly organized county. That meant lawyers and county officials. Some eighty-seven men voted in the first election, choosing the county's first officials. The voters chose J.W. Drury to be the first county judge and rancher-saloonkeeper J.W. Carter to be the first sheriff.

To house the apparatus of governance, the county rented a small frame building for its officers. To meet the need for a jail required a more imaginative step—transporting local felons to neighboring Coleman County. These expedients were only temporary solutions. The county quickly moved to levy taxes in 1879 for the purpose of financing a county building. Late in the year, construction began on a two-story stone building that would house prisoners on the second floor and the county offices on the first. The construction featured iron cannonballs imbedded at strategic points in the masonry, the object being to discourage escape attempts and to strengthen the overall frame of the building. The building was complete by April 1880, and the remaining Taylor County prisoners in Coleman could be transported to their new home.[41]

Frontier justice required the services of lawyers, and several moved to Buffalo Gap before 1880. In the newly settling country, their business was more often land sales than criminal proceedings. Among the more than one dozen lawyers were persons whose names would feature prominently in the history of Abilene—D.B. Corley, Abilene's first mayor; K.K. Legett, namesake of a major street; G.A. Kirkland; M.M. Clack; and others.[42]

The 1880 United States census found Buffalo Gap a thriving village with numerous and diverse business establishments. While many in town called themselves stock raisers, there were others whose occupations stamped them as townsmen—editor, printer, merchant, hide buyer, carpenter, hotel keeper, mail carrier, barber, stonemason, shoemaker, saddler, blacksmith, brick mason, bailiff, sheriff, county clerk, surveyor, numerous attorneys-at-law.[43] Immediately in its future were other signs of civilization and stability—schools, churches, a newspaper, even a college. Between the 1870 and 1880 censuses, Taylor County passed through several stages of the frontier experience and now awaited the next big development—a city.

How Lost Was Coronado? How Lost Was Judge Wagstaff?

Maybe the first Europeans to come near the Place were members of the Coronado expedition . . . maybe. Francisco de Coronado led the first Spanish penetration into the interior of North America in 1540, seeking Quivira, the cities of gold reported by the survivors of the Cabeza de Vaca journey a few years earlier. The men of one Coronado detachment were the first Europeans to see the Grand Canyon. The whole party visited the pueblos of the upper Rio Grande Valley later the same year and then moved eastward onto the plains, still in search of the fabled golden cities. Winter caught the party on the Plains and they passed the season hunkered in a *barranca* (canyon) that protected them from the freezing prairie winds. Most scholars agree that the expedition probably wintered in either the Tule or Palo Duro canyons in the Texas Panhandle before continuing a fruitless search northward to the Kansas plains in the spring of 1541.

However, one dissenting student of the expedition, basing his deductions principally on vegetation evidence, concluded that the canyons mentioned in the journal of the expedition had to be on the North Concho River near present-day Sterling City.

And another dissenter, Abilene lawyer R.M. Wagstaff, convinced the State Historical Commission that the *barranca* in question must have been the Elm Creek valley in Taylor County. There is a state historical marker on Highway 277 southwest of Abilene that says, in bronze, that "the Spanish explorer Coronado is thought to have passed this way." The spot today is called "Coronado's Camp." In a closely reasoned essay, Wagstaff argued that most other interpreters did not take into account the shift in lines of compass declination (the variation between compass north and true north) from Coronado's time and the present. Coronado's recorded compass readings are a major piece of evidence in determining the location of his various camps and Wagstaff thought the readings proved the case for Elm Creek valley. Maybe so, but the Palo Duro thesis still stands as the most likely.

Sources: J.W. Williams, "Coronado: From the Rio Grande to the Concho," in *WTHAYB*, XXXV (1959), pp. 66-98; R.M. Wagstaff, "Coronado's Road to Quivira; 'The Greater Weight of the Credible Evidence,'" in *WTHAYB* XLII (1966), pp. 137-166.

Chapter Three
Planners 1872–1880

The Railroad
The Texas and Pacific

The successful completion of the transcontinental railroad from Nebraska through northern Utah to California in 1869 led some speculators to consider a southern railroad that might avoid the climate problems experienced in the more northern route. To that end, a number of men, all with strong Northern roots, began to plan in 1871 for a southern route to be called the Texas and Pacific. Among the leaders were Thomas Scott, current president of the Union Pacific; Grenville M. Dodge, the chief engineer in the survey and construction of the U.P.; "carpetbagger" governors Powell Clayton of Arkansas and Henry Warmoth of Louisiana; "scalawag" Governor James L. Alcorn of Mississippi; and others.

The first hints that a railroad might come through The Place appeared in the early 1870s when the Texas and Pacific Railway Company began plans to build a line from Shreveport, Louisiana, through Marshall, Texas, and on through West Texas all the way to the Pacific Ocean at San Diego. In 1872, the company named Gen. Grenville M. Dodge to be chief engineer for the building of the new line. Before the Civil War, he was a rising star in the field of railroad construction. During the war, he rose from the rank of colonel to major general and corps commander. After the war, he supervised the construction of the Union Pacific transcontinental railroad. When that task was completed in 1869, the peripatetic Dodge looked for other worlds to conquer—the T&P provided him with that opportunity.[1]

Dodge set to work to do two separate but related tasks in Texas. The first was to lay out and construct two railroad lines: the main one from Marshall to Fort Worth and a secondary line Texarkana-Sherman-Whitesboro-Denton-Fort Worth. This required an "instrumental survey" to identify the specific route from Shreveport to Fort Worth. Dodge's crews finished construction of the line to Dallas in 1873.[2]

Reconnaissance and Delay

The second task was to make a "reconnaissance survey" from Fort Worth west, with an eye toward building the tracks across the continent. A reconnaissance survey would assess the terrain and try to ascertain the general route of the line.

Dodge dispatched a survey team westward in 1874, led by an old comrade, Marshall F. Hurd. Hurd had worked under Dodge as an engineer during the war and then again in Wyoming during the construction of the Union Pacific. He had been a railroad surveyor since his boyhood. Dodge wanted an experienced leader who had seen his share of Indian fights, because "it would be a difficult country and dangerous on account of roaming bands of Indians that were upon it."[3] And the surveyors did have a serious dispute with Indians over access to water at a spring on the edge of the high plains. But they completed the survey successfully, and Hurd went home to Iowa to get married. The team's job was to find and mark a potential right-of-way that would connect Fort Worth and El Paso. The path, which came to be called the "Center Line Trail," was supposed to coincide generally with the 32nd parallel. The trail passed through or just south of

"Unexpected Delay" Drawing by Abilene artist Jody Boren.
FROM THE COLLECTION OF JOE AND MARGARET BOREN

the ruins of Fort Phantom Hill. It followed roughly the route that the Texas and Pacific Railroad would trace in 1880-81 and the Bankhead Highway (first Texas 1, then U.S. 80, and still later I-20) in the 1920s.

It is likely that the "trail" was only dimly marked. A few years later, most people projected the line of the Texas and Pacific in a different manner, suggesting that the Center Line Trail was known principally as a wagon path. The financial panic of 1873 nearly bankrupted the T&P, and the rapid expansion had to slow. Between 1873 and 1876, the line only advanced as far as Fort Worth. National politics again entered the picture at this point. As 1877 dawned, nobody knew who had won the just-completed presidential election. Democrat Samuel Tilden had won the popular vote, but the Republicans believed that their man, Rutherford B. Hayes, might have the most votes in the electoral college. Twenty electoral votes were in dispute, and if Hayes got all of them, he would be president by the margin of one vote. The two parties agreed to a special commission to decide the matter, and out of its deliberations came the "Compromise of 1877." Under the terms of this agreement, Hayes received all twenty disputed votes and assumed the presidency. In return, he would end Reconstruction, make federal patronage available to Southern Democrats, and lend his support to the construction of a southern transcontinental railroad. Hayes was a bit slow to deliver on the third of these points, but in late 1878 he signed a bill authorizing the issuance of federal bonds in support of a southern route.[4] Likewise, the economy was recovering from the problems of 1873. A New York financier and railroad builder named Jay Gould acquired control of the company in 1879. Gould was both famous and notorious for his manipulations, but in this case, he was a builder, not a destroyer. With Dodge again giving overall supervision to the construction, the T&P began to lay rails west from Fort Worth in April 1880. It remained to be seen precisely what line the tracks would follow.

The Route of the T&P

Most people in the new village of Buffalo Gap expected the railroad, when it came, to pass through the Gap. It only stood to reason—it was the natural pass through the hills, an obvious choke point for transportation. Several trails channeled cattle through the Gap, in the path of the buffalo before them. The area had a burgeoning population that would provide a ready market for railroad goods and services. The county seat was already established there. There was a reliable water supply, something steam locomotives always needed.

There were even hints from the company that Buffalo Gap was on the projected path. The local newspaper noted in March 1880 that "the managers of the Texas and Pacific Railway have selected Buffalo Gap as supply depot and headquarters for the engineers on this end of the line. Already their stores and men are coming in."[5] Buffalo Gap was clearly on the path of the railroad. It only stood to reason.

But there was a problem. If it was general knowledge that the tracks had to come through the Gap, such general knowledge meant that anyone could try to buy up the land in the area in the expectation that it would rapidly rise in value when the road came through. So people began making purchases in the hope that the railroad or new settlers would buy them out a bit later at inflated prices. This was a problem for the Texas and Pacific, which preferred simplicity and low prices for right-of-way. Even that was minor, however, compared with the other matter.

The other matter was the cloudy title to all the land in the vicinity. The first platting of the land had taken place almost thirty years before. The landmarks of that survey, mostly trees and the creek bed, had changed. Trees had been cut down; new trees had matured; the creek had meandered. Indians, who recognized surveyors as the harbingers of a white invasion, may have removed some man-made markers. The village grew up with a general idea of how the surveys lay, but no one could quite be certain. A group of men led by S.C. Simmons owned, they thought, the land under the village of Buffalo Gap. When they filed their deeds in the county records, they discovered that another group led by William Heller and Fred Brookreson had filed papers for the same real estate, and a third claimant, J.H. Grant, also asserted rights to the land. Commotion over this problem erupted in the spring of 1879 and continued through the summer. The Simmons group sued both the other claimants. Simmons won, but the Heller-Brookreson group appealed to the state Supreme Court, which eventually upheld the original judgment. That decision came down in 1885, much too late to do Buffalo Gap any good. The cloudy land titles destroyed whatever chance Buffalo Gap might have had.[6]

Several commonsense reasons suggest that Buffalo Gap was never in serious consideration anyway. The first was simple and obvious. Railroads do not build through hills when level grades are easily at hand. A route through Buffalo Gap and into the hills along and above the Elm Creek valley would have been expensive to build and to operate, especially when there was a much flatter alternative only a few miles north. Second, the T&P envisioned building a major city in Taylor County, and the Buffalo Gap area did not provide enough space. When Abilene was laid out, the *initial* survey included almost two hundred blocks. And third, "the railroad . . . didn't want to go through the small towns it found out through its virgin territory. It wanted to create its own cities so it could make money selling town lots."[7] The T&P managed to miss nearly every extant village anywhere close to its path.

Likewise, for reasons not altogether clear, the railroad ruled out the Center Line Trail route through Fort Phantom Hill. Probably the company decided that the terrain was a bit more challenging there than it was a few miles south. Hurd's 1874 exploration had only been a "reconnaissance survey," not necessarily the exact route. Possibly the experience of wagon-borne settlers in the late 1870s played a role as well. The passage through Red Gap (Cisco) and the Mexia Valley in Callahan County represented a much better route. Better yet, the "Baird Hill" provided opportunity for a gentler grade over the Callahan Divide.

Planning "Abilene"

With neither the Buffalo Gap route nor the Phantom Hill route in the picture, the locus of the railroad was fairly well decided. The company then sought to identify a specific spot on the projected line somewhere west of Baird to be the "Future Great City" of West Texas. The choice of the place that became the city of Abilene resulted from meetings held at the headquarters of the Hash Knife Ranch on Cedar

Creek in late 1880. The "founding fathers" of the community were a remarkable group of men, nearly all of them Confederate veterans and nearly all of them significant for other things beyond the business at hand. The first headquarters structure for the ranch was a dugout overlooking Cedar Creek, set up some time in 1874. Later the ranch erected a more substantial above-ground building near the site of the dugout. Tradition holds that the first meeting convened in the dugout in August 1880. The "founding fathers" had already held other conversations on the subject. Most were veteran land speculators. The August meeting brought them together with Horace C. Withers, a track locater for the Texas and Pacific Railroad. John Simpson, twin brothers Claiborne ("Clabe") and John D. Merchant, John T. Berry, and Samuel L. Chalk were the principals in this discussion. Chalk was a surveyor and the junior member of the group. The other men were all ranchers and/or businessmen with interests in Taylor and Callahan counties. All but Chalk were Confederate veterans. Simpson was the founder of the Texas and Southwestern Cattle Raisers Association and later president of the State Fair of Texas and Republican nominee for governor in 1908.[8] Clabe Merchant and John T. Berry were subsequently principal founders of the city of Amarillo.[9]

Claiborne "Clabe" Merchant is usually regarded as the "Father of Abilene." Abilene's Merchant Street and Merchant Park shopping center commemorate his name. COURTESY OF JACK NORTH

The result of this meeting was that Withers accepted a plan to route the railroad through northern Taylor County, bisecting the Hash Knife

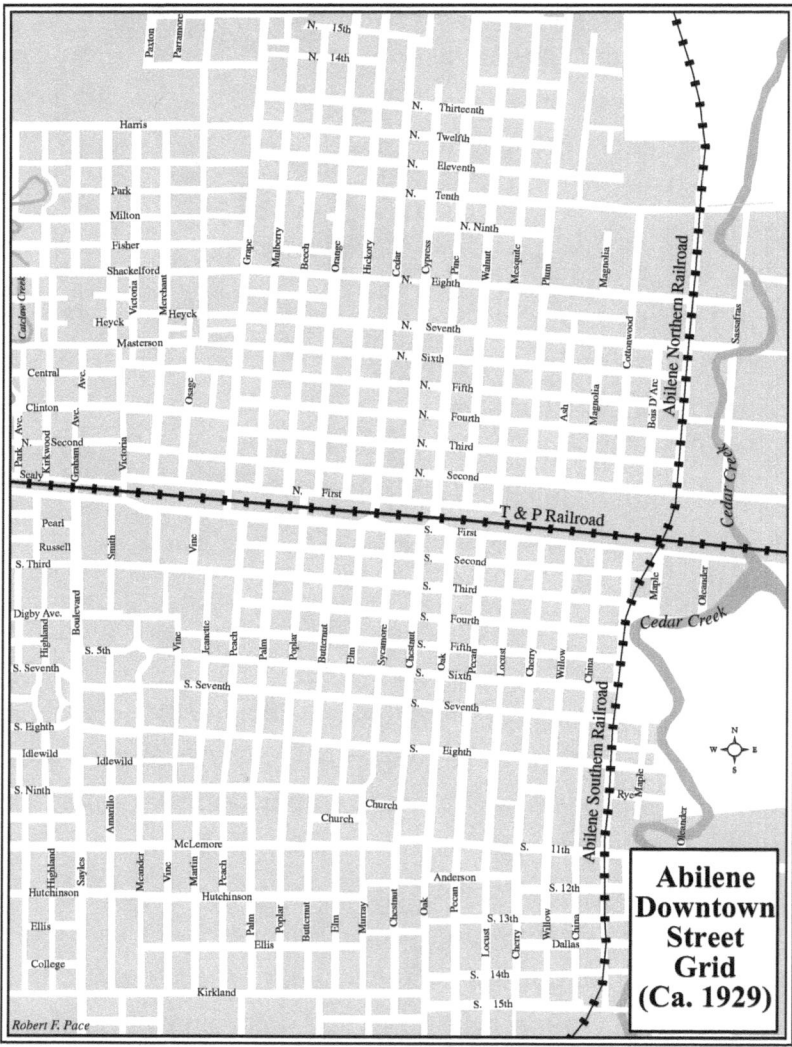

The original Abilene plat was based on the line of the railroad, which slanted slightly to the northwest. Accordingly, the streets that paralleled the line (the numbered streets) also slanted slightly to the northwest. Streets perpendicular to the railroad (named for trees) also ran slightly out of plumb. Note that streets added in later years shift orientation slightly to run true north-south and east-west. The naming of the streets in this fashion was the standard Texas and Pacific practice for the new towns created in the area. It is called the "Philadelphia Plan." Another unusual feature was that the north-south streets did not match up; they are a half-block out of phase where they meet at the rail line. This pattern is seen at Abilene, Clyde, and Sweetwater, and almost nowhere else in the western hemisphere.

range. In return, the railroad would receive title to substantial amounts of land across Simpson's holdings. The group agreed that stock pens and a town site would be provided by the local men, with land to be divided equally between the locals and the railroad.

In December 1880, with the tracks already completed to Baird, the local men met again at the Hash Knife headquarters with J. Stoddard Johnston of Kentucky, a well-connected officer of the railroad. Johnston, nephew of the famous Confederate general Albert Sidney Johnston,[10] was empowered to decide where to site the projected major community along the established right-of-way.

The Merchants and Chalk had been buying up land in the Elmdale area in the expectation that that would be the city location. Withers bought land near Tebo Switch (later renamed Tye), presuming that to be the place. The Merchants and Berry, belatedly realizing that Elmdale would not be chosen, then purchased tracts a few miles westward, adjoining Simpson's holdings. Simpson and his allies persuaded Johnston to designate the city at Milepost 407 (407 miles by rail from Marshall, Texas, the origin point of the T&P) just west of Cedar Creek and about a mile southwest of where they were meeting. Johnston himself also bought up land nearby. His uncle George W. Hancock already owned numerous sections of land in southern Callahan and Taylor counties.

It was not land speculation alone that dictated the site of the new city. Historians of Abilene have often remarked that there was no particular geographic reason for the city to be located where it is.[11] Geography, it was said, dictated perhaps a spot on the Clear Fork or maybe Buffalo Gap. Removing those two routes from the picture would seem to mean that just about any old place along the projected line would do.

But that was not exactly so. Milepost 407 was flat, with the terrain changing barely five feet in elevation over quite a large area. It was near, but not too near, to Cedar Creek.[12] Though the waterway had a propensity for flash flooding, its floods were restricted to a narrow bed, almost a canyon, that a rail line could easily span. A little farther west, the line crossed Elm Creek. Elm Creek, with its long drainage basin, was even more prone to overflowing its banks, and its floods inundated a wide adjacent area. Elm Creek, where the railroad crossed it, had a remarkable characteristic—the neighboring terrain sloped *up* to the creek bed so that when it did overflow, the waters sprawled downhill for a good distance away from the creek.[13]

Access to a reliable water supply was absolutely necessary for a city to develop and was an important factor for the railroad as well. That ruled out Elmdale and Tye. Water wells might have changed that, but nobody had demonstrated that potable water could be found in those areas. Only three creeks on the route between Baird and Merkel could be termed reliable water supplies—Cedar, Elm, and Mulberry. Mulberry Creek meandered nearly west-east along the projected route, threatening frequent washouts of the roadbed. The best water source, Elm Creek, was too dangerous when flooding. Topographically speaking, Milepost 407 was the best site for a dozen miles in either direction. This was not only The Place—this was The *Right* Place.

Johnston asked the local men to select a name. This was a most unusual concession on the part of the T&P. The railroad company claimed the right to name nearly all of the other new communities that sprang up along the right of way. Most sources agree that cattleman Clabe Merchant came up with the name of Abilene, in the hope and expectation that the Texas town would be a cattle-shipping point of similar fortune with the Kansas town of the same name, which these cattlemen knew very well.[14] If so, the community exceeded his hopes, because it is today several times as large as its Kansas namesake. Clabe Merchant is generally called "the father of Abilene."

The "Future Great"
Constructing the Line

The T&P contracted with the "Pacific Railway Improvement Company" to construct its line from Fort Worth to El Paso. The construction company was formed and run by Dodge. Its contract called for rails to be laid to El Paso by January 1, 1882. That deadline made the actual construction of the railway a frantic activity. But there was an even more compelling reason for haste. Collis P. Huntingdon of the Southern Pacific was building eastward from California along the original T&P survey, reaching for El Paso and beyond. As was the case in the building of the Union Pacific and the Central Pacific, each would build until they met. The two lines eventually joined at Sierra Blanca, Texas, ninety miles east of El Paso, in December 1881.

The work crews did the minimum amount necessary to run a viable line, expecting to upgrade it as time went on. The roadbed was hastily and poorly done and often eroded by wind or water after operations began.[15] The first rails were iron with a thin strip of steel welded to the top. Track walkers had to scout the line continuously, looking for defects. Eventually, as the official T&P history noted, "many miles of the road in West Texas which had been built in great haste during the race to El Paso were repaired and improved."[16] Not until 1892 were all-steel rails introduced.[17]

Initially, the line used light locomotives weighing 25 to 30 tons. The engines burned wood, necessitating the deposit of vast amounts of fuel along the length of the line. No more than fourteen freight cars could be pulled by one engine, and at speeds of about 15 miles per hour. Passenger trains, which doubled that speed, usually included the engine, a baggage car, and two coaches. As time passed, the company improved the roadbed, stabilized the bridges, upgraded the rails, employed larger locomotives, utilized coal instead of wood, and provided more comfortable coaches.[18]

Construction included clearing the right-of-way, leveling and building the grade, setting the ties, and laying the rails. Different teams of men performed each of these tasks in sequence moving west, strung out over scores of miles. The clearing and grading crews were in Big Spring in November 1880, though the tracks did not get there until six months later.[19] Callahan County was filled with railroad workers in June 1880, six months before the tracks arrived.

Since few of the trees on this section of the line were suitable, the company hauled the ties from East Texas, where there was abundant timber. Trains carried them to the railhead, and mule- and ox-drawn wagons hauled them forward to be emplaced. In addition to the railway itself, the company also had to provide watering stations, which could include digging wells and building dams. At intervals, the company's surveyors laid out town sites along the tracks, one of which eventually became Abilene.

The workers on the line came from all over the world. Altogether, as many as 5,000 men at one time were deployed along the right-of-way. They were divided into teams, each with a specific task that had to be done in sequence. Many of the workers were Irish, though the western reaches of the line employed Chinese laborers.[20] A substantial majority of railroad laborers in Callahan County in 1880 were native-born Americans, and often Texans. While most were laborers, there were a half dozen who listed themselves as "civil engineers" in this group. Workmen lived in special dormitory cars, tents, or hastily erected rooming houses along the right of way. There were a half dozen boarding businesses dotting the grade in Callahan County in June 1880 and none in Taylor County, so Callahan County was the leading edge of road building at that moment.[21]

Tents housed private contractors who provided meals. A famous pioneer woman, Martha Ann Rogers, and her husband ran a boarding tent: "We went to the T.P. railroad in 1880, three miles east of Eastland

City, and took up a boarding camp. Mr. Rogers and the little boys went to working on the railroad. We had ten milk cows and twelve Wyandotte laying hens. ... I made all the milk and butter we could use for all the boarders and ourselves. We worked along there three months." The Rogerses leapfrogged to Big Spring to resume their business when the final phase of construction was complete at Eastland.[22]

After the contract was let on January 16, 1880, the construction began. The goal was a mile a day at first, but later two miles a day. It was over six hundred miles to El Paso. Construction advanced so that trains were running to Weatherford by June 4, to Eastland by November 13, to Baird by December 14, past Abilene by mid-January 1881, to Sweetwater by March 12, to Big Spring on May 28, on to Toyah on September 12, and finally to juncture with the Southern Pacific at Sierra Blanca on December 16. The midway point between Fort Worth and El Paso was marked by a village named "Midway," later changed to "Midland."[23]

The Founders
Selling the City

Once the founders settled on the name of Abilene for the projected town, railroad promoters in Dallas and Fort Worth began touting the advantages of the site. The advertising slogan was "The Future Great City of West Texas." The slogan was the cause of some derision on the parts of established communities. A Fort Worth newspaper scoffed, "Wonder if someone won't get left behind on this one among so many railroad 'Future Greats.'?"[24] A paper in nearby Fort Griffin noted in February 1881, "The editor visited the town of Abilene, the 'Future Great.' ... Everybody is going to Abilene except our people."[25] And a Dallas newsman wrote, "Abilene is generally looked to as the 'Future Great,' but the writer predicts that Baird in time will be the better point for business." He went on to concede that "Abilene, for a while, will be a great shipping point."[26]

Such doubts notwithstanding, the railroad made plans to make an "instant city" on the plains at Milepost 407. Publicity continued in the east and spread throughout the area around the city-to-be. There was a forty-two-page "homeseekers' guide," numerous handbills, newspaper ads, and more. If advertising had anything to do with it, Abilene was going to get off to a rousing start.

How John and Clabe Got Clabe out of Trouble

In 1874, Clabe Merchant, an East Texas rancher, decided to move his business and his family west. He acquired land in Callahan County and began to drive his cattle westward. As the herd moved through largely unfenced East Texas, a few local cattle occasionally got mixed in with the drive. The drovers periodically "cleaned" the herd, but additional stock still mingled in as the mass of cattle moved along. One farmer in Van Zandt County lost two of his milk cows to the passing parade and quickly swore out a warrant for Merchant's arrest.

Merchant made bond on the charge and went his way. When the Van Zandt County grand jury true-billed him, he returned for trial. The presiding judge asked the complainant to identify the thief. The farmer looked across the courtroom to the defense table where he saw two men sitting. "Clabe Merchant, stand up," the judge ordered. Both men stood. The farmer was unable to point out which one it was, just that "it was one of those two men over there." "Clabe Merchant, sit down," the judge said, and both men took their seats. The process was repeated for the sheriff, and he could not distinguish which was the man he had arrested.

At an impasse, the judge finally directed the jury to bring a verdict of not guilty. Clabe and John Merchant, identical twins, identically dressed, identically bearded, stood together and stalked from the courtroom, never letting on which was which.

Source: R.C. Crane, "When West Texas Was in the Making," in *WTHAYB* XXIII (1947), pp. 46-51.

Chapter Four
Priority 1881–1884

The citizens who poured into Abilene after the auction quickly set about to build a city. They were the first, and they expected to derive major benefits from that. Priority was a significant asset on the frontier. Walter Prescott Webb, in discussing the matter of water rights on the plains, showed that the old English water law that said every owner had equal rights to water along his land did not apply on the Plains. Rather, water rights in the American West belonged to whoever settled a stream bank first; later comers had to settle for what was left. Daniel Boorstin wrote that "the principle of pre-emption, of rewarding the man who got there first, lasted at least to the end of the [19th] century."[1]

That was in law; in practice, priority was even more important. First come—first served! If you were going to make money fast, you had to get in on the ground floor, and it might be necessary to cut a few corners. A best-selling book a few years earlier had popularized the axiom, "It is a good thing to be shifty in a new country."[2] The new townsmen understood that concept.

The Kentucky Connection

One might expect the first settlers in Abilene to be Southerners, and so they were, but in a surprising way. Among the 102 first business and professional people in the community whose origins are identified, seven came from foreign countries. Thirteen came from the North (New England, the Mid-Atlantic, the Middle West), three from California, and the rest from the South. Of those, only eleven were Texans and twenty-three were from the Deep South (North Carolina, South Carolina, Georgia, Alabama, Mississippi, and Louisiana). Forty-five (or nearly half) of the new Abilenians came from the Border South states of Virginia, Maryland, Missouri, Arkansas, Tennessee, and Kentucky. Since Kentuckians were instrumental in building the T&P and situating the town site, it may not come as a surprise to observe that the Bluegrass State was the largest single contributor to the business community, more even than Texas. The Kentucky connection, while not predominant, was strong. Founder J.T. Berry was only two years removed from Kentucky. J. Stoddard Johnston, while still maintaining a residence in Frankfort, was a power in the new town. Though Kentucky never seceded in the late Civil War, the Confederate dimension was the dominant orientation among them.

In thinking about the flavor of the new town, as opposed to the rural areas around it, one might consider then that the cultural, political, religious, linguistic, and other patterns of life reflected more of the Border South than of any other section. The West Texas accent owes more to the Mid-South than to the Deep South.[3] There was no modification of the Abilene speech or cultural patterns because of blacks or Hispanics. Very few African-Americans resided in early Abilene. Even rarer in the town were those with Hispanic surnames. There were, however, a few Chinese who briefly ran laundry services near the T&P tracks.[4]

The Raw Place

Several elements combined to make Abilene an exciting and barely civilized place in the months and first years after the town-lot auction.

Boomtown

The "Future Great City" was, of course, a boomtown, springing into existence almost overnight with all the wildness associated with a boomtown. Not gold, not oil, but the railroad's decree made it an instant city where a fortune might easily be made—or perhaps not. There was no tradition, no established pattern, but there was a sense of urgency. One visitor soon after the auction remarked on the "restless energy of fortune-seekers in that town of tents."[5]

Like most boomtowns, Abilene had a preponderance of young men who were attracted by the possibilities. In the first year, males outnumbered females by a ratio of fifteen to one.[6] Many of the first-comers had limited skills but were willing to try their luck at whatever came to hand—cowboys, hide hunters, bone agents, shepherds, freighters, a few farmers, plus saloonkeepers, gamblers, prostitutes, and miscellaneous adventurers. Railroad construction crews passed through on their way to the track-laying farther west. These people were thrown together in a community that was only beginning to organize itself and had few rules.

At first, it had a temporary look to it. The canvas housing gave way soon enough to hastily-erected simple frame buildings. The frame buildings, typical of the boomtown of the day, slowly were complemented here and there by masonry and brick structure, gradually giving a sense of permanence.[7] In the beginning, though, there were no street improvements and no sidewalks, so that the inevitable wagon traffic routinely turned the streets into a sea of mud after a rain. Early on, someone even laid a single path of stepping-stones to help people go dry-shod across the railroad right-of-way from South First to North First.

Frontier Town

Second, it was a frontier town, bursting forth where there was little population anywhere around or beyond. The county was less than a decade removed from organized Indian raids. Land ownership was still in flux; free-range ranching was the norm; fences were only beginning to appear. There were no roads, only unimproved or abandoned trails. The buffalo trade was still in the process of dying down. And even though the buffalo were about gone, wild game still proliferated in the hills and prairies roundabout—bears, coyotes, cougars, antelope, turkeys. Aside from the path of the railroad, everything west of Abilene was a prairie wilderness.

The Indians may have been mostly gone, but they were not forgotten. Rural people still kept a lookout for marauders. A parade of Lipan Apaches moved through downtown Abilene in the summer of 1881. They were a party of army contract scouts on the Rio Grande making their way back to Oklahoma after the spring campaign. The party included packhorses and women with their children. The squaws, the newspaper noted with raised eyebrows, "rode man-fashion."[8] Late in the year, rumors reached Abilene of the massacre of the "Cox colony" of Quakers in Crosby County, rumors widely believed. They were, it turned out, totally wrong.[9] The Cox colony, which called itself "Estacado," included a physician named Hunt and his family. Dr. Hunt's six-year-old son, James Winford Hunt, grew up to become the founding president of McMurry College.

The Second Abilene

The town's very name suggested wildness. It was modeled on the trail town of Abilene, Kansas, a community notorious for shootings, drunken sprees, rugged lawmen, and the fast buck. It was inevitable that rowdiness would be king in Abilene, Texas, too—at least for a time.

Without anybody quite planning it, Abilene, Texas, turned out to be a trail town like its Kansas namesake. It was supposed to be a cattle town, yes, but everyone knew the Western Cattle Trail passed east of Baird, effectively missing the site of Abilene. In 1886, however, with settlements impinging on the Western Trail, Callahan and Shackelford counties agreed to channel the drives along a particular path. Callahan marked out the existing route, only to find that Shackelford had decided to designate a trail toward Fort Phantom Hill that crossed rough country with limited water. The two paths did not match up, and trail herds passing through Callahan encountered a barbed-wire fence at the Shackelford County line, with no easy connection to the road north. Word of the problem quickly spread back south, and the later herds that spring turned west at Coleman, moving through Taylor County instead. Apparently, the trail ran through Buffalo Gap and along the west bank of Elm Creek to its confluence with the Clear Fork near Fort Phantom Hill.[10] By mid-May, over 22,000 cattle had passed near Abilene during the 1886 droving season. A Baird man lamented that there had been 200,000 head a year moving through his county, but only a few thousand seemed likely in 1886.[11]

In his lightly fictionalized book, *The Log of A Cowboy*, drover Andy Adams told of moving a herd from the mouth of the Rio Grande through Buffalo Gap. Continuing toward the ultimate destination of Montana, the herd drifted past Abilene. A few days later, Adams and his mates heard that they were the twentieth herd to pass Abilene that season.[12]

Railroad Indifference

Nor was there much guidance from the city's creator—the railroad. Abilene was not a company town. The Texas and Pacific was extraordinarily liberal with the community. The company allowed the locals to pick the name of this town, an uncommon practice. Usually, the T&P decreed names for its whistle-stops. These were based on various models, either for early settlers of the area (Strawn, Mingus, Trent, Merkel, Westbrook, Monahans), or for existing designations (Sweetwater, Ranger [Camp], Big Spring, Colorado [City]), or for railroad financiers and construction engineers (Gordon, Clyde, Baird, Roscoe, Cisco). But the founders of the "Future Great" on Cedar Creek had the unique privilege of choosing the name themselves.

The railroad showed no interest in taming the town. The names or titles of railroad employees seldom appear in Abilene's leadership. Indeed, the railroad seemed to have little cultural, social, or political presence in Abilene. Among the occupations listed in the census of 1900, there were only a few identifiable with the railroad. A handful of Abilenians were classed in "minor professional occupations" that were related to the T&P—express agent, depot cashier, railroad agent, railroad cotton clerk, railroad fireman, and telegraph operator. These references suggest that the depot kept a small labor force on hand to handle freight and passenger business. On the operations end, there were listed twelve section hands who found employment in maintaining the roadbed. There were no conductors, no brakemen, no engineers, only the one fireman, no engine or car mechanics, no switchmen, no significant supervisors. Abilene was a major freight stop, but not a maintenance or operations center.[13]

Thus, Abilene experienced little pressure from the company to conform to what the railroad wanted done. The T&P seems to have decided that the residents' own desire to succeed was sufficient cause for Abilenians to create the commerce by which the railroad could prosper, and the tone of the town was of no concern beyond that.

Lack of Organization

Finally, Abilene began as a town in name only. It had geographical structure (e.g., streets and lots) but no political structure. It was a densely populated area of the county, but not an organized or incorporated town. There was little local law, only a justice of the peace and a precinct constable. The county sheriff lived and mostly stayed in Buffalo Gap. The county, the county offices, the county judge, the county jail—all were at the Gap. There was no mayor or city council to pass laws, nor was there a local police department to enforce laws, because the city did not incorporate until 1883. There was no zoning, so anybody could build anything anywhere. There were no local taxes, of course, but that meant there were no services such as road maintenance, garbage collection, water supply, animal control, fire suppression, or any other appurtenances of civilization. The lack of organization was an invitation to rowdiness.

The Rough Place
A Rowdy Town

And rowdiness there was! Abilene developed a bad reputation for the first few years. Andy Adams's trail boss refused to allow his hands to go into Abilene, which "was probably for the best," Adams thought, "for this cow town had the reputation of setting a pace that left the wayfarer purseless and breathless, to say nothing of headaches. . . . it was but natural that he should wish to keep his men from the temptation of the cup that cheers and the wiles of the siren."[14] When prominent businessman Louis Wise brought his bride to the frontier from Virginia, it was with the understanding that he would build her a masonry home for protection from stray bullets.[15]

Saloons abounded in the new town. "You can git two things in Abilene," one oldtimer said, "a ticket to git away and a drink to make you willin' to stay."[16] There were saloons operating out of tents even before the town-lot auction. When frame buildings began to go up, saloons were among the first. Places such as the White Elephant, Ackerman's Delmonico, the Cattle Exchange, the Red Light, and the Arcade drew droves of customers regularly.[17]

The saloons were focal points of continuous trouble, including several early gunfights. In July 1881, a barkeep and a dance-hall bouncer had a shootout over a girl. Both men, it turned out, were equally inept

The "bulletproof" home that Capt. L.C. Wise built for his bride, original portion on the left. COURTESY OF THE GRACE MUSEUM

with a gun—drawing simultaneously, firing at the same time, and missing six times each . . . at which point the relieved witnesses to the scene broke down in laughter at "the worst shots in town."[18] The Red Light Saloon was the scene of another fight a couple of weeks later; again, neither party was injured in the gunfight, but one of the participants then stabbed the other with a knife, inflicting minor wounds.[19] The most serious affray happened in the White Elephant Saloon at North First and Pine in 1884, when three men were fatally shot. One of the men, Zeno Hemphill, was a notorious gambling house operator on South First Street; another, Frank Collins, ran a saloon; and the third, Walter Collins, was a city deputy marshal, the first Abilene lawman to be killed on duty. Hemphill and Walter Collins died on the scene, while Frank Collins lingered for six weeks before succumbing to his wounds. Frank Collins was one of the original town aldermen.[20] Numerous other shooting incidents marred the early history of the town. Weatherman Isaac Cline spent a sleepless night in Abilene in 1885 on the way to his post in San Angelo. His quarters were above a saloon, and "the tramp of cow boys [sic] and the shooting of pistols made it a night of suspense."[21]

Prostitutes quickly showed up to work the town. An 1883 ordinance outlawed in great detail the practice and patronage of the "oldest profession."[22] Dance halls provided slightly less intimate female companionship for the surplus of men coming in and out of the town. Though a highly suspect enterprise, dance halls were not banned by the first laws. The red-light district was located not too far to the northeast of the train depot. One notorious house was near Walnut and North First, allegedly so as to be handy to the train station.[23]

A testimony to the problems Abilene faced in the early days lay in the kinds of city ordinances passed by the first council in 1883. One law made it illegal to discharge a gun within the city limits. Indeed, you could not even *carry* arms, such as guns, oversize knives, razors, brass knuckles, or sword canes. Another ordinance prohibited racing horses on the streets or riding a horse onto the T&P freight and passenger platforms. Also prohibited were any form of gambling, including faro, monte, vingt-et-un (blackjack), rouge et noir, roulette, chuck-luck, keno (a kind of bingo), rondo, and even pool. While the saloon was not yet outlawed, strict rules regulated activities where alcohol was served. The rules were not always enforced.

Other lower-grade crimes included tying tin cans to the tails of dogs; leaving teams hitched to wagons on the city streets; grazing stock within the city limits; and washing, bathing or swimming in Lytle Creek during daylight hours. It should be noted that bathing suits were not considered requisite attire in the West. And swearing or even using "rough or uncouth" language could earn the offender a fine.[24]

The Wire Wars

One of the problems of the countryside invaded the town limits. That was the advent of barbed wire and the opposition to it. Though

Taylor County was not the most notorious hot spot of the "wire wars," neighboring Coleman and Brown Counties were aflame with the issue. Fencing came to Taylor County soon after the railroad. Some "open- range" cattlemen like John Simpson saw the future coming and moved their operations farther west. A few stayed and hoped to retain their ranges unfenced, whether they had legal title to the land or not. Other cattlemen saw opportunity in the wire and began to fence off pastures for their own purposes. Farmers wanted to protect their crops and built fences for that reason. In Abilene, the *Abilene Reporter* (pro-fencing) and the *Magnetic Quill* (anti-fencing) kept the issue before the public in a lively and ongoing editorial debate. And passion over the issue in the city was by no means restricted to the newpapers.

There were two major issues, and many lesser ones, to the fencing of the range. One big concern was that fencing sometimes blocked stock from their accustomed streams and water holes, which were accessible to all on the open range. In drought times, and the summer of 1883 was one such, that could be fatal to beast and costly to owner. As one writer put it, "water, like grass and air, had been considered a free gift of nature to man."[25] The second was that fencers often enclosed the established paths and trails that connected one part of the area with another. Oftentimes, fences went on for miles without a gate, enclosing land that did not always belong to the fencer. This wrought serious hardship on, among others, soldiers who were going about their duties.[26]

The result was an epidemic of wire cutting by travelers in a hurry, or angry "free-range" men, or stockmen with thirsty animals, or rustlers, or organized mobs of night riders. In 1883, with fencing now commonplace in most parts of the state, "wire wars" erupted in several places. In Coleman County, one rancher had forty miles of fence cut between every post. In Brownwood, several dozen fence-cutters took

The Taylor County Courthouse of 1884 in Abilene. COURTESY OF THE GRACE MUSEUM

over the courthouse while their opponents gathered in the opera house, each with the full intention of exterminating the other.[27]

In time, all this cooled down. A special session of the state legislature in 1884 passed emergency laws regulating fencing and fence-cutting. The state laws made fence-cutting a felony but also outlawed fencing land not owned or leased by the fencer, and mandated a gate at least every three miles regardless. Fencing was here to stay, but with limitations.

The County Seat Dispute

About the same time as the wire controversy was reaching its peak, Taylor County experienced another kind of near-war—the county seat election. Taylor County got its first county seat in 1878 when Buffalo Gap won an election over another nearby village, but the result was never formally ratified by the state. The Gap certainly functioned as the de facto county seat for several years thereafter. It met the state criterion that, all things being equal, the county seat should be near the geographic center of the county. It had a solid, permanent fixture, the jail-courthouse.

By 1883, however, Buffalo Gap was far surpassed by the upstart city on the railroad farther north. Abilene citizens, some of them former residents of Buffalo Gap, decided that the county government would serve the citizens better if it were located in the biggest town, and petitioned for an election to move the county offices to Abilene. There was even a block already set aside for the courthouse. The outcome of the election was a foregone conclusion; Abilene won by a wide margin, far in excess of the requisite two-thirds. Cries of fraud emanated from the Gap. Abilene appeared to have cast far more votes than there were qualified voters. Had railroad men, Callahan County cowboys, trainloads of Mexicans, and other ringers been imported specifically to cast ballots for Abilene? The citizens of the Gap thought so.[28]

In late October, the county court met at Buffalo Gap to canvass the returns. Rumor had it that the two southern commissioners would rule that the Abilene votes were so tinged with fraud as to be invalid; that the two northern commissioners were ready to certify the published result as legitimate; and that County Judge John W. Drury might go either way. A number of Abilene citizens, eager to see that justice was done (that is, that Abilene won), took up their weapons and proceeded toward Buffalo Gap. Word of the coming invasion reached the Gap, and the locals prepared an appropriate reception. Clabe Merchant was with the Abilene contingent and persuaded them to wait at Mud Hill while he rode ahead to see if he could arrange a truce. He was successful in his mission, and both sides agreed to disarm to await the deliberations of the county court.

The commissioners voted as expected. Judge Drury cast his vote to certify the published results, making Abilene the county seat. Buffalo

Gap was outraged, and Drury found it prudent to leave town. A mob seized his home and fried up all the judge's chickens as the best retaliation they could muster. It is difficult to see how there could have been any other outcome. Had the court invalidated the election results, Abilene would have simply brought suit for another election, perhaps with Texas Rangers supervising. The result would have been the same. The economic and demographic centers of gravity of the county were on the railroad.

Early in November, the county court rented temporary quarters in Abilene. The word circulating around town was that a $100,000 courthouse was in the immediate future.[29] In a very brief time, the court accepted bids, and the contractor broke ground in February 1884.[30]

Meantime, the commissioners ordered Sheriff Kinch Northington to bring the county records to Abilene. The sheriff refused, saying that there would be bloodshed if he tried. After consulting with District Judge T.B. Wheeler of Graham, Northington went to Austin for further guidance. Governor John Ireland and Attorney General John Templeton advised Northington that the county seat election was valid and that Abilene was now the legal seat, regardless of where the records were. Governor Ireland further directed Northington to obey the orders of the county commission and to remove the records to Abilene. If there was trouble, said Ireland, telegraph him and he would send the Rangers.[31]

After another truce was negotiated, the recalcitrants in Buffalo Gap backed down, and the sheriff finally delivered most of the records to Abilene.[32] When Judge Wheeler returned to Abilene to hold court, he discovered that the county records were incomplete; some were still in Buffalo Gap. Wheeler took a team and wagon and drove alone to Buffalo Gap with the announced intention of getting the rest of the records or else. There was no further debate about the issue; the judge loaded up the remaining files and took them back to Abilene.[33] The county seat was now Abilene, but Taylor County still used that solid jail at the Gap until a comparable facility could be erected in Abilene.[34]

The San Jacinto Day Shootout

Drunken cowboys and angry saloonkeepers were not the only early-day gunfighters. In 1885, the editors of two of Abilene's three newspapers faced each other and shot it out on San Jacinto Day. The duel occurred on a downtown street in front of the First National Bank, much to the delight of the editor of the third paper, who said "they try to prove that the sword is mightier than the pen." The two men had been at odds for some time, taking opposite positions on nearly every controversial issue confronting the town.

In the exchange of bullets, C.E. Gilbert of the *Abilene Reporter* was grazed by a shot across the forehead while W.E. Gibbs of the *Magnetic Quill* was bruised on the arm by a blow from a "loaded whip." "It is an affair which all good citizens cannot fail to regret," the editor of the *Taylor County News* said piously. "Since the trouble occurred, friends of both parties have interfered to bring about peace between them and they have agreed to engage in no further hostilities. An amazing part of the affair is that each party thinks the other beat a hasty retreat."

In fact, both did retreat afterward. Within a couple of months, Gibbs closed the *Quill* and moved on to start a new career as a Church of Christ preacher. The embarrassed Gilbert resigned as Sunday school superintendent of the local Methodist church. Gilbert later moved to Dallas and founded the *Dallas Times-Herald* and then to Austin, where he was again prominent in church affairs. Presumably he had put his Abilene past well behind him.

Source: *Taylor County News*, April 24, 1885.

Chapter Five
Propriety 1881-1891

During all the wild-and-wooliness, the forces of propriety were quietly at work. One analysis of the railroad towns in this sector (Abilene, Sweetwater, Colorado City, Big Spring) concluded that the new communities could be considered domesticated when there was (a) a rock or brick schoolhouse, (b) at least four church buildings, (c) a woman's club, and (d) a civic booster organization. The influence of a more proper and genteel population made itself felt. By 1890, each of the towns had accomplished these milestones and settled down to a more dignified existence.[1]

Political Infrastructure
Organization

It was obvious that Abilene needed to have some kind of organization, but not everybody in town wanted that. Less than a year after founding, some citizens successfully circulated a petition calling for an incorporation election.[2] When the votes were counted, the proposal failed by a margin of twenty-nine votes.[3]

County officials, who were in charge of this sort of thing, called another incorporation election for January 26, 1883. The community had grown to a size that demanded some form of order beyond what a

D.B. Corley became Abilene's first mayor in 1882.
COURTESY OF THE CITY OF ABILENE

county justice of the peace and constable could provide. A careful count found 480 dwellings and seventy-five business houses in Abilene.[4] This time the initiative passed, and a February election for city officials was set.[5] In February, 195 voters chose the city leaders. The newspaper explained the low turnout by citing the extremely cold weather on election day. Thirty-seven-year-old lawyer Dan B. Corley, a recent immigrant from Buffalo Gap, was the first mayor, joined by aldermen Otto Steffens, a banker; M.W. Northington, Jr., a stockman; John Medaris; Frank Collins, who was killed in the 1884 saloon shootout, and C.C. Williams, a butcher.[6] These men represented Abilene's five "wards," electoral districts that each sent a man to the City Council to care for its interests and to make town policy. Equally important was the election of Tom Hill as city marshal.[7]

Corley moved from Buffalo Gap to Abilene with the coming of the railroad.[8] He served very effectively through 1885, at which point the city elected his successor, fellow lawyer G.A. Kirkland. Corley and Kirkland had been roommates in the early days of Buffalo Gap.[9] Kirkland served less than a full term, and was succeeded in 1886 by merchant D.W. Wriston, one of Abilene's best mayors. Wriston held the office through 1891, and after a two-year intermission, again until 1897.[10] Insurance man and former county judge H.A. Porter held the office during Wriston's "break."

Two years later, the Board of Aldermen (also called the City Council) successfully petitioned the state for a new charter designating Abilene as a "city" rather than a "town."[11] This completed the political structuring of the community and provided a firm basis for the imposition of law and order.

An immediate concern was the problem of the town's saloons. A political solution seemed possible in 1887, in the form of a statewide prohibition election. Leading Abilenians rallied to the support of the prohibition proposal. County Judge H.A. Porter published a letter saying that he was for prohibition but that he doubted it would ever work. Though he created a firestorm of protest over the weakness of his prohibition stance, it did not seem to make Judge Porter unpopular with the electorate. They chose him to be mayor of Abilene four years later. Taylor County voted "dry" 535-270, but the "wets" carried the state by nearly two to one.[12] The matter would come up again in the next decade as a countywide initiative.

The U.S. government cast a vote of approval for Abilene's potential when it installed the headquarters of the U.S. Quartermaster Department for Northwest Texas in Abilene. The appointee was a young man with the remarkable name of George Washington.[13] Then, in 1885, the government transferred its West Texas weather station from Fort Concho to Abilene, closer to the region's growing population density. The move was the result of lobbying by J. Stoddard Johnston and Gen. John Sayles and his son Henry, all of whom "were interested financially in Abilene, the new and growing town on the Texas and Pacific railroad."[14] The nation's weather forecasting was in the hands of the U.S. Army Signal Service and its civilian employees at the time. The head civilian weatherman at Fort Concho, Isaac M. Cline, had passed through Abilene only a few months earlier on his way from his previous post in Little Rock. Among the government paraphernalia he brought back to Abilene with him in 1885 was a Bible that the Signal Service (and later the Weather Bureau) used to swear in new recruits.[15] The Army recognized that the growing city on Cedar Creek was going to be the center of population and agriculture in the region.

Cline began attending First Baptist Church and fell in love with the organist, Cora Bellew, the pastor's niece. They married in 1887 and soon were blessed with a baby daughter. In his spare time, the multi-talented Cline served briefly as editor of the local newspaper. Cline's tenure at the Abilene weather station ended in 1889 when he was promoted to the vital post at Galveston, where he would direct all weather operations in Texas. Unfortunately for the family, they were still there in September 1900, when a tremendous hurricane wiped the city out. Over 6,000 people died, among them Mrs. Cora Cline. Isaac and his daughters survived.[16]

As soon as the town developed, the United States Post Office began operations. Post offices existed all over the county as the hinterlands filled up. Buffalo Gap immediately lost its postal pre-eminence to the town on the railroad. One of Abilene's earliest postal supervisors was Mary Houston Morrow, who came to town with her husband in 1886 and became postmistress in 1889, serving until 1911. It probably didn't hurt her in gaining the plum appointment that she was Sam Houston's daughter, and as widely beloved in Abilene as her father had been in Texas in his heyday.[17]

Law and Order

The first peace officer charged with enforcing the city statutes was John Thomas Hill, a Kentuckian. Too young to have fought in the Civil War, Hill nevertheless had gained experience in the U.S. Army on the northern plains. Leaving the army, he took jobs as a peace officer in Baird and Buffalo Gap. Hill came to Abilene and ran for the office of town marshal in early 1883. He was active in public affairs, joining the first volunteer fire department as part of the bucket brigade. A more thankless aspect of his job was collecting the city's taxes. After serving satisfactorily for a time, Hill met a violent end, not in the course of his duties, but as the result of a hunting accident.[18] Law enforcement was a dangerous business, as shown by the death of Walter Collins in the 1884 saloon shootout. But Abilene was beginning to settle down. Despite all the occasional commotion caused by drunken cowboys and jealous saloonkeepers, "Marshal J.T. Hill ran a quiet town."[19] Of course, Abilene still had a few rough edges.

Chief J.J. Clinton, longtime Abilene police and fire chief. Clinton Street honors his memory.
COURTESY OF JACK NORTH

After Hill's untimely death, the city held an election for a replacement. Two candidates sought the job, and in due course, W.A. George won the post. It is likely that his opponent, John J. Clinton, lost some votes for being a Roman Catholic and an immigrant from Ireland. But George found the job not to his liking and resigned, at which time the City Council appointed Clinton to take over. The right man and the right moment had met!

Clinton soon had any remaining rambunctiousness quieted. His credentials were as distinguished as his subsequent performance. Clinton always wore his Confederate veteran's badge, signifying his service in the Civil War. Right after the war, he held the post of deputy marshal in Dodge City during that notorious town's wildest days. As an Indian fighter, he was involved in the scrap that was immortalized in Frederick Remington's painting *Fight for the Water Hole*. Clinton came to Abilene, Texas, in 1884 and signed on as an assistant to Marshal Hill. He had a reputation for being tough and willing to use his gun if need be, but also for being a gentleman. He became a beloved figure in Abilene, serving for over thirty-seven years as city marshal and then chief of police. Clinton, a fearless man, killed only one man during his tenure as marshal and police chief, but that was enough to cause him to quit carrying a gun, preferring to work unarmed. That could be dangerous, as criminals took occasional shots at him and he was stabbed once.

One day a year, Clinton took out his gun for a tradition that began soon after he took office. The new marshal heard that some cowboys intended to shoot up the town at midnight on New Year's Eve. Clinton ordered that the twenty-three Abilene saloons close at that hour. To signal the moment, he stood at the corner of South First and Chestnut and fired six shots in rapid succession into the air. This event continued every year, even after Abilene passed a local-option prohibition law. Indeed, one of his deputies continued the tradition for some years after Clinton's death in 1923.[20]

The tall, erect Clinton worked in collaboration with the Taylor County sheriff, and for most of the early years, that man was 5-foot 4-inch John V. Cunningham. Cunningham was first elected in 1880, and with two gaps (both his own choice), he served continuously through 1908. At one point, when he resigned to become a United States marshal, Cunningham received a certificate from the citizens of the county attesting to the quality of his service by saying no Texas county ever had a better sheriff.[21] He was one of eight West Texas sheriffs produced in the immediate Cunningham family.[22]

Physical Infrastructure
Fire and Water

For most of the 1880s, Abilene was a city built of wood, heated by open fireplaces or wood-burning/coal-burning stoves, and lighted by kerosene lamps. Abilene was a conflagration waiting to happen, and it did not have to wait long. On the evening of August 27, 1881, only five months after the town-lot auction, a blaze erupted in the T.S. Horn Saloon on South First and quickly spread both east and west, destroying large sections of the south-side business district. A volunteer bucket brigade, aroused in the middle of the night, could do little to stem the holocaust. According to the burned-out *Abilene Reporter*, printed in Baird the next day, the crisis was great—"One-Fourth of Town Lain in Ashes."[23]

Fires were an ongoing concern, and the townspeople took steps to deal with them. This took two forms, one organizing a fire brigade and the other securing a dependable water supply. Initially, the men of the town formed bucket companies and used whatever water was handy. Citizens often stored barrels of water in their front yards to be drawn on for all uses. Anybody could pitch in. This obviously was not going to be sufficient, and the prominent young men of the town formally organized themselves as a fire company, electing S.H. Leavell as chief.[24] After the creation of a City Council, tax moneys could be applied to providing equipment for the volunteer organization.[25] In February 1886, the council appropriated funds for a fire wagon, a device that arrived in April. It was needed. A Pine Street building caught fire at 3 A.M. March 12, 1886, but the night watchman, who found it, fired his pistol and aroused enough sleepy men to put it out.[26] Less than a week later, a blacksmith shop on Walnut burned to the ground.[27] And a prairie fire east of town threatened the community in June.[28] With a drought firmly fastened upon the area, there would be more of those.

The fire company began practicing with the wagon, which was pulled by hand or, sometimes, drawn by a quickly drafted horse. Membership in a fire company carried a substantial social cachet, and what Victorian belle could resist a man in uniform? As time went on, more fire companies were organized, and Police Chief Clinton became the fire chief as well.

The second element of combating fire was the availability of water. This was a necessity for more than firefighting. Abilene's proximity to Cedar Creek was a principal reason for its locating the town there. The first attempts to utilize the creek came from the T&P, which dammed it just south of the tracks. This provided a temporary water supply for the community, although no piping system was yet available. Freighters (Dan Foley on the north side, William Campbell on the south side) provided the townspeople and businesses with water by hauling it in wagons to barrels in strategic locations. Likewise, the town built a storage cistern on each side of the tracks. Some people attempted to dig wells, but most were either dry or yielded non-potable water. Other citizens provided their own water from cisterns that collected rainwater from the roofs of houses.

The first reliable public water came from a dam built in 1884 on Lytle Creek three hundred or so yards above its juncture with Cedar Creek (present-day Cal Young Park), creating what was called "Lake Cameron."[29] The city contracted with the Grosscup and Keith Company to lay water mains and find a supplementary source of water. This they did in 1885 by digging a large well on Cedar Creek and installing over 22,000 feet of mains and thirty fireplugs. In 1886, the city

One way of suppressing the dust in early Abilene was to sprinkle water on the streets.
COURTESY OF HARDIN-SIMMONS UNIVERSITY

also erected a standpipe towering to a height of eighty-five feet on "Standpipe Hill."[30] This provided pressure for the system and was filled by pumps located nearby. Operations were transferred from Grosscup and Keith to a local waterworks company in 1886.[31]

Streets

Abilene streets were left pretty much to the care of neighboring merchants or residents. They were dusty most of the time and muddy the rest. During the drought of the mid-1880s, "a large amount of money was subscribed by the businessmen of Abilene to start a sprinkler on Chestnut and Pine Streets."[32] Obviously, that was one of the dusty times. In June 1886, the city attempted some improvements, mainly grading, beginning with the north-side business district and then continuing on the south side. Many of the streets, the council said, were "in bad condition."[33]

A partial solution to the problem of traversing Abilene streets was a trolley system. The City Council granted a franchise for a "street railway" to several leading citizens in 1886, with the proviso that construction begin within two years. It didn't.[34] Wooden sidewalks in front of some businesses helped pedestrians but did nothing for the main thoroughfares, which were plied by water wagons, drays, cotton wagons, bone wagons, wool wagons, and other heavy vehicles, not to mention horses, mules, donkeys, buggies, surreys, chaises, and the occasional hardy pedestrian.

Electricity

Electricity finally came in 1890. A proposal for the introduction of electricity by "an eastern company" came before the City Council in June 1886 but was tabled. J.M. Berry, head of the telephone exchange, introduced the idea.[35] The *Taylor County News* had been agitating for the introduction of electricity for several years.[36] Adolph Heyck, son of Theo Heyck, began tinkering with a generator at a machine shop on South First. It made bulbs glow and "lighted the building and yard quite nicely" in April 1890.

Several local men secured a charter in January for the "Abilene Electric Light and Power Company" and began to implement their dream. They built a generating plant at North Second and Plum, powered by a steam engine. On April 10, the city turned on seventeen arc lamps in the downtown area. By May, electricity was available to homes. It was a primitive system and didn't always work well. It turned off at midnight. Still, it was a major step forward.[37]

Electricity made other services possible. Abilenians needed ice to preserve their food supplies. In February 1886, the town witnessed the groundbreaking for an ice factory. The ice factory "raised steam" on August 19 and prepared to operate at a capacity of 100,000 pounds of ice per day.[38] In 1890, with electricity now available, Henry Pfaff opened an ice plant just across Cedar Creek and north of the railroad.[39]

Also in 1886, the machinery for a steam laundry arrived. It was installed in the Grosscup Building on Pine Street."[40] The waterworks company owned two-thirds of the stock, and the idea was to sell the balance locally.[41] F.W. Grosscup, head of the water company, was also president of the ice company; one of the very few Hispanic names of the era, A.C. Garcia, became vice president.[42] And a month later, local citizens applied to the City Council for a charter for a street railway.[43]

Telephones

Part of the boom of 1885 was the imminent installation of a telephone system. C.W. Roberts was the entrepreneur seeking to introduce this modern device. This would be quite an accomplishment for a frontier town—Alexander Graham Bell had invented the telephone less than a decade earlier.[44] By the end of the year, the newspaper reported that "the Abilene telephone system was almost complete. The telephone was a novelty to a great many citizens."[45] But the 1885-87 drought put an end to that dream, and Roberts had to wait another ten years before it could be realized.[46]

By the end of 1891, Abilene had the rudiments of modern utilities in place. But only the rudiments, the opening wedge—the next fifteen years would see a truly complete system in place to enhance the needs of modern life.

Cultural Infrastsructure
Education

In the original plat, Johnston set aside land for a school on the northwest corner of Third and Cedar. Classes first met in a tent between Hickory and Cedar, under the tutelage of Miss Bell Clark, but a frame school went up on the site in 1883. The building served for various civic purposes, including church meetings.[47] P.M. Barnes, a thirty-year-old Kentuckian, was hired to teach in the school.[48] The 1883 incorporation ordinance gave Abilene a tax base to support schools. Education was still a city government function. That allowed the opening of a second school at North Third and Hickory. The growing town built a primary and grammar school at South First and Chestnut in 1884.

H.A. Tillett held the superintendent's job for a while in 1883 and 1884. Tillett was a young, broke lawyer when he arrived in Abilene. He teamed up with another young, broke lawyer, Joseph E. Cockrell. The school board elected Cockrell, who had been a teacher at Austin College, to the superintendency, but he demurred, suggesting his law partner in his stead. "I told him I didn't want the job," said Tillett, "but he made me take it, for it paid a salary of $125 per month . . . and Joe pointed out that it would keep us eating while he built up the business of our law partnership." Tillett had gone to a military school and soon instilled in the school a military discipline "that was the talk of the town."[49] Boys and girls were rigorously segregated at school, but that did not keep them from walking home together, or perhaps riding home, since most kids, boys and girls, had a burro to ride.[50]

In 1885, Col. J.H. Cole, a Confederate veteran, began a four-year stint as superintendent. He increased enrollment, hired new instructors, and expanded curricula. Did he relax discipline? Probably not. In 1886, the district reported 457 students, and the school buildings were dangerously overcrowded.[51]

Though students were taking high school classes as early as 1882,[52] Abilene's first high school opened its doors in 1887 in a rented building at South First and Sycamore. The building formerly warehoused beer and ice, and the students called it the "Beer and Ice Seminary." The following year, six students graduated from the Beer and Ice Seminary. A second high school building, the first to be erected with that educational purpose in mind, went up at South First and Peach in 1889. It held numerous students and as many as twenty-five teachers. The site continued to serve Abilene's educational needs in later years, when AISD built another high school on the spot, a building that later became Lincoln Middle School.[53]

Simmons College

The time came when Abilenians decided they wanted to have a college. Buffalo Gap, Belle Plain, and Merkel had all had one at one time or other. Religious denominations, not the state, built colleges in that era, and the Baptists, the strongest church in town, were in a position to do just that. But the impetus came in 1888 from Judge Henry Sayles, a Presbyterian. He approached the pastor of First Baptist Church, G.W. Smith, about making a beginning on a college. Smith recruited leading citizens (and Baptists) James Parramore, Clabe Merchant, K.K. Legett, and Will Young to endorse the project. In 1890, Legett and J.S. Williams presented the proposal to the Sweetwater Baptist Association, a loose fellowship of congregations that stretched to El Paso. President R.C. Burleson of Baylor was present at the meeting and spoke vigorously against it, but the resolution passed and a committee was appointed. Otto Steffens, a Catholic, offered sixteen acres north of Abilene and a cash gift of $10,000. Legett drafted a charter for Abilene Baptist College, which was a description, not a name, and trustees were appointed.

Rev. Smith, now between pastorates, worked hard to gather the funds necessary to complete the enterprise. The needed amount seemed slow in coming for the as-yet-unnamed school until a New York Baptist preacher named James B. Simmons heard of the matter and gave a generous donation, sufficient to get the school going. The grateful trustees named the school Simmons College, though the modest Simmons had another name in mind, "Christlieb College."

Rev. James B. Simmons, benefactor of Simmons College. COURTESY OF HARDIN-SIMMONS UNIVERSITY

Simmons added to his initial grant on several occasions and left a sizeable amount of his estate to the school.[54] And it was another Sayles Presbyterian, Gen. John Sayles, who presided at the cornerstone-laying on July 4, 1891. Gen. Sayles was a bona fide Civil War general, former grand master of the Masonic lodge of Texas, author of major books on Texas law, and the town's leading attorney. He led the Masonic ceremony that leveled the cornerstone.[55] It was one the biggest gatherings Abilene had ever seen, and it took three hours to feed the assembled multitude. Simmons soon became the pride and joy of all Abilene.[56]

Churches

The first church organization in Abilene, the Presbyterians, predated the city's birth by a couple of weeks. After meeting in a schoolhouse for several years, the growing Presbyterian congregation acquired a building of its own in late 1884. C.R. Dudley was the first full-time minister. That congregation spun off another group that united with the Cumberland Presbyterian Church (Buffalo Gap College was a Cumberland institution) in 1885. This body erected its own building in 1889 at South Third and Elm.[57]

Before 1881 was over, the Baptists and the Methodists were also in business in the community. A group of Methodists began meeting in mid-1881 and were sufficiently well-organized by November to have a pastor appointed to them, the Rev. G.W. Riley. They acquired a lot on Butternut Street and erected the town's first church building in 1883. Subsequently, they outgrew that modest prairie gothic structure and began a more elaborate building across the street in 1889. They moved into the new sanctuary in late 1890.[58]

A Baptist church was not far behind. Dr. Owen Pope, head of the missions program for Texas Baptists, visited Abilene in December 1881 and, aided by the Methodist editor C.E. Gilbert, whose wife was a Baptist, succeeded in organizing a congregation that included Mrs. Gilbert and the prominent cattleman J.H. Parramore. For 1882 and 1883, the Baptists met wherever they could, including city facilities, schools, and the Methodist building.[59] The congregation grew quickly, including many prominent people, and they commissioned the construction of a building of their own on August 4, 1883.[60] They moved into the new building in the fall of 1883. A wintertime baptism in Lytle Creek made it abundantly clear that an inside baptistry was needed. When it was installed in 1884, it was "the first of its kind in West Texas." Early pastors included M.H. Jones, S.L. Knight, W.A. Whittle, and, from 1886 to 1892, George W. Smith.[61] The Baptists sponsored a revival in August 1885 led by one of their own, Maj. W.E. Penn, which attracted a large crowd who were accommodated in a 3,000-seat tabernacle.[62]

The Episcopalians had had a presence in the area for several years. Itinerant missionary priests served the little Abilene Episcopal group meeting in a school building. But on Christmas Eve 1883, they laid the cornerstone of what came to be called "the little stone church" at North Third and Orange.[63] The property came from J. Stoddard Johnston, a fellow Episcopalian. A major gift from a lady in

Massachusetts enabled construction of the building, with the proviso that the congregation's name be changed from St. Paul's to "Church of the Heavenly Rest." The bishop appointed Dr. George H. Wiggins as first rector. Several ministers succeeded Wiggins over the remainder of the decade before Rev. Robert S. Stewart took over to serve a four-year tenure.[64]

The Restoration Movement emerged from the camp-meeting revivals of the early nineteenth century in Tennessee and Kentucky. Over the years, the membership grew and spread west but also began to separate into two factions, one conservative group calling itself the Churches of Christ and another progressive movement calling itself the Disciples of Christ. Among other issues, they differed over whether to allow instrumental accompaniment to singing in worship services. They landed in Abilene in the mid-1880s, maybe as one group. Early leaders included editor W.L. Gibbs and preacher V.I. Stirman. By 1891, they were two distinct entities, each with its own adherents. The Disciples group flourished better than the other at first and can trace a continuous line back to the 1880s. The Churches of Christ did not function in an organized fashion for some time but more than made up for that in the twentieth century.[65]

There were a number of Roman Catholics among the founders of Abilene, but they seldom had services until 1885, when Father H.D. Brickley was sent to Abilene. The congregation, with aid from other faiths, built Sacred Heart Catholic Church at North Fifth and Beech in 1890. It is worth noting that most of the members were of German or Irish extraction since there was only a tiny Hispanic presence in Abilene in the nineteenth century.[66]

Other denominations contributed their presence in smaller numbers in the latter stages of the nineteenth century. Among these were Lutherans and Northern Methodists, each of whom had a presence in Abilene by 1900. Black Baptists and Methodists also made beginnings as early as 1885.[67]

Women's Clubs

Abilene can lay claim to several "firsts" in Texas. One such was the formation of a woman's study club. An 1883 woman's group called "the Reading Club" metamorphosed the following year into "the Shakespeare Club."[68] A few years later, the Texas Federation of Women's Clubs acknowledged the Abilene group to be the first in the state. If this seems a bit high-toned for an infant prairie town, it may be recalled that Shakespearean productions were routinely presented in the West, and many a cowboy could recite the lines of Hamlet or Lear along with the actors. Another group called the "Hesperian Chautauqua Circle" (Hesperian generally refers to the west, which could be one connotation, but also to the Evening Star, which might imply evening meetings) organized in 1889 and the XXI Club in 1892, with a "Roundtable" in 1895 and others to follow. Finally, the several clubs coalesced into an alliance called "the City Federation of Women's Clubs" in 1898.[69] Women's clubs were a new phenomenon on the American scene. They began in Boston in the early 1870s and spread either individually or in a network of local groups called "Sorosis."[70] The Shakespeare Club was a pioneer in more ways than one.

"There's Nothing to Do in Abilene"

That frequent lament of local teenagers could undoubtedly have been heard around Abilene in the decade of the eighties, but it was no more true then than it is now. If nothing else, one could simply turn out to watch the fires.

Two opera houses and several hotel dining rooms provided facilities for dinners, musicals, balls, and other events, quite aside from the dubious entertainments afforded in the local saloons. A huge masquerade ball was the highlight of the Christmas season in 1883.[71] Firemen's balls occurred annually.[72] Men's lodges proliferated—the Masons, the Knights of Pythias, the Knights of Honor, the Odd Fellows, the Woodmen of the World, later the Elks.[73] Paramilitary drill teams like the Abilene Cadets and a town brass band occasionally performed their marches and concerts. The brass band formed in late 1882, even before the town incorporated. "In the early days [1884], Abilene had a band that won a reputation, and it was composed of splendid musicians." They were sometimes called the "Cow Boy Band."[74] Weddings were often elaborate affairs, as were Christmas celebrations[75] and Fourth of July picnics.[76] Church suppers, baptisms (at least for those denominations that practiced immersion), and revivals were also social spectacles. For those really dull days, you could stay inside and read the old newspapers that were sometimes employed as wallpaper.[77]

Other fads seemed a bit questionable. "The grand jury has raised a rumpus by presenting some of the boys who have tackled poker too often lately. The informer climbed an awning post to catch on."[78] The town was bitten by the horse-racing bug in 1886. In February, the activity was at "a fever heat. Stockmen and jockeys were exchanging money at a lively rate."[79] Then it got even hotter. A match race between "Maggie May" and "Mormus" "resulted in a squabble. It was reported that it will be contested by law." Over $1,500 was at stake.[80] The racing and betting took place west of Catclaw Creek, outside the city limits, where gambling was not illegal. Cockfighting did not seem so obnoxious then as now; it was another forum for betting. Fights were attended by the best people.[81] The fights were held near the stock pens at the end of North First.

The *Abilene Reporter*, in an effort to boost the economy of the county, sponsored the first county fair in 1884 in collaboration with the "Abilene Board of Trade." Unlike later versions of the event, the 1884 fair was located in the second floor of a building on North First Street. It featured agricultural products and a few animals. "Young people looked forward eagerly to the Fair as a time of amusement to break the usual drab every-day existence they knew."[82] This fair featured fruits and other crops, and the first big stand of cotton known in the county. The 1885 fair was on Cedar Creek north of the railroad. This showed more animals, especially fast horses. At first mainly a local event, the fair developed by 1889 into what was called from then on "the West Texas Fair," held for a time at South Ninth and Oak.[83] This one was a major event, complete to a speech by James W. Throckmorton, governor of Texas. The managers of the fair gave prizes for various kinds of stock, several types of fruits, grains, and vegetables, cotton, and prepared food items. The best of these went in the fall to the Texas State Fair in Dallas and reaped for Taylor County the "sweepstakes" award for the best county entry. Tall cotton indeed for a frontier county![84]

Economic Infrastructure
Livestock

The economy of Abilene in the beginning was based on stockraising and agriculture. People had to make a living with the resources available. Grass and fertile soil were two of those resources, but there were others. It took imagination to see that a good profit could be made from picking up buffalo bones, as mentioned earlier.

Abilene was a major shipping center for Taylor and adjacent counties, which was what the T&P had hoped from the beginning. In 1888, the city claimed to have dispatched more range cattle to market than any other Texas shipping point.[85] Trail drives continued to the north to the Kansas railheads and to the Colorado and Nebraska grasslands, but some of the cattle headed north could now be loaded on trains bound for Chicago, Indian Territory or East Texas right in Abilene. The town's founders had promised as part of their agreement with the T&P that they would construct holding pens near the Abilene depot. These were located in the general area around what is now "Frontier Texas."[86]

The wool business was a staple of the Abilene economy during the city's early years. Prominent citizen Theo Heyck was the city's biggest wool merchant, operating a warehouse at North First and Cedar with a capacity of over 4,000,000 pounds of wool. The shipping of sheep into town and of wool out of town was a major element of the railroad freight business. Sheep trains from the west, sometimes as many as four at one time, stopped just short of the railroad's crossing of Catclaw Creek a couple of miles west of town. When the car doors opened and the sheep poured out, it "looked more like water pouring over a long dam than anything else."[87]

Some sheep were trailed into the region overland, sometimes from Callahan County, sometimes from as far as New Mexico.[88] Shearing was usually done on the range, with the wool being hauled into town on huge, high-wheeled wool wagons that could hold three to four tons each. These were drawn by teams of donkeys. On one occasion, it took sixty-four donkeys to pull a single bogged-down wool cart out of a mudhole on Pine Street.[89]

Abilene expected to handle 3,000,000 pounds of wool from the spring clip of 1882.[90] In 1883-84, Abilene claimed to be the largest wool market in the state. The following year that boast was scaled back to a more modest "second wool market in the state."[91] Five years later, the Census Bureau showed that Taylor County was still sheep country with 36,532 sheep and 28,330 cattle. In fact, sheep and cattle were usually present in the county in roughly equal numbers for the first century of the town's existence.

The Distribution Point

Abilene's location on the railroad made it a funnel for all kinds of goods and services. Because Runnels, Tom Green, Concho, Jones, Haskell, Knox, Stonewall, and other counties even more remote were not on the railroad (at least not yet), their goods had to come through

Abilene. Abilene served a vast hinterland, sometimes reaching as far afield as Dickens and Crosby counties.

The federal quartermaster in Abilene served all the way into the Panhandle. Trains dropped off the U.S. mail for distribution to other post offices not only in Taylor but also in the other counties, and picked up the return posts. The bone collectors came from over 100 miles to deposit their treasures at the railroad. Abilene was a communications nexus, with a busy telegraph station. It was so busy, in fact, that a second line had to be installed in November 1882.

Tommie Clack, whose family moved to Taylor County in 1870s. Miss Tommie, along with her sister Miss Bobbie, were long-tenured Abilene educators. Clack Street and Clack Middle School honor the family's memory.
COURTESY OF HARDIN-SIMMONS UNIVERSITY

It was also a commercial center for the same reasons. Further, the town attracted entrepreneurial types from the very beginning, and many of them turned out to be very successful.

As the economic focus of the region, Abilene attracted the country folk roundabout. Though business could bring people to the city on any day of the week, the rural men made sure to come to town for "trade" on First Mondays. A vacant lot in the downtown area was the agreed-upon gathering point for stock trading—horses, cattle, mules, especially. Since there were numerous tricks to this enterprise, it was "buyer beware." First Mondays attracted serious traders, or others who simply wished to swap stories, not animals.[92]

For women and children, Saturday was the big day. Tommie Clack recalled "on Saturday, the horses would be hitched to the wagon and Papa and Mamma and the children, dressed in their best jeans or gingham, as the case might be, were all ready to go to town. Once arrived at the courthouse grounds, Papa and the boys would water the horses at the public water trough and Mamma and the girls would go 'trading.' We never 'shopped.' We 'traded,' often in the literal sense, swapping eggs, butter, vegetables—anything marketable—for goods needed at home. We walked from store to store on the narrow board sidewalks or on the dusty, sometimes muddy, streets, seeing friends or stopping to visit."[93]

Agriculture

Though cotton was not a major crop for the county in the first two or three years, it soon assumed much more significant proportions. By late 1882, hints of a coming boom in cotton began to appear. "An occasional wagon load of cotton was seen on the streets of Abilene, which is quite a novelty here," one of the newspapers commented.[94] Three years later, cotton was no longer a novelty. "The streets of Abilene," the citizens read, "were crowded with prairie schooners loaded with cotton. The staple was remarkably fine and silky."[95] Cotton continued to expand in the county—in 1906, in the earliest statistics available, Taylor County ginned 43,934 bales. It was a boast of the county that it was great cotton country and that it was free of boll weevils and other problems.

Prosperity

So Abilene became the business center of a booming region. All that population growth meant more rail traffic, so that the T&P had to build a new depot in the spring of 1883.[96] Several important wholesaling enterprises got their start in the city, especially the grocery empires of J.A. Radford and H.O. Wooten. People came from miles around for their supplies—ranch goods (saddles, blacksmithing, veterinary supplies), farming equipment and seed, groceries, dry goods, "racket stores," furniture, drugs. They found anything they needed for building—lumberyards, carpenters, stonemasons. They found services—barbers, surveyors, real estate dealers, doctors, dentists, bakers, even confectioners. The traveling salesmen (also known as "drummers") and visiting cowboys found hotels, boarding houses, and saloons. Even before Abilene became the county seat, it had its share of lawyers. That number increased after 1883.

The mood in Abilene in the spring of 1885 bordered on euphoria. It was probable that the population already topped 5,000. The Abilene National Bank formed that spring with a capital of $100,000. It replaced the loosely organized loan and deposit operations of William Cameron and Company, the lumber dealers. J. M. Daugherty was the bank president, and Cameron, whose principal business was his growing lumber enterprise, was the vice president.[97] Well diggers a mile east of town found a mineral that looked very much like silver ore.[98] Workers completed the new Abilene Opera House, and the "magnificent" scenery for its stage was on the way from Chicago. A big brick building with an iron front went up on Chestnut. And the town was abuzz with rumors that the Gulf, Colorado, and Santa Fe Railroad was surveying a route through Abilene, headed for the Panhandle. A telephone system was going in later in the year. A waterworks contract was in preparation for signing in the fall.

Agricultural prosperity kept pace with the maturing city. One shipment of horses bound for Kansas City left by rail from the Abilene pens that spring, numbering over a thousand head. The 1885 wool clip was huge, and the town teemed with buyers. More wool was pouring in from Big Spring, Midland, and other points to be sold at the Abilene market.[99] The June wheat harvest brought yields of 30 to 35 bushels per acre for Red May and Red Mediterranean varieties and 50 to 60 bushels per acre for Nicaragua wheat. "We have the best crops in the state up here," one correspondent wrote. By fall, there were reports of a bumper watermelon crop. R.A. Seay of Lytle Gap harvested 60 bushels of oats per acre, while F.A. Miller got a yield of 80; Thomas Cross had 21 bushels of wheat and 24 bushels of rye per acre, and H. Henderson made 35 bushels of millet. "We grow as fine peaches and pears as they do in Palestine and Tyler," one man boasted.[100] Three years earlier, "nursery stock arrived . . . daily. Nearly everybody was planting fruit trees," and now they were maturing.[101] A newcomer established a vineyard in the area, claiming that Taylor County was superior to California for growing grapes. "He is a native Frenchman and grew grapes in France."[102] "Eastern capitalists," one land man said, had just bought 7,000 acres of land then miles southwest of town at the princely sum of $3.50 an acre.[103]

Drought

But hopes of unlimited growth were soon dashed. The anticipated Santa Fe extension never materialized. The weather, which had blessed the area with adequate, maybe even abundant, moisture and relatively mild temperatures in the four years of settlement turned sour. Thus far, Abilenians had only seen Mother Nature in her benevolent mood. Now they would see her other side, and the contrast was shocking. The region was hit by drought, even though it was really a small one when compared to the dry spell of the 1950s.

The Weather Service did not move its operations from Fort Concho to Abilene until the summer of 1885, so no official records exist prior to that time. The rains ceased in the late summer, though not enough for anyone to pay any special attention. In October, the first month for recorded rainfall, Abilene got 2.61 inches, exactly average for the month. Thereafter, the drought took hold. The dry winter season was even drier than usual. There were nice rains in March 1886, again in June, and over four inches in September. The newspaper exulted: "The once dry west is again thoroughly wet. There were green prairies. There was a renewal of confidence."[104] That was premature—no measurable amount fell in December, and the first three months of 1887 saw very little rain. From the summer of 1885 through the spring of 1887, the rainfall was sparse and usually came at the wrong times. April 1887 saw the end of the dry time. From April through July, Abilene got over twelve inches, a drought-buster. Those spring rains of 1887 continued through the year, and the city ended the year an inch above average. In 1888, the Weather Service recorded nearly thirty-one inches, a good seven inches above normal.[105]

All in all, not too bad—except that Taylor County had nothing to compare it against, only the preceding several good years. Further, the economy depended heavily on agriculture and grazing, and those enterprises were extremely hard hit. It felt awful, even if it wasn't quite as bad as it could have been. One observer wrote years later: "Though the year 1886 was disastrous to farmers, it was not a year of pronounced small rainfall . . . [but] there were frosts in the spring which made the crops late . . . [and] following the rains [in the spring] there was a period of forty-three days with no rain at all [and after a short, heavy June rain] the hot winds came from the southwest with daily regularity. There was no rain from June 7 until July 11, and then only local showers." This precipitated a total failure of crops, whereby a fifteen-county area made from fifteen to seventy-four percent of the usual yields.[106]

The area appealed for help from the outside. Stephens County sent a memorial to the U.S. Congress seeking aid. Ministers appealed to their fellow churchmen in other states.[107] Cries for help went from the region to Austin. The town of Abilene set up a "works program" for the relief of destitute farmers.[108]

There were some responses. The city of St. Louis donated a boxcar full of food. Clara Barton, head of the newly formed American Red Cross, came to the region for several days but found her hands were tied. Nevertheless, she donated $500 of her own money to Texas relief.[109] The state of Texas sent supplies to be doled out by the county judge. "Several carloads of provisions have been received in Abilene during the last week for drouth sufferers in Taylor County. Today Judge Porter has been quite busy dealing out to each man his share of meal and flour." Locals risked their own assets to help their neighbors. Grocer George W. Clayton of Abilene extended credit to his customers to the incredible total of $115,000, much of it borrowed on his own signature from his suppliers. Nearly all of this was repaid when the drought ended.[110]

And people left the area, seeking survival. Methodist pastor Dennis Stark at Lytle Gap (Potosi) wrote in August 1886 that "the drouth and subsequent famine have caused almost a panic among our people. The members of the pastoral charge are scattered from the Gulf of Mexico to the Pacific Coast." In a statewide newspaper, he reiterated the message: "It is exceedingly dry and hot. The stillest weather I have ever seen in this country in March and decidedly the hottest . . . We have had no rain of account here since last September . . . People are very much dissatisfied. Some are leaving the country; others don't know what to do."[111] The population of Abilene, once estimated at over 5,000,[112] did not reach that figure again until into the next century.

Unfortunately, there was not only drought to contend with. Extreme cold conditions for three winters caused a "die-off" of cattle, and those that didn't die scattered before the storms. The fences in Nolan County were all cut to allow the cattle to drift ahead of the blizzards. Some went as far as the Pecos River. In the winter of 1885-86, the county lost ninety percent of its sheep, and "a very large percent of the cattle died or were never found."[113] The *Abilene Reporter* observed in

January 1886 that "the coldest weather ever known here was experienced Thursday, Friday, and Saturday. The thermometer was down to three degrees below zero."[114] That was a bad winter, but worse was to come. For the ninety-six-year span 1885-1980, the record low for a given day in winter was set in 1885-86 only once, that terrible three below on January 8. But 1886-87 set record lows for December 5 and 27 and January 9, and the winter of 1887-88 had record lows for November 27 and 28, December 17, 21, and 22, and January 14, 15, 16, 20, and 21.[115]

Drought nearly wiped out the farmers, and blizzards nearly wiped out the stockmen. The Abilene economy was in shock and began to recover only slowly.

Transportation

Abilene's main connection with the outside world was, of course, the Texas and Pacific. It conveyed people and products in and out of the community. But there were just two eastbound and two westbound trains per day, and these connections did little to serve the needs of local commerce.[116]

A growing road network served the city, with plans for expansion. Informal trails already existed—the Butterfield mail route, bone roads, ranchers' trails. If Abilene was to grow, it had to be connected to its hinterland. It was the U.S. mail center for places as far away as San Angelo and Anson and connecting points. As the country around Abilene filled up, the postal service set up small post offices to serve the rural communities, and these were far more numerous than presently is the case.

The city and county officials expected, by law, that all able-bodied men would share in the maintenance of the roads. This was a common practice; many cities and counties had such laws. Every section line in the county had to be kept free for transportation purposes. The city appropriated funds to build rights-of-way, grades, and the necessary bridges to link Abilene with Anson, Moro, Haskell, and Coleman.

When a railroad reached Brownwood in 1885, community leaders sent a delegation to persuade the line to extend from Brownwood to Abilene, to no avail. Farmers and ranchers in the vicinity needed to bring their produce to market—that is, to the railroad. They needed access to the retail services of the town—medicine, groceries, hardware, clothing, repair services. A road network, not just trails, was essential.

Abilene hoped to be a railroad crossroads. Throughout its early years, the city heard recurrent rumors that a north-south rail line (probably the Santa Fe) would intersect the T&P at Abilene.[117] Tired of waiting, Abilenians in 1886 organized the "Abilene, Wichita Falls, and Kansas City Railroad" which would try to connect to the northern rail network through the new town of Wichita Falls. They still hoped to connect with the Gulf, Colorado, and Santa Fe currently stalled at Coleman. The citizens hoped the inevitable extension of the Santa Fe would come through Lytle Gap or Cedar Gap, but were fearful that the Santa Fe might decide to build through Buffalo Gap and bypass Abilene altogether.[118] In fact, those worst fears came to pass, but many years later.

The Secret of the Chinese Laundry

Tommie Clack recalled that "the path beside the railroad tracks leading from Pine Street to the stockpens was not the most desirable path in the early days, but it was attractive and scenic to little girls; and it was reasonably safe." It went by the shops of Chinese laundrymen.

One Wednesday evening in summer, while their mothers were getting ready for prayer meeting or were otherwise occupied, an older girl named Maude Tarpley persuaded Tommie and Bobbie Clack to sneak off with her to see what the Chinese were really like. They heard rumors about how the Chinese washed and starched the shirts of "the young dudes about town."

Unseen in the gathering twilight, the girls arrived at the huts and peeked in the windows. "There were the men with their long queues hanging down their backs, moving to and fro in the crowded room. On a long ironing board lay the stiffly starched shirts and, from a tin cup, 'Ching' would take a big mouthful of water and spurt it all over the garments to be ironed!" "Next Sunday men would wear their shirts with fronts and cuffs stiff as a board and shiny as a well-honed razor. How did we small girls who had followed Maude's advice feel? Well, we had learned that all that glamour in those shirts had come from a Chinese mouth. It was a sobering discovery." Thereafter, each girl stayed closer to home "and somehow never again took another stroll down the Texas and Pacific before prayer meeting." The Chinese left town when a steam laundry was installed in the 1890s.

Source: Clack, *Pioneer Days*, pp. 220-21.

Chapter Six
Promoters 1892–1907

Abilene began to settle down after those stormy first years. The rough-and-tumble of the frontier town gave way to the development of an economy, a political structure, and a society that were like those in the established towns farther east—but not exactly so. Likewise, the surrounding countryside metamorphosed from an open cattle and sheep range to a fenced land of farms and crops, yielding the abundance of the virgin soil—albeit reluctantly. By the end of the first twenty-five years, Abilene and the Abilene country were firmly rooted in the national culture and economy... with a distinctive West Texas flavor. This did not happen by chance.

The Board of Trade

Abilene's biographers often make the point that Abilene is a self-made town, flourishing because of the booster activities of its people. There is much truth to that idea, and the propensity was visible early on, beginning with the railroad's promotions and Stoddard Johnston's attempts to attract solid settlers. The town newspapers were among the leading boosters of the community. So braggadocious were the townspeople that outsiders dubbed Abilene "the Wind City," and not because of prevailing meteorological conditions.[1] An early form of organized boosterism was the 1888 "Abilene Progressive Committee," a promotional group set up by town merchants, each of whom contributed $25 to get things started. The APC published materials extolling the virtues of the Abilene country and put together exhibits for show at fairs in other cities.[2]

The Abilene Progressive Committee sponsored the first "District Fair" for Abilene in 1888 and publicized it all over West Texas and southern Oklahoma, plus selected other spots across the nation. The committee also fashioned entries for the State Fair of Texas in Dallas, winning a blue ribbon in 1888 and the "sweepstakes award" for the best county presentation in 1889.[3]

In 1890, the boosters changed their name to "Abilene Board of Trade," keeping the same dreams and goals. The modification of nomenclature was the occasion for publication of an advertisement for Abilene that appeared in twenty-seven newspapers across the state. The ad made the rather ostentatious claim that "this section of Texas embraces more natural advantages than any other part of the world."[4] The first Board of Trade chairman was Louis Wise, assisted by a steering committee of some twenty citizens. They adopted the policy of encouraging Abilenians to buy all they could from the local merchants and to hire local workers for their labor supply. This emphasis proved to be fairly successful.[5]

Abilene looked forward to the 1900 census, expecting to validate its claims to being a major city. When the government announced the final tally, there arose a furious outcry from Abilene. According to the feds, Abilene had 3,411 inhabitants, only 217 more than in 1890. There were only two census takers employed to enumerate Abilene's 1900 population. The northside worker was Nannie Mae Sellers, the eighteen-year-old daughter of Dr. Isaac Sellers, pastor of First Baptist Church. Her age and status hardly fitted her for the work at hand, especially when counting saloonkeepers, prostitutes, and the unemployed poor. Charles Malone, the southside enumerator, had better credentials. He was twenty-four, an accountant. Since there was as yet no official arm of government charged with taking the decennial census, the task fell to various United States marshals. They were no better qualified than their two Abilene employees. So Malone and Sellers must have had only the most rudimentary training. It is probable that they made a rather serious undercount.[6]

Certainly the town thought so. Estimates made a little later set the population at closer to 5,000. A school census in late 1900 suggested a total population at close to 5,000; the Sanborn Insurance Company mapped the town in 1902 with an estimate of 5,200. A 1905 city directory also placed the number at over 5,000. Though the Malone-Sellers numbers were certainly low, part of the discrepancy may lie in the fact that Sellers did not count Simmons College students at all, and Malone missed the big home of E.N. Kirby, soon to be Abilene's mayor. Both the college and the Kirby home were at the far edges of town, and perhaps were considered outside the assigned tract. There were clearly other holes in the count.[7]

In any case, an angry Board of Trade set for itself and the town a new objective—a population of 25,000 by 1910. To underscore the dream, they renamed their organization; it now became known as the "25,000 Club." This was a grandiose aim, since the population had officially grown but little in the last decade of the nineteenth century, but certainly worth reaching after.[8]

Political Events
Populism

A great surge of "third party" activity in the United States in the last decade of the nineteenth century was a movement called "populism." It had its roots in postbellum agrarian reform movements like the Grangers and the Greenbackers of the 1860s and 1870s, and the sev-

Abilene 25,000 Club booster band. COURTESY OF THE GRACE MUSEUM

eral Farmers Alliances of the 1880s. The Alliance movement, which began in Texas, had some small influence in Taylor County. It had an innovative political agenda, but at the time, the movement could not interest either major party in its platform. Out of this frustration emerged the People's Party (or Populists), with its strength in the agrarian areas of the South, the Plains, and the West.

In 1892, the fledgling party held a national convention in Omaha, nominating candidates for national offices and building on the Alliance platform. In the fall, its presidential nominee, James B. Weaver, carried Kansas and three other states of the Mountain West, a substantial achievement for a newly organized third party. Populism did not threaten to take Texas that year, but it did build up interest in the party's platform and found some dedicated leaders.

Taylor County was not the center of Populism in Texas, but it was not a minor player either. In the 1894 off-year elections, the Populists won a substantial foothold in Texas, and in Taylor County. The party held a nominating convention in Abilene on April 14 and picked a slate of candidates for most county offices, most state offices, and the U.S. House.

The local Populists endorsed the national party platform, which included a graduated income tax, direct election of senators, civil service reform, the eight-hour workday, and government control of railroads, telegraphs, and telephones. All but the last of those planks came to pass in the next century, and even the last item gained partial success with government "regulation," rather than outright ownership, of most public utilities. The local Populists called for strict economy in government, including reducing the wages of all elected officials. They wanted all paupers who received county assistance to be required to live and work on "the county farm." The county convention boasted that "the Populists have a strong and growing following in this county and the fall election may be uncertain until the ballots are counted."[9]

That ambitious prophecy came true, against rather high odds. The Populist candidate for the U.S. House of Representatives lost the district by only a few hundred votes. The Populists won three of the five seats on the Taylor County Commissioners Court along with a few other county offices. In city politics, usually non-partisan, a Populist gained a seat on the Board of Aldermen.[10]

In 1896, the Populists named William Jennings Bryan, already the Democratic nominee, as their candidate, too, maintaining independence from the Democrats by proposing a different man for vice president. This ploy failed, for Bryan lost to the Republican, William McKinley. The party itself lost traction in the state and local contests, including Taylor County. By the end of the century, the Populist Party had faded to oblivion, save for a few lonely voices across the country.

One of those voices was in Abilene. Just before the 1894 election, a recent arrival in the city named J.L. Hicks went to work for the *West*

Texas Sentinel, a paper published in Abilene for the regional Alliance movement. Though he left the paper with the collapse of Populism in the later stages of the decade, he continued to write columns pushing the Populist agenda.[11]

Except for the brief Populist uprising, politics remained mostly non-partisan, simply because the few Republicans in town could not muster a threat. Thus, the Democratic primary was the place where candidates were chosen and, for all practical purposes, elected. There were philosophical and tactical issues in the Democratic Party, but usually those were subordinated to the politics of personality.[12]

The Splendid Little War

Though it was an isolated, insulated, inland town, Abilene and its population kept an eye on the outside world. When the Spanish-American War erupted in April 1898, Abilene was all for it. Abilenians followed the news from Cuba about the sinking of the USS *Maine* with avid interest. The paper passed on all the rumors that came its way; the rumors were numerous and sometimes even true.

With the outbreak of war, several young men volunteered immediately and were soon on their way to the front. Abilenians W.D. Girard and Jack Cook were sent to San Francisco en route to the Philippines, a Spanish possession at the time. After a stopover in Hawaii, Cook went on, but Girard became ill and was kept in Honolulu. While convalescing, he witnessed the annexation ceremony when the islands became the United States Territory of Hawaii.[13]

The city organized a military company for service as a unit, presumably destined for Cuba. The company elected weatherman Allen Buell captain, with A.S. Hardwicke as first lieutenant and W.A. Minter Jr. as second lieutenant. The initial roster included only forty-five men,[14] but appeals soon filled the ranks to the required 100 recruits. The unit was inducted and sent to San Antonio for training.[15] It became part of the 4th Texas Volunteer Regiment. Buell was promoted to major and given command of the Third Battalion of the regiment.[16] The company got no closer to the war because it was nearly over by the time they got to San Antonio. Eventually all were discharged and sent home.

Facilities
The Lowden Empire—Money, Water, Electricity, Ice, Land

James G. Lowden was a go-getter, an entrepreneur, a wheeler-dealer, a man who dreamed big and followed up on his dreams. He came west from New York in 1885 and went to work as a bookkeeper for the Abilene National Bank when it opened that year. Before long, he was promoted to cashier and then to president and part owner when the first president of the bank, Theo Heyck, returned to his regular interests and left the banking professionals in charge.[17] Lowden entered into partnership with a rival banker, Otto Steffens, to develop utility services for the town. Eventually, they also merged their banks, Abilene National and First National, into a bank called "Steffens and Lowden." As an independent banking enterprise, this answered only to its stockholders, and not to any national or state banking regulators.[18] Later, this became the American National Bank with the same ownership team.

Originally an immigrant from Germany, Otto Steffens came to Abilene from Brownwood with extensive experience in business and banking. Like Lowden, he began as cashier, in his case at First National Bank, and rose to the office of president when J.M. Parramore went back to ranching. Steffens donated the land for the construction of Abilene Baptist College, soon to be called Simmons.[19] The Steffens and Lowden partnership prospered, and they expanded their operations to include banks in El Paso, Merkel, and Clifton, Arizona. With Fred

Cockrell, they acquired and operated an 800,000-acre ranch near El Paso.[20]

Lowden and Cockrell joined with S.P Hardwick in 1897 to develop the beginnings of a utilities operation in Abilene. Water was always a major concern in this section of West Texas. Abilene came to understand that its survival depended on finding better supplies of water than the little that could be impounded behind dams on Cedar Creek. In 1892, it seemed that artesian underground water might be the answer. A citizens committee persuaded the city to drill a well. The drilling finally stopped at 2,223 feet with no potable water. After this failure, the city negotiated for the use of the T&P water supply—small dams on Cedar and Lytle Creeks.[21]

By 1897, the needs of the growing town demanded that a better solution be found. Lowden, Cockrell, and Hardwick secured land and rights near the site of the old Eagle Colony on Lytle Creek and organized the Lytle Water Company. The company began construction of a dam on Lytle Creek a few miles south of its confluence with Cedar Creek and above the existing T&P works. The dam was nearly completed when a major storm dropped enough rain on the watershed to completely fill the lake almost overnight. Lytle Lake and the Lytle Water Company became the city's new supplier.[22]

While all that was happening, others developed different utility services. The city asked for bids for electricity, and in 1891, the winning bidders, General F.W. James and J.P. Massie, opened the Abilene Electric Light and Power Company. Electricity soon illuminated many businesses, several homes, and some city streets.[23]

The Lowden-Cockrell-Hardwick partnership bought up the Abilene electric enterprise in 1898. It had not been very profitable. Two years later, the partners also acquired the ice company. Though now owned by the same men, the water, electric, and ice businesses were never merged into a single entity. Lowden thus had a controlling in-

Power for the new trolley system came from electric wires strung high above the streets. COURTESY OF THE GRACE MUSEUM

terest in a major bank, the waterworks, the electric company, and the ice business in Abilene.[24]

This empire came tumbling down in 1905. The American National Bank went bankrupt, and since Lowden was a principal owner of the utilities, they went under too. It was a massive fiscal catastrophe for Abilene. Lowden and Steffens were indicted for violation of banking laws, to which they were subject by reason of having gone public and national with their bank. Some $145,000 was missing, and the two men, along with W.J. Thompson, were accused of embezzlement and misappropriation of funds. The government also singled out Lowden for making false reports to Washington and false entries in the books. The whole Lowden-Steffens enterprise, banks and utilities, had to be reorganized. Steffens emerged with his reputation intact, but Lowden was convicted in 1908 and sentenced to five years in federal prison. He died a broken man two years later.[25]

Fortunately for Abilene, other businessmen stepped forward to pick up the pieces. W.G. Swenson, George L. Paxton, J.M. Wagstaff, Col.

Steffens and Lowden Bank. COURTESY OF HARDIN-SIMMONS UNIVERSITY

Morgan Jones, Ed Hughes and W.H. Eddleman bought up the utilities and continued to provide services to the town as the Abilene Light and Water Company and the Lytle Ice Company.[26] Swenson, whose family had extensive ranching interests in Jones and Haskell counties, was vice president of the Citizens National Bank, the principal rival of the just-failed American National Bank.

The two new companies picked up where their predecessors had left off under Swenson as president and general manager of each. In 1908, Swenson and some of his partners formed the Abilene Street Railway Company, with Swenson as president there, too. Swenson's efforts at multiple ownership were more successful than Lowden's.

Two Telephone Companies

Neither Lowden nor Swenson had a hand in the telephone business in Abilene. That new invention, only five years older than Abilene, came to town in 1895. An earlier attempt had been thwarted by a drought-fueled recession. But now the town could support a system, and C.W. Roberts received a franchise from the city to begin the service. The first customers were almost all businesses, and their principal interest was in inter-city communication. The company installed a line to Anson in 1896 and to Merkel in 1897. Local farmers and ranchers along the line soon found they could tap in and began siphoning off service and dependability.[27]

In 1900, the city granted permission for another company to operate its system in Abilene. The Northwestern Telephone Company completed its network by the end of the year, with taller poles, and so Abilene had two competing telephone systems. As time went on, residents also began to subscribe to one or another of the companies. Since the two did not interact, many downtown merchants found it useful to subscribe to both of them and to advertise two numbers— one for the Roberts system, called the Abilene Telephone Company, and another for the Northwestern system. J.W. Evans Staple and Fancy Groceries, for example, was 35 on the Northwestern (later Southwestern) line and 298 on the Roberts (later called Independent) line. The Emporium Millinery was 230 on the Northwestern line and 191 on the Roberts system.[28] This state of affairs went on for some time.[29] By 1907, the two companies had 655 customers in Abilene.[30]

Despite complications, Abilene entered the new century with a number of modern services, the like of which was not imagined only a few years earlier. There was even the beginning of gas service in 1906, led by W.A. Minter Jr., but it would be several more years before it was reliable and widely available.[31] Abilene was positioned for growth.

New Institutions
The Federal Court

As a town on the make, Abilene needed a variety of new enterprises to enhance its reputation and its economy. One such seemed to be a federal district court. Abilene began and continued under the jurisdiction of the court in Graham, but as settlement expanded westward, Graham was no longer centrally located. Either the judicial district had to be reconfigured or the seat of the court moved to a more accessible location, like, for example, Abilene.

Abilene sent lobbyists to Washington as early as 1890 to seek transfer of the court, but seemingly to no avail. It took the election of an Abilenian, Judge J.V. Cockrell, to Congress to make the deal, but it finally worked out. The government erected a new federal building in Abilene in 1903 to house the district court and the Abilene post office. The post office, formerly on Chestnut, was presided over by a postmistress, Mary Houston Morrow, youngest child of the Texas hero Sam Houston.[32]

The Epileptic Colony

Abilene also sought a state facility to enhance its status and pad its economy. In 1896, Henry A. Tillett of Abilene successfully ran for the state senate on a platform of securing some such institution. A humanitarian by background, Tillett sought to persuade the state to establish an epileptic colony in Abilene. The malady was so poorly understood at the time that many victims were housed either in prisons or insane asylums. Prison overcrowding was a major motivation for the legislature in finally granting the proposal. The notion of a "colony" plan for the care of those seriously afflicted by the problem was in its infancy but had been successfully pioneered in New York, among other states. The idea was to provide a home for epileptics where they could be cared for with a maximum of individual liberty, not mixed in criminals or the mentally ill. A work program would also help fill the days. Given the imperfect understandings of the day, this proved to be a most effective form of treatment.[33]

One flaw in Abilene's original application was the lack of an abundant water supply. The colony's need was one reason for the construction of Lytle Lake. With the water supply question settled, the next

The Epileptic Colony. COURTESY OF THE GRACE MUSEUM

matter was a site. Citizens managed to gather enough money to purchase a section of land east of Lytle Lake from the ubiquitous J.G. Lowden and Fred Cockrell.[34] Tillett got the ball rolling, but the other local legislators finally pushed the bill through. Heroic efforts by Rep. W.J. Bryan got the legislation passed and the money appropriated in 1900. Governor Joseph Sayers wanted to veto the bill, but Bryan put so much pressure on him that he relented, provided Bryan could get the appropriation re-passed and on his desk by 5 P.M. the same day. Bryan pushed it through both houses and dashed into the governor's office at the stroke of 5, paper in hand. True to his word, Sayers signed the bill.[35]

With a site secured and a water supply settled, work could begin on construction.

Dr. John Preston was the first superintendent of the Abilene Epileptic Colony, and he supervised the construction of six buildings, including a superintendent's home, an administration building, work areas, and inmate residences. The program employed a staff of about two dozen persons to begin with. In 1904, the first residents moved in, and the institution was off to a good start. The good start came to an abrupt halt when the colony's metal water tower collapsed, leaving them without water. But a hastily erected wooden tower served as a stopgap until better arrangements could be made. Before the end of the year, over 200 epileptics were resident in the facility. And Abilene had a nice payroll to bolster the local economy.[36]

The Agricultural Experiment Station

West Texans had been asking Washington for several years for a grasslands experiment station to aid in understanding some of the problems of range grass in the area. Preliminary investigations suggested that overgrazing was a serious problem in West Texas. The Department of Agriculture dispatched C.C. Georgeston, an "agrostologist," to Texas to select a site for an experiment station. Georgeston was looking for a particularly run-down area, and he found it on a section of land owned by Clabe Merchant a few miles northwest of Abilene. The government took a three-year lease on the land, arranging its boundaries so as to include a variety of terrains and soils, much of it with prickly pear and prairie dogs. Abilenians were not really happy to be chosen for having the poorest range conditions. At a meeting called to tout the project, skeptics objected that "none of us know, or care to know, anything about grasses, native or otherwise, outside of the fact that for the present, there are lots of them, the best on record, and that we are after getting the most out of them while they last."[37] Actually, their statement demonstrated the opposite of what they intended.

Several prominent ranchers supported the idea, and the station went forward. The managers divided the tract into several sub-sections, treating each differently. They had to cope with short rainfall, jackrabbit and prairie dog depredations, and other problems. Some of the land was harrowed and seeded, and the experiment appeared to

The new Carnegie Library. COURTESY OF BETTY LOU GIDDENS

be hugely successful in learning how to manage rangelands. "Seeing is believing," said one visitor, "and a half-blind man can see that this range is the best in this section, while before the Government took it over it was one of the poorest." Enough had been proven by the end of the test that the government decided not to extend the program, and the experiments ended when the lease expired.[38]

The Carnegie Library

Three women's groups—the Shakespeare Club, the XXI Club and the Roundtable Club—joined with the newspaper to begin a book collection in 1899. In less than a year, they hired a librarian. The clubs acquired a house at North Second and Cedar to serve as temporary quarters. They applied to the Andrew Carnegie Foundation for funds to erect a modern building on their site. Steel magnate Carnegie had sold his holdings and devoted himself to philanthropy, particularly the funding of public libraries across the nation. His foundation came through with a grant of $17,500 for a new building, and construction began in 1908.[39]

Business
Wholesale and Distribution

Abilene continued to emerge as a distribution center for the area. That meant that wholesalers could make Abilene the base for businesses serving a wide region, towns less blessed with rail facilities or too small to support a large operation, or simply late in getting started.

One such wholesale business was that of Ed S. Hughes, who dealt in hardware to retailers from Ranger to Roswell, New Mexico. He also had his own local retail outlet in a three-and-a-half story building downtown, offering all kinds of hardware and equipment, including farm implements, wagons, automobiles, motorcycles, and bicycles. It called itself the "oldest and largest hardware store in Central West Texas."[40] Another hardware wholesaler, Morgan Weaver, had some sixty employees, some of them local workers, some of them traveling salesmen.

Two of the town's movers and shakers were J.M Radford and H.O. Wooten, both wholesale grocers. Radford came to Abilene in 1882 and began a retail grocery business. In 1893, he expanded into wholesaling and branch retailing. By 1913, he had stores at Abilene, Cisco, Colorado City, Stamford, Sweetwater, Big Spring, Ballinger, Lubbock, and Alpine. His company boasted that "we operate our own cold storage plants, enabling us to handle fruits, produce, dried fruits, cereals, etc. all the year." His credit manager was a bright young man named C.W. Gill, who later founded Abilene Savings.[41] Radford saw the results of fires in Abilene and began to build in brick. Before he was through, he had financed the erection of forty brick structures in the downtown area, plus numerous homes in residential areas. He owned approximately five percent of all taxable property in town in 1923.[42]

Wooten's family came from Tyler to Buffalo Gap in 1879, when Horace was 14. After farming and completing his education at Tyler, he worked briefly there in a general store. He returned to Abilene in 1888, married, and went to work as representative for a St. Louis grocery chain. After two years with the St. Louis company, he went into the grain business for himself. Eight years later, his firm now operating stores on both sides of the tracks, Wooten decided to go into grocery wholesaling. From that start, the Wooten business grew to include fifteen branch houses. Wooten also invested in oil and ranch properties, commercial buildings, and railroads and later built the Wooten Hotel and the Paramount Theatre.[43]

Other firms dealt in candy, dairy products, petroleum products, and other consumer goods. Abilene, with its rail connections, was home base for numerous men who traveled the region on behalf of their wholesalers. They were called "drummers," out drumming up business. The Abilene post office, in a different form of wholesaling, was the distribution center for the United States mail for several surrounding counties.

The Abilene and Northern Railroad

Morgan Jones was born in Wales in 1839, son of a well-to-do farmer. Growing up, he became fascinated with the railroads that were a building across the island of Great Britain and went to work for one, focusing on the construction end of the business. It seemed to the twenty-six-year-old Jones that America was the great new railroad frontier, and so he emigrated just after the Civil War. He gained passage by escorting a shipment of dynamite from its manufacturer in Wales to Gen. Grenville Dodge, then supervising construction of the great transcontinental railroad. Upon delivery of his explosives, he persuaded Dodge to give him a job as foreman of a construction crew building the Union Pacific. After completion of the road, Jones knocked about awhile before landing in Fort Worth in 1876. There he hired on with the Texas and Pacific to try to complete sixteen miles of track from near Dallas to Fort Worth in a month and a half. The T&P would lose a substantial land grant from the state if the road were not done in time. In a flurry of activity, Jones and his crew, aided by volunteers from Fort Worth, pushed the roadbed and tracks westward. Every second counted, and the indefatigable Jones did not change clothes for two weeks. Friends of Fort Worth lobbied the state legislature for every spare second of time. In six weeks, Jones and his crews accomplished the impossible, and Fort Worth had its railroad. Jones was the city's hero.[44]

Jones engaged in the timber business in Louisiana and California before returning to railroading. With Dodge's blessing, Jones began construction of a rail line connecting Fort Worth and Denver, Colorado. Construction went forward from Fort Worth toward Wichita Falls, then pressed on across the Panhandle and eventually to Denver, running the first trains in 1888. Jones became president of the line, while continuing to work on short-line projects across the state. After the turn of the century, Jones built a track south from Wichita Falls to Seymour, the Wichita Valley Railway. In 1905, he extended the line to Stamford. Abilene, noting the construction nearby, was hungry for a second line. There had been high hopes from 1882 forward that the Santa Fe would send a line northwestward from Coleman to Abilene and on toward Colorado. But the Santa Fe continued to vacillate. In fact, as Abilene discovered in 1909, the Santa Fe finally decided to run its line through Buffalo Gap and Sweetwater, bypassing Abilene altogether. There may have been some smiles at the Gap over this—sweet revenge for losing the T&P and then the county seat. Sweetwater could stand a little taller, too.

When the 25,000 Club tired of waiting for an intersecting rail line, it began negotiations with Col. Jones in 1906 to extend the Wichita Valley rails south from Stamford to Abilene. To avoid possible problems with the T&P, the 25,000 Club decided to organize the company itself. The railroad would be called the Abilene and Northern and would connect with the Wichita Valley at Stamford. The group designated W.G. Swenson to be president of the new line. Swenson personally surveyed the route and negotiated with landowners to settle a right-of-way. The club then secured Col. Jones to do the actual construction, with a $40,000 bonus if the line could be finished by the end of 1906.

Despite labor and weather difficulties, Jones and his crews again performed a track-laying miracle. When the tracks reached the Clear Fork of the Brazos, the chief engineer resigned, leaving Jones with the task of getting a bridge across the stream. He asked the Fort Worth and Denver to send him a replacement engineer and was much chagrined when the company sent his nephew, young Percy Jones. But Percy Jones was up to the challenge and constructed the bridge. All the delays caused Col. Jones to fear he could not meet the contracted deadline, so he appealed to the Abilene men to extend the time by a month, in return for a reduced bonus. When they declined, hoping to save the whole $40,000, Jones pushed his crews with renewed fervor and, by cutting a few corners with quality, managed to get a locomotive into Abilene on December 31. Abilene had to pay up, and Jones could go back and shore up the jerry-built sections of track at his leisure. The Abilene and Northern gave the city a second railroad, giving direct service to Wichita Falls and the Midwest. It also gave Abilene wholesalers easy access to new markets. The A&N established its depot at 189 Locust, on the *south* side.

After a peripatetic lifetime, Col. Jones decided to settle down far from his native farm in Wales—in Abilene. He took rooms at the Grace Hotel and used that as his base of operations until his death in 1926. Percy and others of the bachelor railroader's nephews also settled in Abilene. The family gave the town an infusion of energy, money, talent, and service that endured into the twenty-first century. They have been businessmen, community servants, educational leaders, statewide political leaders, and philanthropists without equal.[45]

The Rural Areas Prosper

The town stabilized, but it did not seem to grow much. The hinterland, however, boomed. Taylor and surrounding counties continued to experiment with cotton. Most people thought the area was too dry for cotton, but that soon proved a misconception. Abilene shipped 2,061 bales in 1888 but over 7,500 bales four years later. Cotton became the principal crop of the region.[46] The first gin came to the county in 1888, powered by a sixty-eight-horsepower steam engine. It was capable of ginning thirty bales a day.[47] One positive element was that the boll weevil, which by 1900 was infesting much of the state, had not yet made it to the plains.

Likewise, wheat production was booming, as farmers learned to cope with the low rainfall. By 1893, nearly 6,000 acres of Taylor County farmland was sown in wheat. That supported the introduction of a flour mill, the Pioneer Mills and Manufacturing Company in Abilene, with the promise of a grain elevator a bit later.[48] The company marketed the products of this mill as far as Tucson.[49] But commitment of so much land to these staple crops meant that the county was heavily dependent on prices remaining high, and the 1893 depression soon knocked them down. Some survived by diversifying into milo, corn, maize, and sorghum, and prices recovered in a couple of years.[50]

The expansion of commercial farming implied another trend—the decline of Abilene's dependence on stockraising. Though cattle and sheep ranching continued to be important, farming displaced ranching from the center of the economic stage. Big farm families on smaller tracts replaced the scattered ranchers and their bachelor cowboys, with a much greater population density the result. The city of Abilene may have grown less than ten percent between 1890 and 1900, but the rural Taylor County population nearly doubled in the decade, from 3,763 to 7,088, then more than doubled again in the first decade of the twentieth century. Similar increases occurred in Jones, Nolan, and

Runnels counties, and adjacent counties were not behind. In 1910, Runnels, Jones and Coleman counties all joined Taylor in topping 20,000 inhabitants. The area was filling up, far surpassing the rest of Texas in percentage of growth during the same period.[51] Since Abilene was the commercial center of the area, it meant more business, more wealth, and eventually more population for the nascent city.

The Fairs

To promote Abilene's agricultural products still further, the city decided to host an annual fair. First attempts at a fair in 1888-89 were promising enough that the idea revived in 1897 in a bigger form.[52] After the depression of 1893 faded a bit, Abilene businessmen revived the fair idea with a show in November 1897. It was a relatively low-key affair but featured a parade down North Third Street to the fairgrounds near Cedar Creek. This fair had the effect of stimulating interest in a more permanent and extensive enterprise. In April 1898, a new fair association emerged with plans for greater exposure. The association gave it a name, "the West Texas Fair," secured a permanent facility near the new Lytle Lake, erected buildings and pens, and secured a commitment from the city to care for the grounds in the off-season. "A physical home gives an air of permanency to an institution and keeps its image before the public the year round."[53] It was a whopping success, featuring a promising sugar beet exhibit. This fair also provided a public spectacle, the first parachute jump in Taylor County history—2,000 feet from a balloon!

And the October 1899 fair was even bigger, with larger monetary prizes, races, band concerts, a trapeze act, extensive agricultural displays, even a wedding. As an augury of future fairs, the 1898 and 1899 fairs were marred by heavy rains. The fair promoters may not have liked the rain, but the farmers who displayed their products loved it. More was to come. The fair of 1900 was a fiasco. If the rains of 1898 and 1899 had slowed things down a bit, the deluge of 1900 almost ruined the event. Abilene got fourteen inches of rain in September and October of 1900, and surrounding counties may have gotten more.[54] The West Texas Fair floundered on until 1909, when poor management and weak farming conditions caused its abandonment ... for a while[55].

Culture
Prohibition

Abilenians had been wrestling with each other over the issue of beverage alcohol from the city's beginnings. Saloons were perhaps the earliest businesses in town, and were a major element of the local economy. Also from the beginning, there were those who sought to close them down as public nuisances, the source of much of the town's crime. Suggestions of prohibiting alcohol sales altogether were frequent in the early days, part of a national movement. "Wets" argued that prohibition would simply drive the business underground, or worse, to some neighboring town.[56]

Abilene's predilections could be seen in an 1887 statewide prohibition referendum. Texas rejected the plan by a margin of about five to three, but Taylor County approved with 535 dry votes to only 270 wets. A little later, things were different. Another initiative asking for Taylor County to close its saloons in 1894 resulted in 610 wet votes to 494 dry. The same election saw the city decide whether to go completely dry, and it stayed wet, 464 to 168.[57]

The drys did not give up and, in May 1902, got another item on the ballot calling for a countywide ban on saloons. This time, the matter passed 1,196 to 966, and Taylor County went dry, taking Abilene with it. The ban did not go into effect for another twelve months, but when it did, the city stayed legally dry for three-quarters of a century.[58]

Entertainment

A theater in turn-of-the-century Abilene featured periodic live shows. The Lyceum hosted the touring Columbia Opera Company in "La Mascotte" in September 1907, for example. The performance promised "funny comedians, pretty girls, elegant costumes," so it was not, strictly speaking, the usual operatic performance.[59] Motion pictures had not yet arrived. Edison's first feature film appeared only in 1903, so it was a bit early for Abilene to have the new technology. The Maltbie Opera House hosted plays, concerts, and other programs. It was replaced by an even bigger facility in 1895.[60]

The young crowd, and older people as well, could occasionally enjoy a dance. A dance club was organized in 1890, prompting the emergence of a rival "anti-dance club." The churches were of course opposed, all save the Catholics and the Episcopalians.[61] Nevertheless, dancing continued to be a popular entertainment. The churches countered with activities of their own—ice cream socials, picnics, reading clubs, bazaars, "tacky parties," youth groups. Among the Methodists, a new movement called the Epworth League for young people caught fire in the 1890s and enjoyed great success. Begun in 1890, it held a statewide convention in 1895 in Houston with over 3,000 delegates. Obviously, this kind of program was filling a need. One little-noticed element of the Epworth League was that girls could be officers, and many young women acquired leadership experience previously inaccessible to them.[62]

There were clubs and societies galore to fill the desire for fellowship and amusement. Women's clubs continued to grow and to work, as did fraternal orders. The town baseball team played games with nearby communities.[63]

All in all, Abilene was developing into the town that would later call itself "the buckle of the Bible belt." That description was tempered by a good deal of playful mischief and the occasional evasion of the strict standards of the day. This was, after all, still the Victorian era. To enforce good behavior on the youth, Abilene enacted an 1897 curfew law that prohibited persons under the age of eighteen from being on the city streets after 9 P.M. It proved to be difficult to enforce.[64] Today's aphorism that "nothing good happens after 2 A.M." would have read differently in the 1890s—"nothing good happens after 9 P.M."

The Right Side of Town

Many cities built around a railroad divide into two socioeconomic classes based on the tracks—the right side and the wrong side of the tracks. Abilene's founders did not intend for that to happen. The original layout of the town presumed a business district that would be both north and south of the T&P right-of-way, with space for a school on the north and a courthouse on the south and lot layout aimed at keeping things even on both sides.

By 1900 it appeared that that plan had in fact taken root. A careful analysis of Abilene's socioeconomic distribution by Karen Turner showed that the divisions of Abilene society ran more east and west than north and south. Based on a study of the 1900 census, she concluded that Abilene divided into an upper-class west, a middle-class center, and a lower-class east. Her west-central division line ran between Orange and Hickory on the north and Butternut and Elm on the south, while her central-east division ran between Pecan and Locust on the south and Walnut and Mesquite on the north. Abilene had only limited space to expand to the east. Not far from the downtown was Cedar Creek, with the possibility of occasional flooding. In the east end, the town located its stock pens adjacent to the railroad. The cemetery was a few blocks north. No bankers, attorneys, or physicians lived in the eastern third of town. None of the fifteen highest-valued residences were there, and only one high school graduate. No member of the women's clubs, only two political party leaders, three church leaders, and one automobile owner.[65]

By contrast, the western third had thirty-six bankers-attorneys-physicians, nine of the top fifteen dwellings, thirty-one high school graduates, twenty-eight church leaders, eighteen club members, fifteen political leaders, and ten automobile owners.[66]

African-Americans were the largest ethnic sub-group, and they were scattered all over town. The largest concentration was in the eastern third on the north side, but that group by itself was not a majority of Abilene blacks. A number of blacks lived in the western third, usually as servants to the wealthy white families there. The largest foreign-born group, thirty people, were from Germany, including some of the town's leaders, like merchant Theo Heyck, banker Otto Steffens, and the baker Theo Goedeke. Victoria Street is named for Mrs. Heyck. Most Germans lived in the middle third as solid tradesmen and artisans. Twenty Abilene residents were born in Mexico, but their residences were not clustered except for three who lived along Willow (now South Treadaway). The Hispanic presence in Abilene, which is today quite strong, is of relatively recent migration.[67]

Though there were some small variations, high status in Abilene's social class structure in 1900 could be identified by how far west one lived.

Education
The Baptist College

Simmons College opened with ninety students in fall 1892 with Rev. W.C. Friley as president. Friley's task was to secure a faculty, continue to build facilities, and expand the student body. Friley came to the school from other educational work, most recently in Taylor, Texas. Said one student of the time, "The Friley administration developed the college into a first-class institution. The faculty was selected with great care and was said to be composed of some of the finest educators in the Southwest."[68] In his two years as president, Friley built a men's dorm and expanded the original dining facilities.

After two years, Friley moved on, to be succeeded by Professor George Thatcher. Thatcher served for four years, working hard to build up the student enrollment with only limited success. Abilene was abundantly proud of Simmons, but the school was still stuck with an enrollment of about a hundred students. Nevertheless, Simmons graduated its first students, three young women, in June 1895.[69]

Owen C. Pope, who had fostered the birth of the college, accepted a call to the presidency in 1898. Pope, a talented, energetic, white-bearded man, faced some hard times. The faculty had shrunk, the money was not coming in, there was a revolt from a new faculty member who sought to have Pope fired, the student body consisted mostly of elementary and secondary pupils, and Pope's health was suffering. Simmons did manage to field its first football team in 1897, led by Prof. Karl Krause, who had played at the University of Chicago under Amos Alonzo Stagg. But there was no organized league, and this was an intermittent activity. Finally, President Pope resigned in 1900, but his health continued to deteriorate, and he died the following year. He was buried on campus.[70]

In 1902, Simmons secured the services of a man who seemed eminently overqualified to run a struggling little Baptist college on the edge of the prairie. He was Oscar H. Cooper, a Yale Phi Beta Kappa, a former faculty member at Sam Houston Normal and the University of Texas, former president of Henderson College and of Baylor University, former Texas State Superintendent of Public Instruction.[71] Under Cooper's sometimes-sharp-edged leadership, the school quickly grew. By 1907, Simmons enrolled 340 students.[72] It granted its first B.A. degree in 1907, and it expanded its curriculum to meet the needs of the twentieth-century college graduate. A vigorous building program added badly needed structures for housing and instruction. Cooper assembled a much stronger faculty headed by Dr. Julius Olsen. Literary societies flourished and led to debate competitions as well as study and fellowship opportunities. While student conduct was narrowly circumscribed, student pranks and fun were also part of the college scene. Cooper resigned in 1909, started a prep school of his own nearby, and eventually returned to Simmons to serve out his days as a member of the faculty.[73]

Simmons was clearly a denominational college, and the Baptist influence was quite strong. The major donor, James B. Simmons, intended for the school to be an evangelistic tool, quite in keeping with the understandings of the day in religious education.[74] To that end, Simmons insisted in 1891 that the aim of the college was "to bring young men and women to Christ; to teach them of Christ, and to train them for Christ." A few years later, Simmons amended his charter in a surprisingly tolerant way—"No religious test shall ever hinder any person, even though he be an idol worshiping Hindoo or a heathen Chinaman from entering and receiving instruction in said Simmons College." Without retracting his earlier emphasis, Simmons wanted to open doors to the world.[75] And students of several religious persuasions enrolled there. Despite the sharply drawn theological lines between denominations in 1900, there was an unusual amount of ecumenical feeling. Simmons, in fact, was adopted by all of Abilene as the town's special badge of civilization.

The success of Simmons, out in the country when erected, caused a growth spurt in that direction. A new subdivision called College Heights was one of several new neighborhoods around the college. The spaces between there and town began to fill up with houses, and Abilene experienced a substantial expansion northward. The trolley line connecting Simmons with the downtown area also contributed to development.[76]

Childers Classical Institute

Among the things held in common by the two groups that emerged from the nineteenth century "Restoration Movement" was a rational approach to religion (not, let it be understood, *rationalism* as commonly understood in the day), including an emphasis on higher education. Both had congregations in Abilene. One of the two streams, the Disciples of Christ, had a strong school in Fort Worth called Add-Ran College (later Texas Christian University). The other, called the Churches of Christ, had several small schools operating in Texas when A.B. Barret came to Abilene to preach in 1905. Barret was teaching at Southwestern Christian College in Denton at the time and saw the need for a similar school in West Texas.[77]

After preaching in Abilene and receiving a favorable reception, Barret went on to visit two other towns, Ballinger and San Angelo. He found the quality of water in Ballinger not to his liking, and his reception in San Angelo was decidedly chilly. He thought that might have been because the West Texas wind had blown away his hat, and his limited funds allowed him only to replace it with a cap, leaving him less than credible as a college founder.[78]

Barret settled on Abilene as his choice and, with the support of the local congregation, began to canvass Church of Christ membership in a wide area around Abilene in quest of funds to begin the school. The modest contributions were welcome but not quite adequate to the task of securing land and buildings and staff and students. An Abilene member named J.W. Childers made his contribution in the form of his home at North First and Victoria. He sold it to the school for a pittance and also sold additional land sufficient to comprise a five-acre campus. One condition of the sale was that the school would be named Childers Classical Institute.[79]

Barret hired local attorney J.M. Wagstaff, a Presbyterian and former college president, to draw up a charter for the school and registered it in 1906. The same year, the school opened its doors to the first group of students, twenty-five of whom were resident on or near the campus, with a total of ninety-two enrolled at one time or other during the year. It was not an auspicious start, but it was a start. Barret had scraped together a rather capable faculty to teach a student body whose curriculum ranged from elementary classes all the way through college sophomore work.⁸⁰

A.B. Barret, founder of Abilene Christian University.
COURTESY OF HARDIN-SIMMONS UNIVERSITY

The second year was little better. The Panic of 1907 affected the entire nation, including Abilene, and dried up resources. Before the end of the school year, Barret resigned, and so did several of the strongest faculty. A new president, H.C. Darden of Clyde, would have his hands full just to keep the school alive.⁸¹

The Public Schools

By 1891, the new high school building had to begin sharing classes with lower grades. A new elementary school was an urgent necessity; accordingly, the board built what it called North Ward School near the corner of North Eighth and Orange. Soon thereafter, the board erected another elementary school for southside students. Called South Ward, it was located near the corner of South Ninth and Chestnut. Both were frame buildings, and both were replaced by massive three-story brick buildings in 1902. North Ward was later known as

"Lamar" and South Ward as "Old Travis."[82] These would meet Abilene's educational needs for a while, though a new high school building was in the offing in 1909.[83]

The Galloping Goose Gets Loose

"The funniest thing that ever happened in Abilene," the newspaper called it. The event in question was the inaugural run of Abilene's new trolley system. The Abilene Street Railway System was a necessary response to the sprawling growth of the town. W.G. Swenson, head of the local electric company, was the principal organizer of the trolley system, along with other town leaders. The rail line was powered by overhead electric wires, which snaked through town from Simmons College to Fair Park (now called Rose Park). The last leg was a long run along South Seventh westward from Chestnut.

On the appointed Sunday in November, 1908, the leading men of the town, mayors and merchants, lawyers and ministers, crowded onto the only car the line yet had. They embarked on a ride from Simmons to the end of the line. All was well as they made their way through the downtown, across the T&P tracks, and on to South Seventh. The jubilant crowd, with President Swenson at the controls, looked forward to completing a successful ride as they crested the central ridge of the town just west of Sayles Boulevard.

Then panic struck, for the trolley began to accelerate down toward Catclaw Creek and the president-motorman could not get the brakes to work. As the trolley picked up speed, Swenson shouted for the three dozen dignitaries to jump off. A few did so, but many remained on the trolley until it reached the end of the tracks, plunged forward through posts and fences, and finally overturned in a large mudhole.

The city fathers were strewn hither and yon, eventually emerging covered with mud. Only their dignity was seriously injured, and the rest of the town was delighted. Not least among them were the Simmons students, who had already dubbed the car "the Galloping Goose." The fiasco could not be considered the result of Swenson's inexperience. He was the man who had owned (and personally repaired) the first automobile in Abilene. He had been driving since 1903.

In due course, the company effected repairs and installed proper safeguards to prevent a recurrence. The trolley line, with the addition of more cars, became a major asset for the city and played a significant role in its development. When McMurry College opened in 1923, the company extended a branch line from South Seventh to South Fourteenth along Grand. On hot days, the old tracks peep through the asphalt at South Eleventh and Grand today. The "Car Barn" still stands at 1021 Clinton. The metal building was erected in the 1920s as the second facility of the sort on that property, replacing the original wooden structure. For all the trolley's usefulness to Abilene, most people best recalled its maiden run. The advent of the automobile drove the line out of business in 1931.

Sources: *Abilene Remembered: Our Centennial Treasury Book, 1881-1981*, March 15, 1981, p. 22; Larry Abrigg, *Abilene Historical Landmark* (Abilene: City of Abilene, 1987), p. 11; Duff, *Abilene*, pp. 177-78.

Chapter Seven
Progress 1907-1919

Politics

The Mayor-and-Commission City Government

When E.N. Kirby was chosen mayor of Abilene in 1907, probably no one suspected that he would hold the job for the next dozen years. Abilene mayors seldom served for very long; in fact, Kirby's tenure is still the record, before or since.[1] He successfully confronted a number of serious crises during his time in office. Today, a park and a lake honor his name.

After the hurricane of 1900 made recovery questionable in Galveston, that city experimented with a new form of municipal government, the mayor-and-commissioner system. The idea quickly spread across the United States, coming to Abilene in 1911. Abilene worked under this "mayor-and-commission form" until 1947, when the community adopted the "city manager form."

In 1911, Kirby oversaw the election to allow Abilene to incorporate itself under the provisions of a new state law allowing revised forms of municipal governance.[2] Under the provisions of the law, Abilene could restructure its governance "from an Aldermanic to a Commission form of government with enlarged powers, particularly in the way of improved streets, public parks, new buildings, and a larger water system,

Mayor E.N. Kirby, Abilene's longest-serving mayor. Kirby Lake and Kirby Park are named for him.
COURTESY OF THE CITY OF ABILENE

and taking care of the city by more stringent sanitary regulations."[3] The 1911 plan called for four commissioners, two resident on the south side and two on the north side. However, the whole city voted for each of the four places. Each of the four elected city commissioners would have a specific portfolio of responsibilities for the elements of city operations—one (W.O. Shackelford) would have Fire and Water, one (J.P. Wooten) Police and Health, one (J.N. Ferguson) Streets and Lights, and one (E.H. Boone) Finance and Revenue. The existing system formed the City Council from an elected representative (alderman) from each of the five to eight "wards," the electoral divisions of the town.[4]

The mayor could live anywhere in town. The new structure also expanded the city limits to take in Mayor Kirby's home on South Fourteenth. At the first council meeting of the biennium, the mayor was empowered to designate which commissioner would handle which portfolio of responsibilities. The council met at least once a week, and for at least four hours each time. The mayor and commissioners got six dollars each per meeting, with the mayor picking up an extra five dollars a month as the "chief executive officer" of the city.⁵

This change was not without challenges. A Socialist newspaper in Abilene, *The Farmer's Journal*, contested the decision on the grounds that it favored the wealthy and not the poor. The editor, Joshua Hicks, was a recent convert from populism to Socialism. With support from the national Socialist Party, the periodical briefly attained a circulation of over ten thousand.⁶

Mayor Dallas Scarborough.
COURTESY OF THE CITY OF ABILENE

The recommendation for change came from a handpicked committee chosen by Mayor Kirby. Hicks felt that the committee's makeup guaranteed that the "little man" would not be represented. The committee included "all the ministers of the city," the nine aldermen, and thirty-three others, most if not all of whom represented the business class.⁷ The *Abilene Reporter* favored the proposal, printing comments from proponents but nothing from the opposition.⁸ The charter revision carried easily, 444-116, though the turnout was disappointingly low, suggesting that Abilene did not get very excited about it.⁹

A surprising issue upset the Abilene political applecart in 1919. The popular Kirby had led the city through drought and war, disease and disaster, and seemed politically indestructible. But the latest drought had set Abilenians to thinking about a more reliable water supply. Led by Commissioner Dallas Scarborough, the city passed a bill to underwrite construction of a new dam above Buffalo Gap on Elm Creek. Thanks to Mayor Kirby, the city already owned the land for that lake as well as another site on Cedar Creek south of town. This impoundment, called Lake Abilene, would improve the city's water supply substantially. But Mayor Kirby opposed the matter, not wanting to spend the money. That became a contentious matter between the mayor and the commissioner, resulting in Scarborough challenging Kirby in the 1919 mayoral election. Scarborough also charged that Kirby was too cozy with the electric company. It was a bitter election, and when the dust had settled, Scarborough was mayor by a margin of just 59 votes.[10] The Kirby years were over. It is ironic, but nevertheless just, that the next lake to enhance the Abilene water supply would be named Lake Kirby.

Beyond Local Politics

In state and national politics, Abilene and Taylor County routinely voted Democratic by resounding margins. Voters qualified by being residents of the appropriate precinct and by paying a poll tax. In the 1908 election, 1,706 voters cast their ballots for the Democratic presidential nominee, William Jennings Bryan, and only 177 voted for the Republican, William Howard Taft. Returns for 1912 were incompletely reported, but the margin was 735 for the Democrat, Woodrow Wilson; only 24 for the incumbent, Taft; and 49 for the Socialist candidate, Eugene Debs. In 1912, at least, Socialists outnumbered Republicans in the Taylor County polling booths. The same patterns held, minus the Socialists, in 1916, when Wilson received 2,134 votes to 121 for the Republican, Charles Evans Hughes. This was the old "Solid South" tradition, with large doses of prairie populism mixed in.[11]

The county boasted that "there are representatives of every organized political party in the United States . . . republicans, socialists, prohibitionists, and progressives." But "the democrats are in the majority and elect the public officers."[12] The victor in the Democratic primary could count on winning in the fall general election.

Schools
Simmons Comes of Age

Simmons College just missed tripling its enrollment in the decade of the teens, growing from 330 in 1910 to 982 in 1919. One man, Jefferson Davis Sandefer, led the school as its president from 1909 until the beginning of World War II. He came to Simmons from the presidency of John Tarleton, a junior college in Stephenville. Under Sandefer's enlightened leadership, Simmons prospered in every way. New buildings went up on the campus—Abilene Hall, Mary-Frances Hall, Marston Gymnasium and others. Simmons literary societies competed with similar groups from other colleges and did quite well.

Simmons had been playing football for several years when the death of a player in 1909 precipitated an end to the sport. It was a head injury, and he was playing without a helmet. The outcry against football led to its abandonment at Simmons. The school fenced off the field and covered the stands. In the beginning, it was not missed too much, given the recent consequences. However, in 1914, Simmons joined the Texas Intercollegiate Association to compete against the University of Texas, Texas A&M College, Southwestern, Trinity, TCU, Austin College, Baylor, and Daniel Baker College in a wide variety of sports competitions.[13] Visibly absent from that mix, for Simmons, was football. This contributed in 1916 to considerable agitation among students and alumni for restoration of the program. In 1917, the trustees agreed to resume football, though President Sandefer made it clear this was a probationary period. "It took several years," Professor

Simmons College football, ca. 1898. COURTESY OF HARDIN-SIMMONS UNIVERSITY

Rupert Richardson remembered, "for the college to develop a football team that could make a creditable showing."[14] Meantime, other sports, including track, basketball, tennis, and baseball, flourished among the men, along with basketball for the women.[15]

Abilene Christian College Survives

Childers Classical Institute grew from 200 in 1910 to 234 in 1920. That may seem like a small increase, but the infant Church of Christ school struggled mightily through the early years of the decade. In the beginning, there was an almost annual turnover in the presidency, and there were some lean crop years so the institute was consistently in debt; the enrollment for 1911 dropped to thirty-five.[16] But in 1912, the school secured the services of Jesse P. Sewell as president. He found a brick classroom building and the Childers home as the total assets of the school, along with a modest debt. He also found a school that officially bore one name but unofficially went by another, Abilene Christian College

Sewell went to work and wrought a renaissance. The little school at North First and Graham slowly grew. It began to offer college classes and received junior college accreditation in 1914. Though the school's regimen of discipline was strict, increasing numbers of students found it attractive. Sewell and the trustees had to expand their building program. By the time Sewell resigned the presidency in 1924, there were twelve more buildings, so the campus was getting a bit crowded. The school received state recognition in 1919 as an accredited four-year college, though the elementary and secondary programs continued. So "Childers Classical Institute" no longer accurately described it.

Besides, public usage had long since dropped the name. An advertisement for the school in 1913 touted "Abilene Christian College" and the word Childers did not appear once.[17] The school's athletes already went forth with "A.C.C." emblazoned on their uniforms. "Abilene Christian College" appeared in the school's catalogs and other official publications, though the name on the charter remained undisturbed.[18] In 1920, the school changed officially and became "Abilene Christian College," a name that brought fame to the school and to the city. The renaming was not without rancor. The Childers family, noting that the original grant of land was contingent on the Childers name being preserved in the school's title, disputed the new designation. The school was able to negotiate a cash settlement that resolved the matter. ACC may not have grown much in enrollment, but it was many degrees more mature in 1919 than it had been just a few years earlier.[19]

The postwar years looked like the beginning of a new era for ACC. The college fielded its first intercollegiate football team in 1919. That was also the second year of a tradition that would grow in importance from then on—the Bible Lectureship, an event that attracted visitors from all over the state and beyond.

New Buildings for AISD

Public school attendance grew from 1,856 in 1910 to 2,236 in 1920. The city constructed a modern red brick high school building in 1909 at South Third and Peach for $40,000. Four elementary schools served the town—South Ward at South Ninth and Elm; North Ward at North Eighth and Orange; Central Ward at South First and Peach; and a "negro school" at North Second and Plum. Central Ward was a new school in an old building, taking over the old high school structure. John H. Bennett (1908-15) and J.L. Brooks (1915-17) led the district as superintendents through the period, giving way in 1917 to an experienced school man, R.D. Green, who would oversee the AISD for the next twenty years.

On the north edge of the city, near Simmons College, there was a "common school district" called North Park, which had been established in 1902 in a two-story brick building. It came under the county school system and had an enrollment of nearly 250 students. It became part of the Abilene system in 1950, by which time the city limits had completely encircled it.[20]

While the enrollment in Abilene schools did not rise spectacularly in this period, the physical and managerial framework developed substantially.

Construction
The Joyful Ring of the Hammer

A central theme for this period of Abilene's history was construction, though the real expansion lay in the decade to come. In 1909, the newspaper observed that "about the loudest, most continuous, yet withal musical, sound now breaking the stillness of Abilene is the joyful ring of the hammer and the merry buzz of the industrious saw."[21] The article went on to list numerous residential construction projects around the city, especially in College Heights. There was a major upgrading of the Alexander Sanitarium. W.L. Beckham's new hotel on North First was a $75,000 job "rearing itself into the sky as days go on." Beckham expected completion of the building, which he called the "Grace Hotel" after his daughter, by July 1.[22]

Track crews were laying track southward from the newly chartered Abilene and Southern Railroad's new roundhouse at South Ninth and Rose. The concrete laying for the roundhouse was nearly done, looking to a building that could handle six locomotives. Despite cold weather, the only hindrance to track-laying was the slow delivery of rails and ties from the east.[23]

At the same time, the newspaper noted that the new Carnegie Library was just about complete on the exterior.[24] Crews razed the existing structure and replaced it with a two-story brick building with a tiled roof. On July 7, 1909, with great fanfare, the city accepted the new building and its contents from the proud founders and agreed to operate it as a civic facility.[25]

In the decade following the turn of the century, the United States Congress appropriated funds for the construction of about twenty new Weather Service stations across the country. Abilene was one of the lucky recipients of a new building. Heretofore, the service had operated out of rented facilities in downtown buildings. Work began on the new building at North First and Beech in 1908 and was completed in late 1909. The new facility provided observation and work stations, public space on the first floor, and quarters for the chief forecaster's family. While the weathermen were moving in, the chief forecaster, James W. Watson, fell down the stairs and was killed. But operations began in early January 1910 and continued there through 1944, when the Weather Bureau moved to new quarters at the municipal airport.[26]

New church buildings were going up, especially in the downtown area—a Methodist church worth $45,000, a Baptist church worth $50,000, and a Presbyterian church worth $30,000. These were substantial sums—the Methodist building's value equaled the cost of the new library and weather station combined.[27]

Likewise, there was talk of a new courthouse. The county court deemed the existing structure to be unusable, and in early 1913 it moved the county offices to the first floor of the Grace Hotel, abandoning the courthouse. The district court operations went to the federal building.[28] Buffalo Gap took advantage of the move to lobby for a county seat election, hoping to reverse the decision of 1883. The newspaper editor said that no one should object to that, for Buffalo Gap had that right. But, he went on, it was patently absurd to move the seat out of Abilene, where half the county's population lived.[29] A bond election to raise funds to build a new courthouse *in Abilene* went before the voters in March, and it passed easily with support from the newspaper. "The new building should be fire proof," the editor said, "to last and to save insurance."[30] In the Abilene precincts, the bond initiative passed 894 to 30.[31]

Public Improvements

Once that matter was settled, the county commissioners let bids to raze the old building. C.A. Clayton of Sweetwater won the contract with the understanding that the building would be demolished and the debris hauled away within forty-five days. The commissioners also agreed to continue in the Grace for the time being, since bond prices were weak. In the interim, they made permanent the temporary designation of the Grace as the official county courthouse, until bond prices got better and the building could be erected.[32]

Road improvements in the city also created commotion. In the four years 1909-1912, the city paved "all the principal business streets."[33] Pavement was what they called "bitulithic" or "macadam." In 1913, the city began work to extend the macadamized roads into the residential areas. Paved sidewalks were also part of the general improvement of local transportation.[34] The city expected to expand its improved street system out to meet the improved county system.

Abilene began to think about a park system. There were already informal gathering spots around town, like the Cedar Creek area north of the tracks, or the oak grove where Simmons College was built. The newspaper led calls for some type of urban green space in 1913. The town of Temple had such a public park, the paper said, and it was well used. "The Reporter has about given up on Abilene ever owning a park, but we have not given up seeing other towns get them."[35] The creation of a public park in March 1914 on the T&P right-of-way off North First was a small start toward answering this call. It was called "Everman Park" and simply recognized a place where people gathered anyway for special events related to the railroad. Private citizens did most of the maintenance and beautification for Everman Park. In July 1914, the city acquired another plot of park land. Located on the southwest edge of town, this was the forty-acre tract called "Fair Park." The city owned and maintained it but leased it to the West Texas Fair Association, which undertook responsibility for grandstand, track, and building construction.[36] Mr. and Mrs. H.H. Cobb of Fort Worth donated twelve acres on the north side of town for a city park in 1919, but it was not developed until later.[37]

Another Railroad

Though Abilene prospered by its location on the T&P and on the Abilene and Northern, citizens still wished for a connection leading south. They kept hoping the Santa Fe would be that connection, but the line kept stalling, and indications were that it would bypass Abilene altogether when and if the company ever decided to build. Abilene was left to its own devices. With Col. Jones leading the way, and Ed Hughes and J.M. Radford in strong support, a state charter was granted in 1909 to the Abilene and Southern Railway Company to

Col. Morgan Jones, railroad entrepreneur and founder of an Abilene family dynasty of service.
COURTESY OF THE GRACE MUSEUM

build a line from Abilene all the way to Sonora, where it could connect with the Southern Pacific. Outside investors, including Grenville Dodge, signed on, but it was really a Morgan Jones operation. He built the tracks, and he ran the business.[38]

Construction began at Winters and Ballinger even before the company was organized. Track-laying began in Abilene almost simultaneously with the granting of the charter, with a depot on South Third across the street from the Abilene and Northern depot and the tracks paralleling Cherry Street on the way south. In September, the line was complete and began passenger and freight service all the way to Ballinger and a connection with the Santa Fe through that town.[39]

Jones had in mind to run the road farther south, across the hill country to San Angelo and Sonora and on, perhaps, to San Antonio. Eventually, threats of a "war" with the Santa Fe over these plans convinced him that Ballinger was far enough. He called the Abilene and Southern "the best little road I ever built." Certainly Abilene liked it.[40]

In 1910, it seemed likely that Jones would build another line. The Abilene and Central would aim toward Waco, and Jones drummed up some local support for it. When he changed his mind, he lost a bit of his hero status in Abilene, and some local men sued him to force him to go through with the plan. Jones and the committee compromised when the builder offered instead to connect a spur line from Anson on the Abilene and Northern to Hamlin. This would expand trade territory somewhat and would perhaps soothe the failed ambitions of the Abilene men. Despite opposition from Mayor E.N. Kirby, that was precisely what happened. The strange part was that the spur would be part of the Abilene and Southern network, using the Abilene and Northern tracks from Abilene to Anson to make the connection.[41]

Economic Developments
Agriculture

Cotton was king in Taylor County; after setbacks in 1917 and 1918 caused by drought, production reached the 40,000-bale mark and continued to hold steady. World War I created such a strong demand that cotton and wheat farmers could sell everything they could produce, and at good prices. Cotton prices and rainfall totals were front-page news in Abilene through the teens; a major share of the city's economy depended on the cotton harvest. Cotton-picking time came in the fall; in many West Texas communities, the cotton harvest meant that school was let out so the children could go into the fields. Often, the teachers would join them as hired laborers. When the crop was done about a month later, everyone resumed classes.[42] In 1923, Bronte schools delayed opening the fall term until October "to give the children a chance to aid in gathering the cotton crop which is just now getting into full swing."[43]

The idea of a fair, dormant since 1909, popped to the surface again in 1913. The Chamber of Commerce, the city leadership, and local

Cotton became a major product for the Abilene country. Wagons shown near the new Federal Building. COURTESY OF HARDIN-SIMMONS UNIVERSITY

businessmen combined to resurrect the fair idea. With an eye to the enhanced transportation provided by the streetcar system, the city leased to the new Fair Association a tract of forty acres on the southwest edge of town at the end of the streetcar line. It would be called Fair Park. The association leased the land for twenty-five years, with the understanding that the lease could be voided if the fairs were not held. The new organization, which called itself the "Central West Texas Fair Association," assembled a capital sum of $20,000 and began a massive building program—a 500-foot midway, an exhibition hall, a woman's building, a poultry building, a racetrack, a 1,800, seat grandstand, and a fence around the whole, all aimed at opening the renamed "Central West Texas Fair" in October 1914. Though the fair still featured the region's agriculture, it was changing more into a spectacle and less into a platform for promoting the farming prospects of the area. The whole thing made a modest profit in 1914, encouraging still more construction. The affair got bigger and bigger, attracting circuses and daredevils and other professional entertainers over the next couple of years. But drought and war in 1917 sapped the local economy and enthusiasm, so the fair could not be held in 1918 and the idea lapsed again . . . for a while.[44]

Petroleum!

Texas was stirred in 1901 with the advent of the Spindletop oil field in the Beaumont area. It was stirred again in 1911 and 1912 with massive oil discoveries in Wichita County at Electra and Burkburnett. Could it happen around Abilene? The first whiff of possible petroleum prosperity came in 1914, with Abilene on the consuming, not the producing, end. Natural gas discoveries in Moran, about thirty miles east, began in 1910. By 1914, the Moran field was producing enough gas to sell, and the market was Abilene, the nearest sizeable town.

Workers laid a gas pipeline from the Moran wellheads above ground across the prairie to Abilene, to the T&P Park at South First and Oak. On May 7, 1914, the city laid on a major celebration to mark the event, with Mayor Kirby, a brass band, a huge crowd, and roman candles to ignite the gas. There was some problem getting the gas lit, but it soon produced a highly satisfactory flare. It lasted only a few minutes before the pipe produced a stream of water that extinguished the flame. Hereafter, Abilene had a gas supply, but it was not as reliable as hoped because water in the lines froze in cold weather, precisely when the demand was greatest. Burying the pipeline solved that problem, and the gas supply was thereafter more dependable.[45]

The possibility of a major oil find seemed even brighter in 1916, when an experienced oil operator named Frank Fox began to drill near Cedar Gap a few miles south of town. The derrick became something of an attraction, with citizens riding out to see the action. But the well found nothing down to 2,000 feet, and the operator announced he was abandoning the attempt. "Not so fast," said some of the town's leaders, who promised Fox a bonus of $2,000 to keep drilling another thousand feet. He went a little further and got a trace of oil at 3,200 feet. The Chamber of Commerce manager went out to the rig and triumphantly returned to town with two quarts of oil. But that was about it, and Fox again began to shut down.

This time Abilene leaders formed a company to pursue the matter. For lack of a better name, they called it "The Hunch Oil and Gas Company," with banker George Paxton as president. Fox drilled again nearby and found a little better showing at 1,890 feet, but only a little better. In August, the third well struck a commercially viable pool that could produce twenty-five barrels a day. Nice, to be sure, but not the bonanza everyone hoped for. Within a year, Hunch Oil shut down its operation and sold its drilling assets.[46]

Although Taylor County seemed out of luck, some neighboring counties soon hit it big. A major strike at Ranger in late 1917 created enormous excitement, followed the next year by another huge strike at Desdemona and yet another at Breckenridge. Though these communities were some distance removed from Abilene, the oil boom necessarily impacted the region's biggest commercial center.

Good Roads

Inter-city transportation at that time and a decade later consisted principally of trains. Thus, travelers' accommodations were invariably hotels or boarding houses located near the railway station. A road network existed, to be sure, but it was poorly marked and even more poorly maintained. Roads were narrow paths in the best of times, and when it rained they were simply long mudholes. In many cases, travelers embarked across the unmarked prairie with wagons and teams to arrive at their destinations.

Regular ice delivery was an essential utility for early twentieth-century Abilene.
COURTESY OF HARDIN-SIMMONS UNIVERSITY

Abilene knew that a good road network was vital to economic prosperity. The city passed a bond issue in 1910 for Road District No. 1 to the tune of $150,000. Originally forty-five miles of roads emanating from Abilene were improved, mainly by grading and graveling—eight miles toward Buffalo Gap, seven miles toward Anson, ten miles toward Hamby, six miles toward Elmdale, twelve miles toward Potosi. Workers macadamized four and a half miles of the Elmdale Road and three miles toward Hamby. The roads were sixteen feet wide, with an additional eight feet on each side as graded dirt. The plan was that people should use the shoulders in dry times and the improved center only when it was wet.[47]

This served well enough until 1917, when Abilene joined in a new movement to build even more roads. An Abilene delegation met with sister cities of the Fort Worth-El Paso Highway Association at Big Spring in January 1917. The object was to encourage counties to im-

The perils of modern traffic, ca. 1909. COURTESY OF HARDIN-SIMMONS UNIVERSITY

prove their portions of the proposed pathway.⁴⁸ Maintenance was not very professional. Counties had construction bosses to oversee the roads, but citizens supplied the labor as a way of paying their road taxes, a long-standing practice throughout the country. Apparently, local citizens did not comply too well. The Taylor County Commissioners' Court found it necessary to remind everyone in 1917 that men subject to road work must be made to put in their full five days each year.⁴⁹ Various districts of Taylor County, though not on the planned path of the proposed highway, wanted improved roads, too. Tuscola and Ovalo voted for road bonds by large margins in 1918, with Buffalo Gap not far behind.⁵⁰ Taylor County was then ready to extend roads from Abilene through Cedar Gap to Tuscola, Ovalo, Guion, and Bradshaw to the Runnels County line; from Abilene through Caps to View; from Abilene all the way to Buffalo Gap; and, perhaps, through Cedar Gap to Lawn and on to the Coleman County line.

In 1918, the good road movement caught fire across the state and nation. Texas identified Highway No. 1 as the road from Texarkana to

El Paso. Another, Route No. 30, went from Wichita Falls to Paint Rock. Route No. 30 was the southern extension of what was called "the Ozark Trail." Highway #1 was part of projected transcontinental highways called "the Dixie Overland" and "the National Highway." There was talk of a new national route to be called "the Bankhead Highway" after its principal booster, Alabama Senator Bankhead. That road would be *paved* all the way. Both passed through Abilene. The route was finally improved to Trent, "thus completing this county's section of Texas Highway No. 1."

Captain Eddie Gets Stumped

Roads were an increasingly important element of West Texas travel in the early days of the twentieth century, but they certainly needed improvement. A young automobile salesman from Ohio found himself in Abilene in 1909 trying to sell his stock of Firestone-Columbus cars. He hit upon a wonderful sales gimmick when he discovered that the famous William Jennings Bryan, the three-time Democratic presidential nominee, was in town. He went to Bryan and offered to chauffeur The Great Man around town in one of his demonstration cars; Bryan accepted the offer.

A rancher named Hutchinson came into town to hear Bryan. He also saw the car, was intrigued by it, and offered to buy three of them—if the young man could drive him out to his ranch and back without breaking down. That seemed simple enough, and he agreed to the challenge. It was only after they set out that the salesman discovered that the ranch was some eighty miles away.

"A few miles out of Abilene, the road became simply a wagon track cut through sagebrush and mesquite." After a couple of flat tires as the only problems and the ranch house in sight, the salesman reported that the car hit "a big stump, at least six inches in diameter, sticking right up between the wagon tracks. It had bent the axle. I was sick. There went three sales flying right off with the angels."

But the rancher only laughed, and after the axle was heated and hammered back into shape the next day, he bought the three cars anyway. Ten years later, that young salesman was one of the most famous and admired men in America. He went on during the next decade to become a famous race car driver, the first ever to average a mile a minute at the Indianapolis time trials. Altogether he drove in four Indy 500s before World War I intervened. When the United States entered the war, he entered the flying corps and became the American Ace of Aces with 26 enemy planes shot down. His name was Captain Eddie Rickenbacker.

Source: Edward V. Rickenbacker, *Rickenbacker* (Englewood Cliffs, NJ: Prentice-Hall, 1967), pp. 48-50.

Chapter Eight
Peril 1911-1919

Destruction
The 1911 Storm

The heavens opened on July 31, 1911, to devastate central and south Abilene. Though no one reported a tornado, the result seemed just as bad. A severe thunderstorm blasted the city with high winds (in excess of sixty mph for ten minutes, in excess of fifty mph for an hour, the Weather Bureau said), nearly four inches of rain, egg-sized hail, and numerous lightning strikes. This storm was part of an overall rain event in West Texas and Oklahoma, but nowhere was there damage like that in Abilene.

One man was killed when his barn collapsed on him. Another was in his house when it blew off its foundations into Lytle Lake. He extricated himself and managed to swim to shore. Hail broke four-fifths of the recently installed streetlights. There were long lists of damaged buildings downtown, including the new Elks Lodge. Two tall smokestacks on the oil mill were toppled; the Baptist mission church was a total wreck; First Baptist suffered $5,000 damage and St. Paul Methodist about the same; the Epileptic Colony lost windows, pumps, and a barn; one man was struck by lightning but survived with serious burns; people who were away from shelter were battered by the hail;

Fire at Radford Grocery wholesale house on South First and Oak.
COURTESY OF HARDIN-SIMMONS UNIVERSITY

winds took the roof off the Radford Building; phone service was down; the City Hall roof was "completely wrecked." Altogether, the city estimated damages at over $200,000, no small sum in those days. It took weeks to clean up the downtown. The paper called it "the worst visitation in Abilene's history" and lamented "the damage done, the misery occasioned, the dreadful scenes enacted."[1]

As time went on, it didn't seem quite so bad. "In a short time," the paper said optimistically, "people will readjust themselves to the situation and the business life of Abilene will go on as though nothing in the nature of a storm had even made its presence felt." People felt that the beneficial rain almost made up for all the chaos.[2]

The 1913 Dam Break

Two years later, heavy rains occasioned another near-catastrophe for the city. The earthen dam across Lytle Creek southeast of town had stood since its construction in 1897. Behind the dam, Lytle Lake was the city's principal water source, although the city had sold bonds to

Storm waters cover the railroad in 1911. COURTESY OF JACK NORTH

finance another, larger lake to supplement the supply and provide a capacity sufficient to support a city of 50,000 people.[3] On November 23, 1913, heavy rains fell in the Lytle Creek watershed and filled the lake to capacity. Water began seeping under the center of the dam, and then "the impetuous waters"[4] burst forth in a full-scale break that released 800,000,000 gallons of water down the creek bed toward the T&P railroad bridge and beyond. The bridge held, and the Lytle-Cedar Creek gorge contained the flood. The major damage was to the intake pipe that fed the standpipe in midtown. Total losses were estimated at $20,000.

The "fire calliope" spread the news throughout the community that something had happened, and hundreds of spectators flocked to the creek banks to watch the passing flood. With Lytle Lake draining to a few pools, fishermen waded into the mud to pick up fish marooned by the receding waters.

The city vowed immediate replacement and summoned an engineer from Dallas to consult on building a better dam. He arrived within a day. Men wanting jobs in the cleanup and rebuilding processes swarmed the city offices. Many of them were put to work as soon as the rains ceased.

Of course, the city water supply was shut off because the standpipe held only so much storage. The valley of Lytle Creek between the dam and the railroad held a modest supply, sufficient for eighty days' consumption. That basin had long been called "Lake Cameron."[5] The city re-rigged an intake pipe in Lake Cameron, and water service resumed by 4 P.M. the following day.[6]

The 1919 Power Plant Fire

The disaster-filled decade ended in 1919 with one final blow—the destruction by fire of the electric generating plant on April 18. The fire began on the roof of the boiler room on a day with a "brisk south wind" and totally destroyed the plant's operating ability. Also lost were a diesel generator, three ice machines, and the D.C. converter for the Abilene Street Railway Company.[7] Since the plant was already engulfed when the firemen arrived, they fought the flames mainly to keep them from spreading to the nearby Continental Oil and Cotton Company oil mill.[8] The loss was valued at over $200,000.

The catastrophe meant that (1) there would be no electricity, because there was no national grid to pick up the slack; (2) there would be no ice, at a time when most people kept their food in iceboxes; (3) there would be no water, because the city's pumps were electric; (4) the telephones would be down; and (5) the electric streetcars would be out of service. Much of Abilene's infrastructure was deactivated in one quick moment.

Mayor E.N. Kirby and the city's political and economic leaders immediately began work to ease the crisis. Fire trucks pumped water into the standpipe, thus assuring some water service. Boxcars of ice came from Dallas to meet the immediate cooling needs. The electric company ordered backup generators from Big Spring and Stamford. One would power the water pumps, and the other would provide a small amount of electricity for the town. Initial estimates were that the electricity would be fully back on line in ten days, the ice-making in thirty days, and the trolley system in several weeks.[9] In the meantime, Abilenians were asked to limit their water, telephone, and electric usage, particularly in the evenings. A generator brought from Snyder powered the telephone system temporarily.[10]

Of course, not everything went smoothly. The huge generator from Big Spring was too big for the railroad, so it had to come overland, via dirt roads and weak bridges. Just east of Sweetwater, "it went through a bridge . . . and was stuck in a creek."[11] Eventually, the 11,000-pound generator made it to town and was soon on line. There were two more units coming from Snyder and one from Ballinger. Between them, they had a capacity of 450 kilowatts, which authorities believed would be sufficient to meet the needs of Abilene and Merkel. That proved to be optimistic; three days later, the company asked the townspeople to shut off their electric signs, electric fans, and other non-essential uses.

A streetcar was stranded by the blackout on the south side of town. The local Cadillac dealer agreed to tow it back to the trolley barn on the north side with one of his cars. It was great advertising, and a large crowd lined the route to watch the "rescue." The electric company vowed to build a bigger and better power plant, one that would be fireproof. And, in due course, things got back to normal.

Dangers
Drought

The period 1916-1919 hit Abilene with four major problems in addition to the 1919 power plant fire. The first was a serious drought that affected the whole region. Rainfall for the twenty-four-month period beginning in July 1916 and ending in June 1918 totaled 22.29

inches, when an average rainfall would have been about 47 inches for the period.[12]

The water shortage soon became acute, and Abilene began to plan for ways of resolving the matter. Water was an issue in the 1917 mayoral election. Candidate A.M. Robertson wanted to leave it to a public vote but asserted that without some kind of solution, "we will be subjected to the most severe ordeal in the way of a water famine that the city has ever suffered."[13] It was obvious that the Lytle Lake water supply was inadequate. Mayor E.N. Kirby and Commissioner Dallas Scarborough pushed for a new dam, this one owned and controlled by the city. The city acquired land for the proposed new lake on Elm Creek upstream from Buffalo Gap and paid for the construction with bonds approved in a bond election in 1918.[14] Even in the midst of this debate, the city aided its neighbors by building a pipeline to Baird to help keep the roundhouse and railroad repair facilities operating.[15]

The city decided to build the new lake, and construction of a dam on Elm Creek began while the drought continued. In the summer of 1918, abundant rains fell and began to ease the problem, but the dam went on. A construction camp called "Camp Clinton" went up near the dam site. In September 1918, crews began the concrete slab that would line the central spillway, but estimated completion of the impoundment to be called "Lake Abilene" would take another twenty months.[16] That estimate proved to be a bit pessimistic, and the facility began operation in 1919. That would solve the problem for the next few years but did little to help in the short run.

The Methodist Episcopal Church, South transferred Rev. O.F. Sensabaugh to be presiding elder over the Abilene District in November 1916. He remembered that "it was in the middle of one of the worst droughts that section ever experienced. Pigs died; chickens and turkeys starved; young cattle starved; homes were deserted; preachers suffered. I came to Dallas [whence he had just left] and secured between eight and nine hundred dollars to carry them through the year. I would drive to the parsonage, take the preacher in my car and often pick up a steward and take them to the seat of the Quarterly Conference. In the second and third rounds I took nothing for [my] part except in three or four charges. I would figure out my part, then give all to the preacher. Frequently I met a family struggling to return to where they came from and one or both horses or mules would be down by the roadside unable to get up and go. Of course, but little remained in my pocketbook when I left them. Many left to secure work. Frequently I saw men leading the last milk cow into town where they would take any amount they could get for them."[17]

Private efforts like those reported by Sensabaugh helped, and some public monies were forthcoming. A state drought relief fund sent Taylor County $1,000 to be doled out for food and clothing to devastated families. The county decided no more than $25 would be granted to any one family.[18] The federal War Finance Corporation arranged for emergency loans to drought-stricken cattle raisers in West Texas.[19] Much of this kind of aid came too late to help much, and West Texans simply had to endure the best they could.

Losing the College

A second problem came during the drought. As West Texas filled up with population, its citizens came to believe that they deserved a branch college of Texas A&M. Agitation for such a school began right after the turn of the century, but it was not until 1917 that the legislature approved a bill establishing a "West Texas A&M College." Various towns lobbied hard for the school—Amarillo, Lubbock, San Angelo, Snyder, Sweetwater, Ballinger, Haskell, Abilene. Whoever got the school could look forward to great things, even in the midst of the water shortage. Governor James Ferguson appointed a five-person selection team, with himself as chair, to visit and review the proposals

Dr. O.H. Cooper, distinguished administrator, teacher. Namesake of Cooper High School.
COURTESY OF HARDIN-SIMMONS UNIVERSITY

from the towns. Abilene chose three prominent citizens to present her case—Will Minter, Dr. O.H. Cooper, and Judge W.F. Cunningham. The rumors began to spread that Abilene would be the first choice, with Kerrville second. On June 29, 1917, Ferguson announced that Abilene was indeed the winner.[20]

The *Abilene Reporter* carried the news in a headline in what was irreverently called "Second Coming print," saved only for the end of a war or the Second Coming of Christ—ABILENE GETS A&M COLLEGE: BIG CELEBRATION SATURDAY. Abilene was beside itself with joy. The city blocked off all of downtown for "a humdinger" of a celebration. "There will never be such scenes again until Uncle Sam beats the Kaiser." Ten thousand people turned out to hear the speeches and join the festivities. The fire whistle went off and the fire trucks ran up and down the streets with sirens blaring, people danced (in Abilene!) in the streets, bands played.[21] When the three triumphant lobbyists got off the T&P, they were carried around town on the shoulders of the crowd.[22]

The A&M College Board met to decide how to apportion funds between College Station and the Abilene school.[23] President W.B. Bizzell of A&M announced that Abilene would be a cavalry ROTC.[24] A separate Board of Trustees was set up for the new school, with Judge John I. Guion of Ballinger as chair.[25] "Work will start on a beautiful site south of Abilene within sixty days," the newspaper announced. The land was a 640-acre tract—the Burchard farm on Buffalo Gap Road.[26] It was all set, and prosperity was just around the corner, regardless of the drought.

Then, a slight sliver of doubt crept in. The first reports of the selection meeting said that Abilene had two votes on the first ballot, with Haskell, San Angelo, and Kerrville each getting one vote. The second ballot went three for Abilene, said the source, and two for Amarillo, with a third ballot making it unanimous.[27] However, there were reports that the vote had not gone that way at all. When such reports became public knowledge, Governor Ferguson and committee secretary Thompson said that the vote was correct and there would no further discussion. But Commissioner of Agriculture Fred Davis, one of the five, said he voted for Snyder on both ballots. Lieutenant Governor William Hobby said he had voted first for San Angelo and then for Amarillo, while Speaker of the House F.O. Fuller said he voted for Haskell first and for some other town, but not Abilene, on the second.[28] Confusion reigned!

Abilenians placed blame for the problem on the press, namely the *Dallas News* and one of the San Antonio papers, both of which presumably hated the governor and wished to embarrass him.[29] Sweetwater Judge H.C. Hord got some blame, too, when it was alleged that he opposed Abilene on the grounds that the city was not in West Texas, an accusation he said was a misquotation by the *Dallas News*.[30] Eventually, the four committee men joined with the fifth member, State Superintendent of Public Instruction W.F. Doughty, a strong Abilene supporter, to issue a joint statement: "Regardless of what has been said or done or is contemplated to be hereafter done, we desire each and every one of us to state that the said location and selection of the said City of Abilene for the location of the said College was in all things regular, honest, and square and it is beyond all human probability that there could have been an error; consequently we do not think it prudent to re-open the question." Hobby and Davis, having signed the document, then equivocated, saying they believed this to be true but would withdraw their support if at least three of the five did not sign affidavits saying that they had voted for Abilene.[31] The euphoria dwindled, and little more was heard of the matter. The mix-up was never explained, and Ferguson was impeached on other charges before anything more could come of it. The next legislature repealed the authorization. The West Texas Chamber of Commerce besieged Austin with protests, but the matter lay untouched for the next few years. Abilene was deeply disappointed. When the college issue was revived in 1923, the choice fell on Lubbock for home of the renamed "Texas Technological College."[32]

War

The third crisis was the Great War. Abilenians paid little attention to the news of the assassination of the Austrian archduke in 1914 and had only marginally more interest in the war that ensued. Local attention focused more on the Mexican border, where the ongoing Mexican revolution sometimes spilled over into the United States. When Mexico proved incapable of suppressing the rebel activities of leaders like Pancho Villa, President Woodrow Wilson sent American troops across the border into northern Mexico in an attempt to prevent further incursions and punish Villa and others for crimes against American lives and property on both sides of the border. This incursion, under Brig. Gen. John J. Pershing, dragged on without much result until American entry into the European war made it necessary to concentrate resources elsewhere.

As it became apparent that the U.S. might be involved, Abilenians became increasingly belligerent. As good Democrats, they supported President Wilson's policies. They lived in the most warlike section of the nation. They believed stories of German atrocities, some of which were true. When the Congress declared war, Abilene approved wholeheartedly and began to pay much more attention to European events.

The war quickly became personal for Abilene. UT law student Robert Wagstaff, son of a prominent Abilene family and a member of the Texas National Guard, was activated and saw service on the border during the problems with Pancho Villa. When war with Germany broke out, the Army sent Wagstaff back to his hometown to recruit a Guard company. Capt. Wagstaff set up headquarters in Fair Park and successfully signed up well over 100 young men for service. Initially called Company I, Texas National Guard, the unit went into federal service as Headquarters Company, 142nd Regiment, 36th Infantry Division. The company went to Camp Bowie in Fort Worth in September 1917 for equipment issue and further training. During training there, an accidental mortar explosion killed Lt. Alan McDavid and three others. Wagstaff's company went to France in July 1918 and saw heavy action. In the early fall, the local paper began to report Abilene casualties.[33] Another company of draftees left Abilene for Camp Travis in San Antonio in September 1918 under Capt. Morgan Covington, but these did not see action.[34]

Some of the young men at Simmons College joined early on and contributed to the casualty figures of 1918. As the Army's ranks filled and the need for leaders grew, the War Department set up a program called the Student Army Training Corps on campuses across the nation. One such was located at Simmons College, under the leadership of a retired general, a veteran of the Indian wars. Simmons President Sandefer asked a young faculty member, Rupert Richardson, to take charge of the Simmons contingent that was dispatched to Illinois for

Dr. Rupert N. Richardson, Abilene's premier historian and educator.
COURTESY OF HARDIN-SIMMONS UNIVERSITY

preliminary training. The Army gave Richardson a commission and sent him back to Abilene to work under Gen. Hare at the college in the fall of 1918. Of the 167 men in the unit, forty-two were ACC students. "Formal flag-raising, reveille, retreat, and the bark of drillmasters became part of campus routine."[35] Schoolwork and military discipline went hand in hand. The war ended just as Simmons was alerted to begin sending their SATC men to active duty. Four hundred Simmons alumni went into service, and thirteen of them were killed in action in France.[36] Altogether, thirty-two men from Taylor County died in "the war to end all wars." By the last week of the war, Taylor County had dispatched 886 men to the services, 560 via the draft and 326 as volunteers.[37]

Anti-German feeling rose throughout the country but was not in much evidence in Abilene. Unlike other places, locals did not extend their anti-German feeling to their neighbors of German descent, especially when the list of local wounded men included names like Otto Faust.[38] Some of the prominent founders of the town, the Theo Heyck family, for example, were German. However, the German-descended citizens of Brandenburg in nearby Stonewall County found it prudent to change the town's name to "Old Glory," a name the village still has.[39] New Braunfels briefly considered changing its name to "Pershing."[40] The Abilene papers were full of war news, including a special daily series of lurid tales of German atrocities and outrages in Belgium. Abilenians regularly referred to them as "the Huns" to emphasize German barbarism. Still, that antipathy did not extend to locals.

Doing their part at home, Abilenians oversubscribed their quotas for the four Liberty Bond drives activated to help finance the war effort.[41] They endured without complaint occasional shortages, such as sugar. Men registered for the draft, a law Abilene public opinion supported.[42] Initially aimed at men between the ages of twenty-one and thirty-one, the draft extended eventually to include all men ages eighteen through forty-five.[43] People put signs on their cars and buggies announcing that they would give a lift to servicemen.[44] Homes with boys in the military placed "service flags" in their windows.[45] Churches prayed for the troops and for the success of American arms. The front pages of the newspapers carried extensive reports on the progress of the war.

Epidemic

A fourth major crisis, perhaps deadlier than the war, was the outbreak of the "Spanish influenza" in the fall of 1918. The influenza epidemic of 1918 was a worldwide catastrophe. 1918 was the only year in the history of the United States, ever, that the population total decreased, and the troop losses in France were only a very small part of it. To fight the epidemic, cities across the nation banned public gatherings, shut down schools, mustered health care facilities as best they could. The Abilene region did not escape. The "flu" hit the neighboring small town of Lueders so heavily that the sick were tending the sick. Those few that did not catch the disease feared that they might and avoided contact with the sufferers. One heroic pastor and wife earned the gratitude of the whole community by defying the odds to minister to the physical needs of their members and neighbors day and night for several weeks during the outbreak.[46]

First hints of the crisis came in September 1918 with word that the flu afflicted about a hundred merchant seamen just returned to a Massachusetts port from Europe. "Strenuous effort is being made to prevent the spread of the disease," the local paper reported.[47] But it was to no avail. Soon the epidemic engulfed the states east of the Mississippi and made its way west. By early October, the disease, had reached Abilene. The opening of the public schools had to be postponed. "Many homes in the city are affected by the widespread malady, which is now sweeping the entire United States . . . [it hit] Central West Texas pretty hard, although no deaths reported. . . . The Abilene Reporter has especially been victimized by the 'gentle' plague, its entire work force practically being placed without the horizon of activity."[48]

Public events and gatherings were cancelled or postponed in Abilene. Some people continued to work even though ill, which probably did not help much. Schools were seriously affected. ACC lamented that "the recent epidemic of influenza has made it very difficult for [the ACC faculty] to keep their organization intact."[49] Military camps were especially hard hit across the nation, as well as overseas. Camp Travis in Brownwood boasted in early October that it had not yet had a case, but that record did not long endure.[50]

Abilene mobilized to meet the crisis. The local Red Cross chapter, already operating at peak efficiency to meet the demands of wartime, appointed an "Influenza Committee" chaired by Mrs. Joseph Daly. They helped distribute drugs, food, and ice to victims, they ran errands, they provided child care, and they even washed clothes for afflicted families. The Boy Scouts distributed 2,000 pamphlets door to door on "How to Prevent Influenza." Volunteers organized transportation for victims. Mayor E.N. Kirby donated the use of his horse and buggy for two days to set the example. The Red Cross set up beds in the county courthouse to accommodate people visiting the city to see about loved ones.[51]

By November, the epidemic had about run its course. The Army's surgeon general said that only a few new cases were being reported at mid-month, mainly in the far west.[52] Even in late October, Abilene was beginning to breathe easier. Simmons President J.D. Sandefer exulted on October 20 that Simmons was now clear of the disease. President Sewell of ACC announced that his school, too, was influenza-free.[53] On November 10, Abilene Public School Superintendent R.D. Green noted that school attendance was back up, averaging 98.5 percent overall and in no school under 95 percent.[54]

Lubbock was not quite out of the woods, though. The Hub City still forbade all public meetings, so that the Methodist Northwest Texas Annual Conference set there for early November had to be cancelled. Rev. O.F. Sensabaugh, head of the Abilene District of the denomination, and pastor James W. Hunt came to the rescue, offering to host the conference in Abilene. Sensabaugh recalled: "[My] second year on the District, through the marvelous assistance of the pastor of St. Paul Church, J.W. Hunt, when Lubbock could not entertain the Conference on account of a flu epidemic and only three days away, we wired 'Abilene will entertain the Conference.'"[55] Abilene was still a little nervous about the epidemic. "The city fathers allowed us only three days' stay [November 6-8, 1918 - RWS] with no special city rallies."[56]

End of an Era

When the 1920 census showed that the city had grown only slightly, from 9,204 in 1910 to 10,274 in 1920, many could look back over the preceding few years and wonder whether there was a permanent dark cloud hanging over the town and its prospects. But if Abilene did not come close to the longed-for 25,000 mark, at least the total was now in five figures, and the coming years would prove that pessimism was unjustified.

Signs of the next decade were already apparent. One of them was traffic—automobile traffic. Abilene hired a policemen to do nothing but traffic law enforcement. Officer Frank Ferrier was outfitted with a motorcycle with which to enforce the traffic laws.[57] Was this necessary? Officer Ferrier demonstrated that it was when he counted 696 cars passing North Second and Pine in one hour on a Saturday night.[58] Chief Clinton, still serving the town after nearly four decades, vowed strict enforcement of the laws, which included a fifteen mph limit in residential areas. He was also concerned about "open mufflers" and lack of headlights "on the unimproved streets of Abilene."[59] This was a statewide trend—the newspaper said that "Texas students of economics [in Austin] are wondering whether the automobile is not now beginning a revolution in Texas that will in the end equal that brought about by the railroad." Indeed, increased use of the auto was already reducing railroad profits.[60]

Abilene's first auto arrived in 1903, and the use of the contraption grew as time went on. One sign of the transition from horse power to engine power was the advertisement in the 1913 *Taylor County Yearbook* for the Lion Harness Company, which offered its services for "harness, strap goods, auto and carriage tops."[61] A similar ad touted the services of Ed Northrup and Sons, "general woodworkers," who said that "auto tops and boddies" [sic] were their specialty, but also "wagon, buggy, and implement work promptly done."[62]

Another sign of the coming decade was a rising divorce rate. Alarmed by a bump in this trend, Abilenians heard that "the divorce record in Taylor County has been trying to approach the numbers of marriage licenses issued over the past thirty days."[63] The concern was premature, since the divorce rate in the county, while rising through the '20s, did not reach even the twenty percent mark against marriages in that span.[64]

Probably Abilenians, looking back over the past few years, filled with crisis and peril, expected that the decade opening before them would have to be better. All the bad stuff was surely behind them, and they had survived more or less intact. There was a sense that, with the Great War over and done with, a page had been turned.

Losing The Normal School

During the 1911 legislative session, the Texas House and Senate considered a bill affecting Abilene, a law written by Sen. William J. Bryan of Abilene to establish a state normal school in the city. "Normal school" was the term applied to a college intended principally for teacher training. Abilene sent W.J. Cunningham to Austin to lobby for the bill, and he sent back encouraging reports. Rep. Thomas J. Barrett of Anson, whose district included Jones, Callahan, and Taylor Counties, carried the legislation through the House with minimal dissent, and it went up to the Senate in early March. There it met some resistance. The Abilene newspaper alleged that the principal opposition came from partisans of Sweetwater, Brownwood, and San Angelo. Nevertheless, the Senate Education Committee reported favorably on the bill, and it went on the agenda.

Two things eventually stopped the initiative dead in its tracks. One was the opposition of Governor Oscar Colquitt, who announced that he would veto any normal school bill (there was another pending for Waco) because the state already had too many of them. The second problem was the approaching end of the term. In a flurry of last-minute debates on a multitude of bills, it was to be expected that the Senate would not get around to one that the governor had promised to veto. The legislation died with the adjournment, not to be resurrected.

Sources: *ADR*, January 31, 1911, p. 3; February 27, 1911, p. 1; March 8, 1911, pp. 1, 4; March 12, p. 1.

Chapter Nine
Prosperity 1920-1929

After a brief postwar slump, the American economy embarked on an unprecedented boom fueled by the rise of the automobile industry, with the concomitant government spending on transportation infrastructure—streets, highways, bridges, signage, law enforcement, vehicles. Paralleling the auto expansion was the emergence of electric services—household appliances, street lighting, electrification of industry, entertainment (movies, radio), generating, and distribution services. At the end of the decade, overindulgence of private and public capital in those enterprises would cause a great readjustment, as the economy could not digest the changes. That readjustment was the Great Depression, when public and private debt overwhelmed the flow of money.

In the meantime, the businessman became the great American hero. The best-selling book of the decade, *The Man Nobody Knows*, was a biography of Jesus written by an advertising executive, Bruce Barton.[1] One chapter had the title "The Executive," and another was "The Founder of Modern Business." "The business of America," proclaimed President Calvin Coolidge, "is business."

The Great Expansion
Population Growth

Abilene shared in all of this, beginning with the boom of the '20s. The town's population more than doubled in ten years, from the 1920 census figure of 10,274 to 23,175 in 1930.[2] That was not quite to the level of the old Abilene 25,000 Club dream, but it represented a doubling and then some. In 1923, a local headline read, "Thousands Are Moving to Abilene." The article went to list the advantages that would draw newcomers—colleges, climate, conveniences, churches, hospitals.[3]

Everything grew—the number of telephones in Abilene from 1,672 in 1920 to 5,010 in 1929;[4] the number of motor vehicles registered in the county from 4,656 in 1922 to 14,072 in 1929;[5] college enrollment from Simmons's 962 and ACC's 234 in 1920 to Simmons's 1,391, ACC's 517 and the new school, McMurry, with 593, as of 1929.[6] It amounted to a population explosion for the sleepy town on Cedar Creek.

And population numbers are only part of the story. Where was the city going to house all those newcomers, and where were they going to work and shop and worship and play? The answer, of course, was the construction of numerous new buildings, perhaps the most impressive expansion of any period in the city's history, excepting only 1881. The city annexed several large tracts toward the south and southwest. Anticipating the opening of McMurry, Abilene took in an area of about twenty blocks just to the north of the new college in 1923 and annexed the college area itself the following year. When ACC announced in 1928 that it would move to the northeast edge of town, the city promptly annexed the area. The city fathers incorporated into the city limits a large chunk between Catclaw and Elm Creeks and between South First and South Twelfth, including the neighborhood that came to be known as Elmwood. Construction crews had their hands full in Abilene in the '20s.

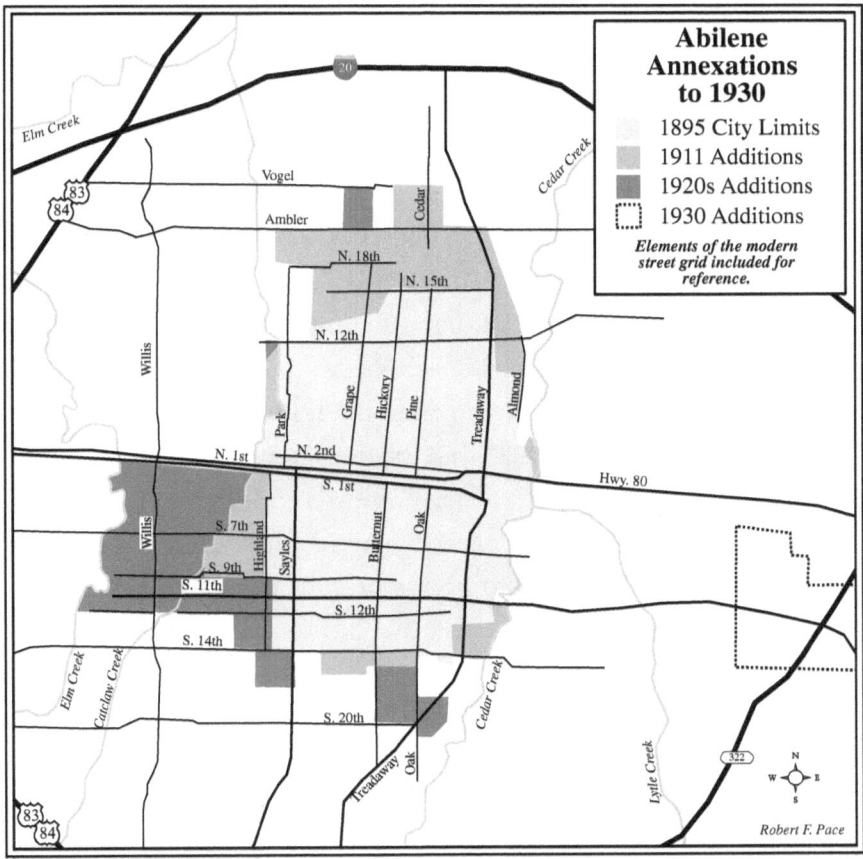

The city expanded substantially to the southwest in the 1920s. Numerous annexations through the decade sought to keep pace with the growing residential areas.

Educational Construction

McMurry College began operations in 1923 with two major buildings and several lesser ones. Simmons moved into the new Caldwell Fine Arts building in 1922 and into Ferguson Hall in 1925.[7] Abilene Christian transplanted to new facilities on "The Hill" in 1929, with several brand new buildings waiting for them.

The public school district also went on a building spree to house maybe three times as many students from one end of the decade to another. It began for AISD with the construction of the "Americanization School", eventually called "Houston," in 1920. The following year, the district built another elementary school on North Sixteenth called "College Heights." South Ward School (Travis) was increasingly decrepit, so the district replaced it, also in 1921. In 1925, twin schools went up on the north side and the south side; they even bore similar names—Alta Vista (Spanish for "High View") on South Eleventh and Valley View on North Eighth. The Locust Street School was built on South Eighth in 1927, and Fair Park Elementary was built on South Sixth in 1929. The new northside schools were intended to keep elementary students from having to cross the railroad.

The district decided in 1923 that the fourteen-year-old high school needed to be replaced with a larger, more modern facility. The old school, at South Third and Peach, burned a bit later and was out of use for a time before it could be restored to use as an elementary school. The new high school was two blocks north, on Peach and South First. Completed in 1924, it served Abilene as the high school until 1956, when the current Abilene High building on North Sixth and Mockingbird came on line. The railroad problem for northside students was solved by a tunnel under the tracks. From 1956 to well into the twenty-first century, the building housed Lincoln Middle School. A gymnasium dubbed "the Eagles Nest" was added in 1929.[8]

Commercial Buildings

Most of Abilene's skyline, the downtown business area, went up in the 1920s. The tallest buildings were usually hotels. A consortium of Abilene businessmen led by George Paxton, president of Citizens National Bank, decided in 1926 to erect a first-class hotel. Among the investors were famous Abilene names like Guitar, Swenson, Fulwiler, Hanks, Wagstaff, Ely, Minter, and Wooten. Pooling their resources, they underwrote construction of a ten-story hotel, which they proclaimed the best between Fort Worth and Los Angeles. The consortium hired a young hotelier from Cisco named Conrad Hilton to open the facility in 1927. They allowed him to name it the Hilton, and it became the first piece in the great Hilton Hotel empire.[9] Wholesale grocer H.O. Wooten was so taken by the hotel business that he financed and opened one of his own in 1930—the sixteen-floor Wooten Hotel. The old Grace Hotel at North First and Cypress added a fourth floor and other improvements in 1924.[10]

And not all the lodgings were in the downtown, for times were changing and some hotels catered now to the automobile trade rather than to railroad passengers. The route of the main road through town, eventually called the Bankhead Highway, hosted several hostelries. In 1922, J.M. Radford built the Tourist Hotel at Second and Oak, featuring a full-service garage and filling station.[11] Modern tourist courts included the Ponca Motel, built in 1928 west of town on South First, and the Abilene Courts on South Eleventh.

The downtown building boom produced new stores and offices in profusion. Grocery magnate J.M. Radford constructed the Park Office Building at South First and Oak in 1922, housing, among other enterprises, Abilene Building and Loan and the National Business College. Across the tracks, Dr. J.M. Alexander commissioned construction of an office building, a seven-story edifice at North First and Pine. When completed in 1925, it was, at least temporarily, the peak of Abilene's skyline. The Alexander Building was home to the Abilene State Bank and other shops on the ground floor, with offices above.[12] Radford named his next enterprise, a three-story structure at South Second and Chestnut, after the recently deceased Chief John Clinton. Brooks Dry Goods Co. and others moved into the Clinton Building in 1925.[13] Numerous other buildings, some tall and some not, completed the growing downtown. The Mims Building (1926), the Johnson-Gorsuch Building (1929), the Compton Building (1923), and the Fulwiler Building were among them.[14] The *Abilene Daily Reporter* built a new home for itself in 1921 and expanded it in 1928. Waldrop's Furniture held its grand opening at 220 Cypress in September 1923. The event featured "free souvenirs to the first 600 women at the opening."[15] Also in 1923, Mead Bakery began operations in a new facility on Pecan, a building 50 feet by 100 feet.[16]

While there were already several theaters in the city, more sprang up. Workmen completed the Palace Theatre on Chestnut in 1922. Also on Chestnut, the American Theatre featured vaudeville productions beginning in 1921. The name was later changed to the Oasis. The Majestic opened on Cypress Street in 1925 with *Charley's Aunt*. The Majestic had a new air-cooling system based on water evaporation. The Rex on Chestnut opened a few months later, also with a cooling system and 650 seats.[17] H.O. Wooten erected the enduring centerpiece of Abilene's entertainment business on Cypress next door to the Wooten Hotel in 1930. Intended as a partner to the hotel, the Paramount Theatre was a marvel of the day, with exotic exterior styling and an interior that featured artificial clouds and stars on the ceiling.[18]

It was a dream of Dr. Millard Jenkens, pastor of First Baptist Church, that Abilene should have a hospital in addition to the existing private "sanitariums." Jenkens even turned down a call to a bigger church to pursue that vision, especially after the flu epidemic of 1918. He recruited the assistance of President Sandefer of Simmons, other local Baptist pastors, and several laymen to assist in the effort. Mr. and Mrs. J.M. Caldwell of Breckenridge donated six acres of land just south of Simmons for the establishment of the West Texas Baptist Sanitarium. The building cost $150,000, an enormous sum for that day. Medical personnel and patients began to utilize the facility in September 1924. The five-story structure boasted seventy-two rooms and handled over 800 patients in its first year.[19] Abilene ended the decade with three hospitals: the West Texas Baptist Sanitarium, the Alexander Sanitarium, and the Abilene Sanitarium.[20]

Butternut Fire Station, 1926. COURTESY OF HARDIN-SIMMONS UNIVERSITY

Public Buildings

Numerous churches went up in the city during the 1920s. Prominent among them was a new building for Sacred Heart Catholic Church on South Eighth. The architecture drew from several sources—Spanish, Gothic, Moorish, and Romanesque. Fundraising for the church began in 1924, with construction beginning in 1930.[21] First Methodist Church put up its new building in 1925 on Butternut at the cost of $100,000. The city also built a striking new fire station on Butternut in 1926. The Abilene Traction Company, proprietor of the city's streetcars, upgraded its car barn on Clinton Street in 1928. This involved tearing down the original wood-framed barn in favor of a metal-framed structure. Since the streetcar service ceased to operate only three years later, it did not see much service under the original intent.[22] After much promotion by Editor Frank Grimes and the newspaper, the city built the Fair Park City Auditorium on South Seventh Street in 1927. It became the site of numerous city events, concerts, athletic contests, traveling shows, and the like.[23]

Other Construction

After the dam failure on Lytle Lake in 1913, the city cast about for a more reliable water source. With the proceeds from two major bond sales, the city bought land above Buffalo Gap on Elm Creek and began construction of a dam. In January 1921, the massive project neared completion. Steam shovels were busy excavating the last portions of the planned lake. The 3,000-foot-long dam was sixty feet high in the middle and 320 feet thick at the base. The concrete spillway, "unlike that at Lytle Lake, is similar to the overflow system of the modern bathtub."[24] Then, as the lake began to form, a major problem arose. A geologic fault under the dam began to leak water out of the lake. A large chunk of the dam dropped eight feet into the gap. Engineers pondered the matter and could come up with only one idea. They would dynamite the fault. Mayor Dallas Scarborough, undoubtedly holding his breath, ceremonially pushed the plunger to ignite the explosion. "The blast pulverized the underground clay and dropped it into the fissure. Workers then pumped water into the crack for two weeks to puddle the clay into solid mass."[25] And the mayor could breathe again.

Even the new lake could not solve all of Abilene's water needs. A short but severe drought between October 1927 and April 1928 caused Lake Abilene to go dry, forcing the city to sink water wells in the area to make up the shortfall. In May of 1928 the city received over twelve inches of rainfall, beginning to refill the lake. But the lesson was already learned, and the city leaders sought another source. That same year, they built a dam on Cedar Creek south of the city to impound yet more water, a lake they named for a former mayor, E.N. Kirby.[26]

In 1920, local golf enthusiasts began to seek a place to play. A committee consisting of merchant G.L. Minter, entrepreneur H.O. Wooten, architect David Castle, publisher M.B. Hanks, insurance man Charles Motz, and others laid plans for a golf club of nine holes on Cedar Creek "on land owned by the city on Potosi Pike, some three or four miles south of the city."[27] By March 1921, the plans had matured, and the "Abilene Country Club" was set to go on 160 acres "between Cedar Gap and Buffalo Gap Pikes."[28]

Architect David Castle, "the man who built Abilene." COURTESY OF THE GRACE MUSEUM

Homes

To all the public and commercial construction must be added an impressive array of houses, ranging from mansions to more humble dwellings. The city expanded in every direction, but especially south and west. Homes continued to rise in the area between downtown and Simmons, mostly in the blocks close to the trolley line. College Heights continued to build up around Simmons, and some development took place north of the school as well. The same phenomenon occurred in the southern part of town. McMurry, built beyond the far edge of town in 1923, quickly attracted numerous homes north of South Fourteenth and a few around the campus. When Abilene Christian moved to the hill northeast of town, development began south of the school and between the campus and Cedar Creek, even before the new buildings were occupied.

Henry Sayles worked hard at developing the "Sayles Boulevard district." Most of the homes on Meander, Amarillo, Sayles, Highland, and Santos sprang up in the 1920s all the way to South Fourteenth. Sayles also sought to build an elite addition bordering Elm Creek, an area called "Elmwood." One of the first stone houses in the area (1041 Elmwood Drive) was built in 1929.[29] Other additions went west from Grape Street in the northwest. An impressive array of other houses that are considered major Abilene landmarks also trace their beginnings to the 1920s, in several areas of town.[30]

Dimensions of the Construction Boom

The city granted construction permits in the '20s in record numbers—270 building projects in 1920 were estimated to total nearly one and a half million dollars. The rush slowed slightly in 1921, at 210 permits and $1,297,244, but reached over $1.5 million in 1922. The city issued 389 permits in 1923, 453 in 1924, and 643 in 1925. The building surge crested in 1926 with 1,079 projects totaling over four million dollars in value. The high rate of construction continued to the end of the decade, but the numbers declined slightly after 1926, reflecting, perhaps, a weakness in the agricultural arena. Abilene ranked in the top ten in Texas for construction during several of these years.[31]

The County

Outside of the city (could we call it that now?), Taylor County also increased in population by more than 4,000 from 1920 to 1930.[32] The decade of the '20s was the all-time peak of cotton production in Taylor County, with the fluctuating totals averaging just under 40,000 bales a year.[33] The internal combustion engine showed some small impact—while production was increasing, the number of horses and mules employed on the county's farms began to decline slightly. The weather cooperated. Temperatures were seasonable throughout the decade and the rainfall, if not abundant, averaged about an inch and a half above normal.[34]

Modernization
Radio

Abilene was not far behind the curve in radio broadcasting. The first public broadcast came from KDKA Pittsburgh when the station gave the results of the 1920 presidential election. The following year, the federal government began licensing stations; the *Abilene Reporter* secured a license for WQAQ in 1923.[35] WQAQ carried mostly local talent but also played dance records, which provided entertainment for anyone who had a set. The station could occasionally be heard as far away as Maine and California.[36] The studios were in a tall building, to give maximum antenna height. One day a gospel quartet was performing when the accompanist went through an unfamiliar door and somehow fell down the elevator shaft to her death. That ended the station in about 1925.

Three years after that, the newspaper leased another license and moved a private operation called KFYO from Breckenridge to studios on the first floor of the Grace Hotel. Young Grant Turner got a job playing his ukulele and singing, plus answering the telephone to take requests for records to be played. Other live acts included locals like "Cowboy Joe"—a McMurry student named Stuart Hamblen (a Methodist preacher's son who gained national fame as a singer-songwriter); Sam Redwine, a local tailor who played "a mean ragtime piano"; and the Free Sisters. Among out-of-town acts were W. Lee O'Daniel and the Light Crust Doughboys and Jimmy Rodgers. Eventually, the Breckenridge man who owned the license decided to move to Lubbock and took KFYO with him.[37] The paper got the license it needed in 1936 and started Abilene's first permanent radio station, KRBC.[38]

Comparable to the emergence of radio was the continued development of the phonograph. No longer hand-cranked, no longer amplified by a horn, these devices now featured electric drives and electric loudspeakers. Electricity allowed automation—Hall Music Company advertised its newest "Automatic Orthaphonic Victrola" in 1929. It could play twelve records nonstop, changing them automatically![39]

Automobiles

The rise of the automobile led to a demand for many kinds of goods and services. As highways improved and motor cars became more numerous, automobile tourism emerged as a possible source of revenue for Abilene. The city's advantage was in its location as the gateway to the west. It sat squarely astride the Bankhead National Highway, which incorporated portions of other roads in the days before highways were numbered—the Dixie Overland, the Ozark Trail, the Tex-O-Kan, the Colorado-to-Gulf. One enterprising citizen implored the City Council to set aside land for a "tourist campground" to attract still more automobile tourists. "Seven or eight years ago," the citizen argued, "an occasional motorist would pass through; five or six years ago, the occasional motorist had increased to respectable proportions, and last summer [1920] the tourists formed almost a continual procession through the city, bound in all directions." The campground would attract more visitors by offering camping spaces with free wood and water. It could be advertised by roadside signs for "many miles around."[40] That never happened for Abilene, but Vernon, Texas, did it a few months later.

Automobiles would never be successful without the proper support system. This grew slowly but surely—garages, dealerships, streets and highways, traffic signs, "filling stations," and tourist camps. The latter were an advance over the outdoor camp mentioned above. They were located, not near the rail station like the hotels, but on the edges of town where main highways entered. One type was a free-standing frame hut with a bathroom and running water, plus a parking place next to it, six or more in a line with another half dozen facing them. One such endured on east South Eleventh into the 1980s, though long since abandoned. Abilene Courts still stands on South Eleventh as an example of an upgraded facility, a tourist *court* (the rooms arranged in a hollow square, or courtyard) rather than a tourist *camp*. Toward the beginning of World War II, such facilities were upgraded even more and called "motor hotels," a term that soon telescoped into "motel." The tourist court-motel, situated along automobile routes toward the edges of town, sought to combine something close to hotel luxury with easy automobile access.

The *Abilene Daily Reporter* carried a regular weekly column after the war called "Live News from the Automobile and Motor World." It simultaneously published a comment about the public facility known as "the Oak Street Water Trough" for horses.[41] These newspaper features showed that 1921 was the time of transition from "horse-and-buggy" to automobiles. In early 1921, dealers sponsored a "spring motor car show" that sold fifty-six automobiles, and that was not counting "second hand cars."[42] The same issue announced the opening of SSS Motor Co., selling Packards, Hudsons, and Essexes in the new Radford Building on South First between Sycamore and Elm. The dealer offered sales and servicing for his products.[43]

Automobile sales in Abilene skyrocketed. Taylor County's registration of vehicles went from 4,656 in 1922 to 14,072 in 1929. Most sales were new cars, since many families were shifting from horse-drawn to self-propelled vehicles for the first time, and dealers did not much want to accept "Ol' Dobbin" as a trade-in. City streets built to accommodate what was called "the carriage trade" now had to handle scores of cars, with their increased rate of speed and frequency of accidents. The state set speed limits of twenty mph in residential areas and fifteen mph in business districts; enough motorists ignored this to provoke a scolding editorial in the *Daily Reporter*.[44]

The automobile demanded better paving; in fact, most Abilene streets were unimproved at the end of the war. The city commenced to improve its streets, moving outward from the downtown business area. By the end of 1922, most of the downtown was paved. Much of this was a weak surface called bitulithic, but some streets received brick paving, Hickory being the first and Grape having that surface well into the 1960s. Sayles received concrete as a boulevard (lanes of traffic divided by an esplanade), one of several eventually laid down in the city. In 1925, the city completed paving on Pine all the way to Ambler and the Simmons campus. Suburban streets, such as South Eleventh, were paved in the late 1920s, with the homeowners abutting the road picking up a large share of the expense, usually in the form of a city lien on their property until their assessment could be paid. A one million dollar bond issue in 1927 underwrote paving of eighty-two miles of county roads, a task completed in 1929. It marked the completion of one of the last unpaved stretches of the Bankhead Highway.[45]

Downtown congestion sparked a demand for better regulation of traffic. At first, warning signs were sufficient, but soon traffic lights guided the flow at major intersections. Pine and North Second was the first to get a light in 1924. The following year, after that test, the city added eight more lights downtown.[46] School zone warnings went up around the public schools and colleges.[47]

Parking congestion was another problem, but then it always had been, from the horse-and-buggy days. Leading citizen J.M. Radford proposed that parking be banned from Pine and Chestnut streets ("the two main streets of Abilene," in Radford's opinion) between First and

Third streets. A law about this had been on the books since 1915 but not enforced. Radford said, "When this town was laid out, Walnut and Oak Streets were intended to handle the heavy traffic and that is the reason they were made one hundred feet wide... [It] was intended to take care of the farmers' wagons and to become their hitching places. While we have changed largely to automobiles, from a traffic standpoint the situation remains the same."[48] The City Commission did not follow Radford's suggestion, but it did seek to improve access to downtown businesses by setting one-hour limits for parking in the area in 1927.[49]

By 1929, the automobile reigned supreme in Abilene. The machine allowed suburban growth in areas not served by public transportation. It provided employment for scores of new occupations. It began to erode the business and social institutions of the countryside by making access to town so much easier so that the farmer or rancher could now move to town and have city amenities such as electricity, living in town while still tending his farm. Those who continued to reside in the country could now worship in a larger city church, buy their supplies at better-stocked stores, have quick access to an array of medical services, and send their children to bigger schools. The pages of the newspaper teemed with advertisements for automobiles and automobile products. Abilene dealers offered a bewildering array of vehicles— Dodge Brothers, Studebakers, Buicks, Chryslers, Essexes, Hupmobiles, Paiges, Whippets, "the new President Eight," DeSotos, Plymouths, Packards, Hudsons, "the All-American Six," Chevrolets, Oaklands, Oldsmobiles, Cords, Cadillacs, Flints, and Fords, Fords, Fords.[50]

Aviation

Abilene Aviation Co. set up shop two and a half miles west of town on "the Merkel road." The proprietors were an English father and son named Locking. Lt. E.A. Locking, late of the Royal Flying Corps, and another man would be the pilots of the two aircraft. The objective was to teach flying, to provide air service to any point, and to service any other planes that might come along. They called the facility "Pioneer Field" and had about three hundred spectators for the grand opening, at which time several persons took rides.[51] Barnstorming pilots flying World War I surplus planes visited the area from time to time, but the city had no regular facility to land or service them.[52]

The U.S. Navy dirigible *Shenandoah* passed over Abilene in 1924, making a huge stir among the population. Since the itinerary of the airship had been widely circulated, there was great anticipation in town. The fact that headwinds delayed its expected arrival by a short time simply heightened the expectation. Everyone in town, it seemed, turned out on streets and rooftops to see the spectacle. The public schools dismissed their classes for the occasion. *Shenandoah* passed back through the area a few weeks later, but after dark, so that only its ghostly lights could be seen.[53]

Dr. M.T. Ramsey made the first enduring steps toward aviation in Abilene. With a partner, Ramsey bought land east of town in 1925 and set up an airfield, which they called "Kinsolving Field." The field was ready in 1927 when Charles Lindbergh came to town. In May 1927, the young pilot captured the imagination of the world by making a dramatic nonstop solo flight from New York to Paris. After returning to the United States, he made a tour of the country. In September, he flew the *Spirit of St. Louis* into Kinsolving Field for a very brief visit to Abilene. A triumphant motorcade took him to the bandstand beside the post office for a short speech. Cheering throngs greeted him and his official hostess, Abilenian Mildred Paxton Moody, wife of Governor Dan Moody. After a few words downtown, he was whisked back to Kinsolving Field and soon took off. His visit lasted less than two hours, yet it became one of the most memorable events in Abilene's history. Even visits from presidents and ex-presidents never stirred such interest.[54]

Charles Lindbergh visit, 1927. COURTESY OF HARDIN-SIMMONS UNIVERSITY

Lindbergh's visit further stimulated the town's interest in flying. Ramsey hired L.E. Derryberry to be his chief pilot and airport manager. A few other pilots hung out at the field and gave flying lessons to daring Abilenians, including women. The voters overwhelmingly approved a 1929 bond issue that allowed the city to purchase Kinsolving Field and make it a public institution with upgraded facilities and services. Abilene was one of the first Texas cities to have its own municipal airfield.[55]

Electrification

Construction on a new power plant began in 1920 but took two years to complete. The plant was located just east of Cedar Creek off Highway 80. The plant would burn either oil or gas. Its smokestack, competed in 1921, was visible for miles around. It was 187½ feet from base to top and thirty-four feet in circumference at the top. The American Public Service Company, which operated the facility, included an ice plant that could turn out fifty tons per day and store 2,000 tons. The generator came on stream in the fall of 1921. It soon became apparent that Abilene's demand for power was growing, so another unit was added in 1926.[56] In 1923 the electric service industry in Abilene reorganized under the name West Texas Utilities, providing a brand that endured into the twenty-first century and allowing a structure that could meet the exponential growth of electric needs.

The City Commission decided in 1923, that the newly available power could be used to make the city prettier and safer. They authorized a street lighting system that would be called Abilene's "White Way." It would make the community's "paved streets and boulevards the best lighted of any city in her class in the Southwest." The overhead lights illuminated over seven miles of Abilene streets. When the system was turned on, 5,000 people showed up at the post office lawn for the lighting ceremony. On the evening of May 20, 1924, Mayor Charles Coombs ordered, "let there be light!" Public works commissioner W.D. Mayfield threw the switch, and behold, there was light . . . at least in the paved parts of town.[57]

The class that benefited most from electrification was the housewife. Her workload was immensely simplified and eased by the addition of electrical appliances. Dealers in Abilene were happy to supply these devices. West Texas Utilities entered the retail market in these items, selling, for example, electric stoves—"it's reliable and produces delicious meals."[58] The utility also provided lighting fixtures[59] and a vacuum cleaner called "The Premier Duplex." In dusty West Texas, a vacuum cleaner was a godsend, vastly superior to the traditional feather duster, which merely rearranged the dust.[60]

The most onerous of household chores were clothes washing and ironing. WTU offered a washing machine called the "Fedelco,"[61] which would wash the clothing with a powered agitator and wring the items out using an electric mangle. Electric dryers were yet over the horizon, so clothing had to be hung on a clothesline to dry, but even so, the advantage of the electric washing machine was incalculable. Mondays would be much easier. Ironing was an even worse task, involving heating flatirons on a stove and then using them to flatten out the wrinkles in cotton fabrics. In wintertime, this hot task was perhaps tolerable, but ironing in summer included heating the stove in addition to standing over the hot iron. An electric iron could make the whole business much more comfortable so that Tuesdays, too, would be easier. It might be noted that air-conditioning, like electric dryers, still lay in the future. But even here, electricity was invaluable—it could turn the blades of the new electric fans. Many homes in Abilene possessed such appliances by the end of the decade.

One electric appliance that would become a necessity in ensuing decades was slow to gain acceptance in the '20s, but it was one of the few products that would grow in sales even during the depression. It was the refrigerator. Heretofore, the most advanced method of food preservation was the icebox, which kept food at cool temperatures through the melting of ice.[62] Abilene's ice plant was a thriving business, but that was about to decline in the face of the new technology. By 1929, a few Abilene homes had refrigerators, purchased from West Texas Utilities or one of its retail competitors.[63] The proper name for these devices was "refrigerator," but people of that generation continued to call it "the icebox" for decades.

Education
Colleges: Lose One, Gain One

The desire for a state technical college in West Texas did not die after the fiasco of 1917. The West Texans continued to lobby hard for a school, and the legislature finally passed the needed bill to authorize a school. Once again, towns submitted bids to host the new college. Abilene may have felt it had the inside track after being

James Winford Hunt, founder of McMurry College.
COURTESY OF MCMURRY UNIVERSITY

disappointed in 1917. A state selection committee visited some thirty-seven applicant towns, including Abilene, before accepting Lubbock's bid in 1923 to be the site for the new "Texas Technological College." [64]

But there was some consolation for Abilene in that its third denominational college opened in the fall that same year—the Methodist school named McMurry College.

James Winford Hunt had been a cowboy, newspaperman, and minister during his colorful career. The son of an Army contract doctor, he was born in the Kaw Indian camp in northern Oklahoma. The family moved to the high plains of Texas in 1881, joining a Quaker colony called Estacado. Later he became a Methodist, then a Methodist minister, holding churches all over Northwest Texas. Hunt succeeded to the presidency of the denomination's Stamford College in 1916 and led the faltering school until 1918, when a fire destroyed the administration building. At that point, the trustees decided to end the school, and Hunt returned to the pastorate of St. Paul Methodist Church in Abilene, which he had left to assume the reins of Stamford College.

The dream of a college did not die, and Hunt began to agitate for construction of another Methodist school, maybe in Abilene. When the church's regional governing body, the Northwest Texas Conference, expressed interest in renewing its commitment to higher education, members at St. Paul and other Abilenians began to make plans. Stamford and other towns also wanted the school, so a bidding war of sorts began. In 1920, Abilene won by offering 25 acres of land on the city's far south side, a substantial sum of cash, streetcar connections, and free city water. The land and much of the money came from four men —Presbyterian Henry Sayles, Jr. Episcopalian Ed Hughes, Baptist K.K. Legett, and Methodist J.M. Cunningham. Denominational loyalties did not stand in the way of promoting the growth of Abilene.

Bishop William F. McMurry, presiding over the Northwest Texas Conference that year, appointed Hunt to be commissioner for the new school, with the obvious intention that he would be president when it materialized. Hunt's work was rewarded in 1923 with the opening of the new school. At first, it provided an "academy" (a high school) and two college grades. By 1926, it was prepared to offer its first baccalaureate degrees for four years of college-level work. It engaged in sports and debate and other intercollegiate activities from the very beginning, taking the nickname "Indians" in respect for the founding president's roots. The school retained that name until 2006, when it was forced by the NCAA to disavow the team name and related symbols for athletic purposes.

Growth of the Public Schools

During the 1920s, Abilene High School moved into a new facility; the district added several elementary schools; and AHS football teams achieved statewide success, including two state championships.

Those seemed to be the big happenings of the decade for the public schools. But buildings and sports were only part of campus life. One of the really significant events of the decade came with the hiring of Raymond T. Bynum as band director in 1926.

When Bynum came onto the Abilene High School staff, the administration expected him to diversify the school's music program from its current state, a variety of vocal ensembles and choruses. What Abilene High needed was a boys' band, and Bynum was just the man to deliver it. Abilene had had bands before, dating back almost to the founding, but they were town bands, not school groups.

October 15, 1926, is the birthday of the AHS band, the day Bynum gathered twenty boys and their miscellaneous instruments together to begin once-a-week practices after school. They developed into a nice little group and hoped to have uniforms by the following year. "Many ... believe them to be the nucleus of a well-trained high school band," the school yearbook said hopefully.[65] And so it happened. With uniforms, the band expanded to twenty-nine players in the fall of 1927, and the "boys stepped out in their black and gold" as a marching band.[66] It claimed to be the first high school marching band in the state, the vanguard of thousands to come. It was a sign of the times that the band was still all-male. Eventually, there developed a parallel "Girls Band," and this arrangement continued until 1947. After twenty years as an all-male group, the AHS band "integrated" by merging the two ensembles into one band. "This year for the first time," the yearbook proclaimed, "the Eagle Band consists of both boys and girls."[67] Bynum left AHS after the 1945-46 school year to begin the work of awakening the McMurry College band from its wartime hibernation. The Eagle Band was one of the most distinguished ensembles in the state, and its graduates went on to significant careers. Some were killed in World War II.

A second tradition at AHS began in 1925, when the school initiated publication of a campus newspaper. Since the "Eagle" logo was just

The first Abilene High School marching band.
COURTESY OF HARDIN-SIMMONS UNIVERSITY

catching on and since the yearbook was already called *The Flashlight*, the student paper became *The Battery*. In various forms and under generations of sponsors and student editors and staff, *The Battery* has been produced with distinction ever since that time.

The numerous new elementary schools were necessary to meet the growing demands of the town. School-age population (6 to 20 years) increased from 2,990 in 1920 to 6,320 in 1930, about the same rate as the overall city population.[68] Further, an increasing percentage of young people began seeing their education all the way through, from first grade to eleventh grade.[69] School overcrowding became so severe that the local Lion's Club, which studied the matter in 1924, told the school board that "based upon the average increase in attendance for the past four years, the City should provide one ten-room building per year for the next five years."[70]

Responsibility for managing this vast expansion fell on the shoulders of the superintendent, and Abilene was fortunate to have one man in that post throughout the decade. He was Roland D. Green, who served from 1917 to 1937. One observer remarked of Green: "His contributions are many but his legacy is best remembered by the system's aggressive building program of the 1920s, which relieved pressures that rapid growth generated." Green also added vocational, shop, and home economics classes to the curriculum.[71]

Among the continuing concerns about overcrowding, the school board busied itself with teacher qualifications. Those were partly dictated by the state, but local policy could also apply. For example, the board allowed only unmarried women to serve as teachers in the Abilene system. When the case of a married woman came up in 1927, the school board voted unanimously to enforce the standing regulation that required a female teacher to resign immediately if she married. The same policy, of course, did not apply to male educators.[72]

The Man Who Built Abilene

On the record, Abilene was already three years old, and even had some brick and stone buildings, when David Castle was born. But David Castle was really the man who built Abilene, even though he never set foot in the town until 1914.

Among his designs still standing as Abilene landmarks are the Oldham Building, the Park Building, the Windsor Hotel, the Wooten Hotel, the Paramount Theater, the Minter Building, the current Post Office/Federal Building, Old Main and President Hall at McMurry, several buildings at ACU and Hardin-Simmons, the former Abilene High-Lincoln Middle School, Alta Vista and Valley View schools, the Abilene Woman's Club, and numerous other public buildings in West Texas. He planned most of the West Texas Utilities offices in the region and all of the Radford grocery chain wholesale buildings. There were Castle-designed hotels, high schools, courthouses, businesses, and churches all over West Texas. Castle also planned private homes using multiple styles—718 Victoria (Prairie), 1642 Swenson (Prairie and Eclectic), 1545 North Fifth (Prairie), 2102 Swenson (Spanish Mission Revival), 346 Mulberry (Gothic Revival) and others.

David S. Castle left his Michigan home at age fifteen and worked his way through an engineering education in Chicago. Working for the Chicago Telephone and Telegraph Company, he developed a specialty in designing telephone office buildings. This talent brought him to Texas to work for Southwestern Bell and then into private practice with a Fort Worth architectural firm. The Fort Worth business sent him to Abilene to open a branch, and he went out on his own the following year. An avid golfer, he was one of the founders of the Abilene Country Club.

Though he has been gone from the scene for decades, his mark is still very much on the city in many of its signature buildings.

Sources: Donald Frazier, Robert Pace, Steve Butman *Abilene Landmarks: An Illustrated Tour* (Abilene: State House Press, 2008) features ten Castle-designed buildings among its hundred choices; Larry Abrigg, *Abilene Historical Landmarks* (Abilene: City of Abilene, 1987) includes a dozen or more Castle designs among its seventy-five selections; see biographical sketch in Hugh E. Cosby, ed. *The History of Abilene* (Abilene: Hugh E. Cosby Co., 1955), pp. 256-259.

Chapter Ten
Positioning 1920-1930

When people think of the 1920s, they think less about the business boom, and more about prohibition and bootlegging, "flaming youth" in flivvers, the Jazz Age, the Ku Klux Klan, the flight of Charles Lindbergh, the rise of spectator sports, the evolution controversy, and scandalous behavior in the movies.

This was an era of culture clash, when the values and traditions of an older, simpler America seemed to be challenged by a new, complex world based on the standards of the city. From biblical times, rural folk have been suspicious of urban culture and the traps it holds for the unwary and the unsophisticated. In the early '20s, the United States crossed from being a predominantly rural society to a predominantly urban one. That was true in West Texas, too; sometime in the decade, the population of the Taylor county seat surpassed the population of the rest of the county.[1]

Urbanization was only one element of the culture war. Another cause was the presence of a large number of unassimilated immigrants who arrived on our American shores from Southern, Central, and Eastern Europe between 1900 and 1914. They brought value systems totally foreign to the traditional American patterns. Few of these immigrants had penetrated to the Southwest, but they were coming to dominate popular culture—music, humor, motion pictures, radio, magazines, newspapers—in the Eastern cities and in Hollywood. And yet another challenge to traditional values came from the veterans— "How you gonna keep 'em down on the farm after they've seen Paree?"

The reaction to all this went in two sharply divergent directions. One group of Americans fought against change, seeing the face of evil in the growing independence and iconoclasm of "flaming youth" and those who influenced them. This movement produced a wide range of reactions, seeking means of preserving the culture of the past, even if it meant going outside the law to do it. Another group of Americans plunged headlong into the new scene, rejoicing in a new freedom and reveling in hedonism, the pleasure of the present moment. Both of these were present in Abilene.

Pursuit of the Past
Nativism

In 1920, ten percent of American residents were foreign-born. Most of that migration stayed in the Northeast, but it upset the cultural status quo sufficiently to prompt a reaction called "nativism." Nativism was an attempt to preserve the traditional white Protestant Anglo-Saxon culture against the influences of the Irish, Germans, Slavs, Jews, Italians, and others who threatened it. These "others" did not observe the Sabbath properly, they were "wets," they were frequently dark-skinned, they did not speak proper English, they were often Roman Catholic or something even more exotic, they were poor, their standards of sexual morality seemed different, they did not assimilate easily. "Americanization" was an attempt to facilitate rapid assimilation to traditional American values and patterns and was a widely used term across the nation.

The passions raised in the United States in World War I carried over into the postwar period in the form of xenophobic isolationism that lasted for much of the decade. The manifestations of this xenophobia included race riots, lynchings, isolationist foreign policy, prohibition, opposition to presidential candidate Alfred E. Smith, all summarized in the re-emergence of the Ku Klux Klan. Did nativism reach Abilene? Absolutely! To be sure, the community had no race riots as such, and Abilene supported American participation in the League of Nations, but all the other elements were present.

The Ku Klux Klan of the 1920s can be distinguished from the Klan of Reconstruction and the post-World War II manifestation of the hooded order in several ways. First, it was widely supported, claiming as many as five million adherents nationwide. It was national, with some of its strongest influences in Oregon, Indiana, Massachusetts, and Oklahoma as well as in the South. The Klan involved itself prominently and visibly in politics, often endorsing and publishing a list of acceptable candidates. Membership came from the basic middle class—lawyers, ministers, physicians, bankers, merchants, teachers— as well as from its usual stronghold in the lower middle and lower classes. It was anti-black, like the Klans before and after, but also actively anti-Catholic, anti-Jewish, and anti-immigrant. The Klan attempted to enforce prohibition where the law could not reach it; to warn and punish wife-beaters, adulterers, prostitutes, and their patrons; and to protect the community against lawlessness of any form (except its own, of course). Klansmen saw themselves as a bulwark against a modernist assault on Christian moral, cultural, and intellectual standards, and rejoiced that they were not bound by legalities in the righting of wrongs.

The Klan came to Abilene in 1921. Without revealing its membership, the Klan approached the newspaper by telephone, asking the editor to seek permission for a downtown parade from Mayor Scarborough. The newspaper agreed to do that, thereby making itself a partner of the hooded order while maintaining an appearance of

Fair Park auto race. COURTESY OF HARDIN-SIMMONS UNIVERSITY

neutrality. Mayor Scarborough granted permission, and the paper printed his response. On Thanksgiving Day, some 225 hooded Klansmen paraded through the downtown streets before a large throng of spectators lining the way. After dark, the city's lights went out, and the Klansmen continued the march with burning crosses and other small lights. Eventually, the lights came back on and the event ended.[2] Obviously, the Klan had active support from the newspaper and the city government. When the Klan wanted to use Fair Park for a ceremony in 1922, it had free rein to do what it wished, including burning a forty-foot cross in the racetrack. Later that year, the hooded order had permission to do the same things in connection with the West Texas Fair. Other Klan activities, often only hinted in rumors, continued in the city through 1922.[3]

Although the Klan was supposed to be anonymous, prominent citizens lent their prestige to the hooded order. Editor Frank Grimes gave, at the very least, tacit support to the Klan. If President Jefferson Davis Sandefer of Simmons was not a Klansman, he was clearly a Klan sympathizer. He proudly noted that his father had been in the post-Civil War Klan. The president's brother was one of the few who could be identified as a current member. President Jesse Sewell of ACC had a visitation and donation from the Klan during a service at College Church of Christ. He accepted the donation, apparently without comment. Klan visitations at First Methodist and First Baptist had similar outcomes.[4]

The Klan held another giant rally in Fair Park in April 1923. Three to four hundred hooded men and about fifty hooded women paraded past the grandstand and eventually burned a cross. The spectacle included a Klan brass band (one has to wonder how they could blow their horns through a hood), tableaux on the football field, and even an airplane emblazoned with a scarlet cross overhead. The Klan speaker denounced San Angelo as an un-American city for denying the Klan a permit to parade there but was "glad a progressive city like Abilene accorded them that right."[5]

Very few people initially opposed the Klan, partly because the earliest Klan pronouncements seemed reasonable and in line with the standard values of the town. But as time went on and the Klan's influence became more pervasive, misgivings and then outright opposition emerged. Like the national Klan, the Abilene Klavern went into politics, endorsing candidates who appeared favorable to it. (Non-partisan, of course; in Texas in that day, there was only a choice between Democrats). That sparked some resistance, even from the newspaper. Editor Grimes's opposition was belated (1926, by which time the Klan was in general disrepute) and lukewarm.[6]

The real resistance to the Klan came not from the churches, not from the colleges, not from the businessmen, not from the newspaper, not from law enforcement, but from the local legal community, especially J.M. Wagstaff. Wagstaff and fellow attorneys J.F. Cunningham, E.M. Overshiner, and Harry Tom King organized an anti-Klan rally in late 1924, centered on the gubernatorial campaign in which the Klan had endorsed a candidate. Wagstaff debated Rev. Lewis Stuckey of St.

Judge John M. Wagstaff, lawyer, college president, bank president, state representative, churchman—the man who beat the Klan in Abilene. COURTESY OF JACK NORTH

Paul Methodist Church over the issue in Baird. In the public debate, Wagstaff challenged Stuckey to deny that he was the head of Abilene Klan Chapter 139. Stuckey evaded the question.[7]

After 1924, Klan influence quickly waned in Abilene and across the nation. Sex scandals involving Klan leaders nationally (and, reputedly, locally as well) undermined the Klan's credibility as the bulwark of the American home. Most members soon tried to forget all about it.

A last gasp of '20s nativism occurred in the 1928 presidential election. The Democrats nominated Governor Alfred E. Smith of New York, a Catholic who was associated with the notorious Tammany Hall political machine, who looked and sounded like the New York Irishman he was and who advocated repeal of prohibition. Loyal Democrats in Taylor County wrestled with their consciences over Smith; could they vote for him, who stood for everything they opposed, or could they hold their noses and vote for the Republican Herbert Hoover? In November, Taylor County voted Republican for the first time ever, and the last time for another twenty-four years. Taylor County abhorred Smith even more than Texas did; he got only thirty-one percent of the vote in the county while winning forty-eight percent statewide.[8] But Abilenians were not turning Republican just yet; in the same election, over eighty percent of them voted for the Democratic senatorial and gubernatorial candidates.[9]

Minorities

The number of blacks in Abilene took a substantial drop between 1910 and 1920, if the census figures can be believed. There emerges the suspicion that they cannot; Abilenians of the day constantly disputed the census returns, feeling their population was seriously under-reported. If that were indeed the case, it would go double for the black population. The census found 602 blacks in town in 1910 but only 410 in 1920, while the black population grew to 1,403 by 1930.[10]

Their lot was not much better than it was in other portions of the southern United States, save that their small numbers made them less of threat to "white supremacy." The local Ku Klux Klan, despite its disavowal of violence, engaged in sporadic terror attacks on the black community. Porters in local hotels were especially vulnerable, often being suspected of pimping or bootlegging. The Abilene press reported several instances of abductions and beatings in the spring and summer of 1922.[11] This intimidation climaxed in September when masked men shot and killed Grover C. Everett at a hotel in the black section of Abilene. No one was ever charged, although Judge W.R. Ely pushed local law enforcement hard to solve the case. The judge publicly alleged that the failure to find the culprits was directly attributable to foot-dragging on the part of the prosecutor and the sheriff, whom the judge believed to be Klansmen. Even Ely was no champion of blacks, saying of the murdered man, "Of course, he was just a negro . . ."[12]

Segregation and white supremacy were the order of the day in Abilene. Editor Frank Grimes of the *Abilene Daily Reporter* published several editorials supporting white supremacy in no uncertain terms. He took it as an unassailable fact that whites were superior. "The main difference between the races is that they are in different stages of evolution."[13] "The Caucasian is the dominant race . . . its brains, natural ability, commonsense, rule the earth." He even lamented that Cau-

Judge Walter R. Ely, jurist, highway commissioner, namesake of Judge Ely Boulevard. COURTESY OF JACK NORTH

casian medical advances were keeping the death rates down in foreign lands, and that might come back to haunt the West. And trade with the underdeveloped world might do the same, enhancing the survival of races whose needs were "beyond what can be supplied by their own acreage and natural resources. However, nature's law of the survival of the fittest is not going to be repealed."[14] Grimes reflected fairly closely the opinions of most of his readers.

Blacks lived in a segregated section of northeast Abilene. With the exception of a few ministers, teachers, and other professions serving the black community, they engaged in menial tasks. They patronized a segregated business community. There was a segregated Masonic and Eastern Star lodge. They worshipped in segregated churches, Mount Zion Baptist (1885) being the oldest.[15] Their children attended segregated schools. Their schoolbooks, their supplies, even their buildings were hand-me-downs. The city put up a one-room school for black children in the 200 block of Plum in 1890. When this became too crowded, the principal, a man named Harvey, moved the classes to a nearby Baptist church. In 1902, the city moved the North Ward school building to North Seventh and Treadaway as the facility for black education, while a new North Ward school was erected for the white students. In 1921, the district constructed a new building for College Heights and moved the existing structure to the North Seventh and Treadaway location as the "new" "Abilene Colored School."[16]

The white community associated their black neighbors with vice. Whites alleged that gambling, prostitution, and bootlegging were rife in the black section. A sting operation in 1918 netted nineteen black bootleggers. In one arrest, federal, state, and local lawmen "accosted a negro, spoke a few words—and right before the astonished eyes of the officers, the negro accepted pay for the booze and passed over the pint."[17] The *Reporter* also railed against prostitution, locating it in the black community and saying the women should be put on a chain gang and their white patrons should be publicly exposed. "The Reporter has referred to cleaning out 'nigger' town several times, but it don't [sic] seem to do any good . . . 'Nigger' town in Abilene is a public disgrace and will result in hardships for the good and worthy negroes of the city unless there is a change."[18] Black leaders felt the same danger. A few years later, L.D. Glover, principal of the black school, called for a cleanup of "the largest bunch of sorry negroes just lying about town" because sometime soon, one of them might commit some egregious crime that would bring the down the wrath of the white community on all black citizens.[19] Nationwide, the absolute low point of relations between the races from emancipation to the present was the time right after the First World War. That appeared to be the case in Abilene, too.

Evidence of a quiet population shift began to emerge in 1920. Heretofore, Hispanic names had been very little in evidence in Abilene, but more and more people were moving in directly from Mexico, many pushed out by the revolutionary violence of 1914-20. Others were only a generation removed from Mexico. This created some problems in the schools, with the result that the AISD set up a special campus called an "Americanization school" in 1920. There was a national trend toward "Americanization" prompted mainly by the influx of European immigrants between 1900 and 1914. The census of 1920 did not differentiate Hispanics, but it can be seen that the combined totals of Abilenians who were either foreign-born or had foreign-born parents was still quite small. The "Americanization school" was for children who spoke mainly Spanish, and it operated only five months a year "due to agricultural demands."[20] In 1925, the school moved to new quarters as "the Mexican School."

Pursuit of Pleasure
The Jazz Age

The Jazz Age came to Abilene through the media, first the movies and then the newspaper. The titillating titles and subject matter of the motion pictures early roused a storm of protest in an Abilene not all that long removed from the Victorian era. Many of that generation would not pronounce the word "leg," substituting "limb" in its place, which seemed awkward when they referred to the "limbs" of a table.

Early on, the ministers of the community mobilized to deal with the movies, which were silent films with written subtitles. Movies were a popular entertainment in Abilene, with several theaters to choose among. They had been part of the Abilene scene for at least a decade.[21] The notices for these features received prominent mention in the newspapers, and the ads and articles suggested somewhat risqué programs. One among many in 1921 was *The Girl with the Jazz Heart*, about a young woman who was seeking love advice from another woman who was "a devotee at the shrine of Jazz."[22] Observing films of this sort, the city attorney, B.A. Cox, served notice that he would draw up and ask the City Commission to pass an ordinance establishing the office of censor for Abilene. Some films, he said, were "a disgrace to OUR civilization and shocking to the refined moral sensitivities of our girls and the motherhood of our land."[23]

Cox rallied public opinion to his side, receiving endorsement from most of the local ministers and a church woman's group. Dr. Jenkens of First Baptist said that censorship "is a thing that must come, not only for Abilene, but for the whole country." Jenkens did not like crime movies or those featuring "loose relations between the sexes."[24] Despite resistance from the local motion picture operators, the ordinance passed after several delays, mostly occasioned by the practical matters of getting the process to work. In February, Mayor Dallas Scarborough appointed a five-person Board of Censors, Chief Clinton and four local women. They did not meet as a board to do their work but instead rotated through the job, one person reviewing films each week. The full board served as an appeals panel.[25] A questionable film could be banned altogether or shown only with the objectionable scenes deleted.

Apparently, not everyone agreed with the board's decisions. Enough complaints surfaced, mainly from the clergy, that the city named a ten-member censorship board in 1925. Complaints continued to arise, and the commission named yet another board in 1928. These boards also censored live shows, mainly by telling producers to delete or amend certain features from future versions of the performance. The censorship continued into the 1930s.[26]

Movies were not the only threats to public morals at the time. In 1923, the *Abilene Daily Reporter* began carrying a series of syndicated articles of a sensationalist nature. One such was headlined "How 'Vamps' Are Used in Modern Business." "Vamping," the article said, "has become a recognized profession. As in olden days, the modern vamp preys upon impressionable men, luring him with her smiles, fascinating him with her beauty, and separating him from his money. . . . Today, instead of being freelance in the wide open battlefields of fortune, she works for a regular salary, and is employed by big business . . . Are you a 'born' vamp? Then don't fritter away your gifts in useless flirtations. Big business has a job for you."[27] A charming young woman with a good knowledge of stocks and bonds or of automobiles, the ad suggested, could outsell the best male salesman in the world, but it sounded worse than that. Mothers shuddered when they saw their daughters being recruited for such roles.[28]

The male form of vamping was "mashing." "Masher" referred to a man who attempted to force his attention on women by various forms of bizarre behavior. The city sought to pour cold water on its "flaming youth" by outlawing vamping, mashing, and all other forms of flirting. Sometimes the language of the anti-flirting ordinances went to ridiculous lengths and, in the end, probably had little effect on human nature.

Dancing was another problem, involving as it did close physical contact between the sexes. When some of the local World War I veterans wanted to have a street dance on the Fourth of July 1919, public outcry led by Dr. Jenkens of First Baptist Church and other ministers forced its cancellation. When the Masonic Lodge sponsored a 1921 street dance, blocking off Cypress between North Second and North Third for the event, Jenkens was there again to protest the misuse of the public domain. Dancing was of course forbidden at the three local colleges, a stance that endured until McMurry broke down and allowed it in the late 1950s. But dancing went on, especially because phonographs were becoming increasingly popular and because the radio broadcast dance music was a staple of its programming.

Violations of the prohibition laws happened in Abilene, as they did all over the nation, though Abilene had no overt gang wars over the matter. There appeared to be no organized criminal conspiracy in town. Bootleggers were much more likely to be isolated amateurs seeking a fast buck. Much of the illegal beverage alcohol came in from other places. But there was domestic production as well. Police found an illegal still at North Fifteenth and Pine, run by two white men. They confiscated three quarts of whiskey and fifty pounds of mash.[29] This was likely only the tip of the iceberg.

Since Abilene had been officially dry since 1902, the passage of the national prohibition law had little effect locally. It did expand prohibition enforcement to include federal officers, and it cut off neighboring liquor oases. Probably some Abilenians found ways of circumventing the law, but that sort of thing seldom gets recorded.

Sports

The decade of the 1920s is sometimes called the "golden age of sports," the time when spectator sports of all kinds found their archetypal heroes—Babe Ruth, Bobby Jones, Bill Tilden, Red Grange, Jack Dempsey, Gertrude Ederle. Sports had been important in Abilene for a good while, but now the city began to share in the national sports craze, though Abilene's really golden age lay ahead in the 1950s.

One element of Abilene's sports awakening was the advent of semi-professional baseball. Abilene had a team in the West Texas League beginning in 1920. The team, called the Abilene Eagles, was successful from the start, winning the league title over the Ranger Nitros in 1920 and over the Sweetwater team in 1921. The ownership was a local consortium.[30] The *Abilene Reporter* promoted the team with purple prose—the paper hailed shortstop W.M. Etheridge as one who "wields a wicked smash of the pill," while outfielder John Bechtol "held down the center garden for the Eagles . . . grabbing 'em off and covering the terra firma."[31] The Eagles finished sixth in the six-team league in 1922, after which the league disbanded. When the West Texas League resumed in 1928, Abilene's team did not fare as well. After two seasons, the depression caused the league to fold again.[32]

The other Abilene Eagles, the high school team, had substantial football success in the decade, playing in three state championship games and winning two of them, led by a dynamic little coach named P.E. "Pete" Shotwell. The nickname "Eagles" did not apply to AHS teams before 1923, not even to the 1922 state finalist football team.

Coach P. E. "Pete" Shotwell.
COURTESY OF MCMURRY UNIVERSITY

That team lost the state championship to Waco, 13-10, on the strength of a drop-kicked field goal in the closing minutes. Waco was the only team to score a touchdown against the Abilene eleven that season. Photographs of those games show some of the players in action without helmets, while the others wore thin leather head-coverings. Team stars were Earl Guitar and Bob Estes.[33]

The next season, AHS acquired the "Eagles" nickname, which may have been the inspiration for their return to the state championship.[34] Once again, they faced their old nemesis, Waco. This time, Eagle captain Pete Hanna provided the only score of the game with a field goal of his own. The 1923 team beat Dublin, 104-0, and Fort Stockton, 95-0, in bi-district during its championship run.[35] Nine of the 1923 Eagles won all-state honors—left guard Tubby Hembree, center Dick Bryan, right end Herring Bounds, right halfback Dub Wooten, and fullback Roy Stevens on the first team; and left tackle J.T. Watson, right guard Bill Rathmell, quarterback Chili Wells, and left halfback Hanna on the second team.[36] It was a pleasing reward, though not intended that way, for these players to enter their new high school building just two months later.[37]

After a few off years, the Eagles were back in the playoffs again in 1927. Under new coach Dewey Mayhew, they went undefeated until they lost in the playoffs to, of course, Waco High. Fullback and captain Aultman Smith, guard Dan Salkeld, quarterback Esco Walter, and tackle Don Burger earned places on the all-state first team.[38] The 1927 success paved the way for the 1928 season, when the Eagles captured their second state crown in football in six years.[39] The 1928 version of the Eagles walloped Port Arthur, 38-0, in the championship game.

The Goo-Goo Eyes Ordinance

The term "goo-goo eyes" had been in common parlance from the turn of the century and was the theme of a 1923 popular song, which had a refrain "Barney Google, with those goo-goo-goo-ga-ly eyes." No one could be quite sure how to define the look, but it was supposed to be an intensely flirtatious expression. The city fathers of Abilene, however, gave it legal definition in a 1925 ordinance outlawing "any person who by word, sign, gesture, wink, facial expression or look shall seek to attract the attention or form the acquaintance of any person of the opposite sex other than a friend or acquaintance for the purpose of making a mash or flirting." The term "making goo-goo eyes" was part of the ordinance. The law further denounced "lascivious, lewd, [or] indecent" acts between the sexes on the streets or in an automobile.

The ordinance made Abilene the laughingstock of the nation for a while. Newspapers all over the country gleefully recounted how the West Texas hicks had tried to outlaw something no one could even define. But the city was in earnest! In the first six months after passage, eleven men and one woman were convicted of mashing and were fined accordingly.

Sources: Tate, "Abilene's Golden Era," pp. 92-93; Paul D. Lack and Gerald McDaniel, "Did the Jazz Age Come to Abilene?" DVD in the Abilene Public Library Centennial Series, October 20, 1981; the woman might have argued that she wasn't mashing—she was vamping, an offense not covered by the ordinance.

Chapter Eleven
Poverty 1930-1939

The stock market crash of 1929 made no immediate impression on Abilene. The area had already entered into a mild economic decline, and "hard times" were not unusual to rural West Texans. Most people thought it was a matter that affected only a few New York investors. That proved to be a miscalculation.

One characteristic of depression was that everything slowed down. The mark of a depression was not so much what happened as what did *not* happen. There were no long bread lines in Abilene, nor were apple sellers and bootblacks thronging Pine Street.[1] Instead, the downtown in a depression simply showed a lack of activity, a lack of people, an aura of abandonment. The town seemed vacant. There were plenty of parking places, and the stores were nearly empty.

Life went on, to be sure. People got married, though not so frequently. Babies were born, though not so many. The years 1932-34 produced the smallest cohort of American children of any comparable period in the twentieth century. People still died on a regular basis, perhaps even a little faster. Farmers grew crops, but with less profit.

When, at its nadir, unemployment hit twenty-five percent in 1933, that still meant that seventy-five percent of workers had jobs. When depression survivors are interviewed, they will often say, "Well, we knew some folks who were unemployed, but Dad always had a job," or "we were hard up for a while, but Papa caught on with the WPA and things worked out." People muddled through somehow, but it wasn't easy.

The Ordeal of Depression
The Public Crisis

The statistics of the depression are . . . well, depressing. The value of building permits for Abilene, which was annually in the millions in the 1920s, dropped precipitously. The figure got up to $4,000,000 in 1926 before subsiding slightly.[2] Compared with that, only $183,000 worth of construction went up in 1931, and the trend bottomed out at $54,741 for the whole city in 1933. That was just over one percent of the 1926 figure. By 1936, the industry was recovering, reaching $383,151 and then climbing up to $781,674 in 1938, before succumbing to the "Roosevelt Recession" in 1939 and 1940.[3] The 1935 recovery, while not all the way back, made Abilene eighth in the state for building permits that year, behind only Dallas, Houston, Austin, San Antonio, Fort Worth, Galveston, and Tyler.[4] These numbers were a pretty fair indicator of how the depression went nationwide—worsening precipitously through 1932, bottoming out in 1933, rising slowly through 1937, sliding backward in 1938 and then climbing again with the onset of wartime spending.

Under the headline "Recovery in Abilene nearly attains normal level—few lines of business not all the way back," the *Daily Reporter* painted an optimistic picture of Abilene's economic health as 1936 began, overly optimistic, in fact. The indicators showed not only an upswing but also the depths to which the town had fallen. Postal receipts, for example, were $184,000 in 1929, dropping to a low of $138,000 in 1932, then rising slowly to $160,000 in 1935.[5]

The numbers of utility customers showed a similar profile. There were 6,748 electrical subscribers in 1930, 6,341 in 1932, and 6,261 in 1935. Telephones, which could viewed as less of a necessity, reacted more sharply. Abilene phone users were 4,700 in 1930, down to 3,875 in 1933, but recovering to 4,911 in 1935. Natural gas hookups fell from 6,127 in 1930 to 5,000 in 1932, before rebounding to 6,097 in 1935.[6] Active water connections stood at 5,529 in 1930, then fell and did not regain that level until 1934, from which point they continued to rise.[7]

The public school enrollment, which boasted 5,832 pupils in 1929, dropped to 4,248 by 1932, then began to recover, reaching 5,057 by the fall of 1935.[8] The three colleges, with substantial student populations from outside Abilene, lost more significantly in the short run. Simmons dropped from 1,391 students in 1929 to 792 in 1932, after which it began a slow recovery. ACC's enrollment went from 517 in 1929 to 405 in 1931 but rebounded thereafter. McMurry lost from 1929's 593 down to 339 in 1932 before stabilizing. Simmons and McMurry did not reach their pre-depression enrollment levels until after the war, but Abilene Christian's student body actually grew larger.[9] Two contradictory factors were at work in college attendance, the first being that parents with diminished incomes could not pay for their children's education during the depression. On the other hand, high school graduates with no immediate employment opportunities could find in college a beneficial alternative to fruitless job hunting. Maybe jobs, better jobs, would be more plentiful after four years for people with enhanced credentials.

The numbers indicate that 1933 was rock bottom for Abilene, after which things began to improve slightly. It is likely, judging from the utility and school numbers, that the population declined. Certainly the lost college enrollments would have diminished the count. But most Abilenians were still in town, hunkered down and trying to last out the crisis.

Part of the recovery after 1933 has to be attributed to the infusion of federal money into the economy, compensating to a degree for the radically diminished private-sector investments. It should also be noted that states, counties, and cities spent heavily on roads and other improvements in the 1920s, but those expenditures were now ended, and the debts remained. The city's bond indebtedness in 1931 stood at almost $4,000,000, much of it owed on infrastructure improvements from the '20s. The city had to resort to "shotgun refunding," whereby bondholders would refinance their bonds at a lower interest rate. The "shotgun" here was that the city might go bankrupt, in which case nothing would be paid.[10]

Government spending was not up all that much in the depression; but *federal* funding in the 1930s replaced the extravagant *state* and *local* investments of the 1920s. And Abilene made sure to get its fair share of federal funds—the CCC, the NYA, the PWA, the AAA, the WPA, and other federal anti-depression agencies all poured money into the city's economy. It could be argued, in view of Camp Barkeley and Dyess Air Force Base in the near future, that Abilene developed a dependency on federal investment during the depression. That observation is not entirely fair, perhaps, but not entirely wrong either.

The Personal Crisis

An editorial in the *Daily Reporter* at the beginning of 1935 showed something of the spirit of mutual assistance. The editor noted that "unemployables," which meant the aged, the infirm, and the handicapped, could no longer qualify for either state or federal aid. "The problem . . . has been placed squarely on the shoulders of the county and municipal governments. . . . It is a duty that must be discharged. There is no getting away from it."[11]

People helped each other where they could. There was a donation-supported Free Milk Fund. Well-to-do women created the Sunshine Nursery. Mrs. Morgan Jones Sr. founded a Negro Day Nursery. The city's welfare office, headed by Mrs. Benno Schmidt, worked tirelessly.[12] Mrs. Schmidt became the conduit for numerous anonymous contributions from Mr. and Mrs. Tom Hendrick.[13] Families helped families, neighbors helped neighbors, sometimes strangers helped strangers. Motorists developed the habit of picking up hitchhikers, a courtesy that became a patriotic duty during World War II. There was the sense of a brotherhood of suffering.

Churches helped where they could. Rector Willis Gerhart of the Episcopal Church of the Heavenly Rest gained a reputation that stayed with him through the years for generosity and caring.[14] The historians of many of the Abilene congregations did not record evidence of soup kitchens, handouts, clothing banks, and the like, though perhaps such existed. Like everybody else, churches were just trying to survive.

Tom Hendrick, benefactor and namesake of Hendrick Medical Center and Hendrick Home for Children. COURTESY OF THE HENDRICK HOME FOR CHILDREN

Abilene was situated on the main east-west rail line between Southern California and the South. The trains were filled with "hoboes," some of them inveterate tramps, some desperate fathers, some young men looking for a job anywhere else. The old American instinct to go west when things were not satisfactory at home continued to assert itself. When these transients dropped off the trains in Abilene, they would often go panhandling door to door, mostly back doors, at a time when yards were not usually fenced. Oldtimers tell numerous tales of beggars with sad stories, and most Abilenians were willing to help out. It was told around town, and perhaps it was true, that there were secret signs chalked on curbs and light poles indicating where one could likely get a handout. Homes within a few blocks of the rail line could expect a knock on the back door from a shabbily dressed man seeking help. Seldom was there any danger from these hoboes, and local folks generally obliged if they could, usually with a sandwich and a glass of milk, which were wolfed down on the spot.[15] Abilenians learned to offer food rather than money; a few tramps, turned down for cash, would depart in a huff rather than accept merely food. But most beggars were truly desperate, and it was the feeling of the town and the nation that this was a crisis that required mutual assistance where it was possible.

Sometimes the hobo would ask for an article of clothing. One Abilene housewife received such a request, thought about it a minute, and brought out a well-worn suit for the man. Later, when she told her husband what she had done, he exploded, "But that was my best suit!" She replied reasonably, "You haven't taken it out of the closet in three years and, besides, it had worn-out elbows." "BUT IT WAS MY BEST SUIT!" He walked away muttering about female "logic," or the absence thereof, while she stood there grumbling to herself about male "reasoning," or lack of same.

Others, traveling through in dilapidated automobiles or overloaded trucks, sometimes broke down with no funds to effect repairs. The location of Abilene on the Bankhead Highway meant in the 1930s that the town would accumulate a certain amount of human debris stranded by events in this obscure corner of West Texas. When this happened, the community helped as well as it could. There is the story of a traveling band that got "stranded" in Abilene without funds and had to play for room and board, and nothing more, just to survive.[16]

While most breadwinners had jobs, many did not. Day laborers, particularly those in the construction trades, were especially vulnerable to layoffs. James R. Horn, an Abilene contractor, awoke each morning to find his front yard full of men looking for a day's work. He made it a practice to pass the jobs around so that everybody got hired occasionally.[17]

People tightened their belts and eliminated luxuries. One year, Abilene High School ordained that boys would not buy corsages for their senior prom dates.

The Institutional Crisis—Businesses

Banks were among the institutions that were most vulnerable to the depression. In August 1931, the Abilene State Bank failed. The bank managers knew it was coming but gave little warning. In fact, the October district grand jury indicted bank president A.C. Pool and vice president B. Miller on theft charges. Apparently they had accepted deposits from several customers even after they knew the bank would not be able to honor drafts on those deposits. The October trial was postponed because of Pool's illness.[18] Other banks would follow, if not so ignominiously. On October 1, 1931, the First State Bank of Cross Plains shut its doors.[19] Pool was convicted and sentenced but exonerated on appeal. In 1933, the headline read, "A.E. Pool freed by appeals court—conviction reversed and case dropped." Pool's attorneys proved that the bank, after balancing out assets and liabilities, was in fact solvent, so there could be no fraud.[20] The same day, the paper announced that a Baird jury had acquitted the Cross Plains bank president of similar charges.[21]

The New Deal started prematurely in Texas. Even before President Roosevelt could be inaugurated in March 1933, new Texas Governor Miriam A. Ferguson declared a five-day bank holiday in Texas in an attempt to stop runs on banks. "Bank holiday taken calmly," the paper said. Most banks complied, though some towns, like Coleman and Austin, allowed limited activity despite the decree. The two surviving Abilene banks shut down completely, not even accepting deposits.[22] Three days later, the newly inaugurated President Roosevelt did the same nationally by executive decree, citing a national emergency as the justification for his unprecedented action. Editor Grimes and the *Daily Reporter* affirmed FDR's action and others he proposed, saying "it is impossible for an American citizen not to feel a glow of pride as he contemplates this rededication of a great people to the task of preserving democratic government [and] . . . to give every man his share in the New Deal."[23] A limited reopening of banks was authorized almost immediately "to meet essential needs of business and citizens."[24]

When all was said and done, Abilene was fortunate. Two of the three Abilene banks were left standing. One was Citizens National Bank, run by longtime Abilene business leader George L. Paxton. His bank survived because he personally gave of his own wealth to make it endure. Even so, it had to reorganize in 1935. The other was Farmers and Merchants Bank, which later became First National.[25] Bank deposits, a measure of the city's economic health, stood at just over five million dollars in 1930. That figure dropped slightly in 1931, perhaps reflecting the failure of the Abilene State Bank, but rose in 1932 back to post-depression levels, dropped slightly in 1933, and then jumped to nearly eight million in 1935. The number remained near that point until 1939 saw the figure rise to just over ten million.[26]

West Texas Utilities Company was part of a large utilities conglomerate held by Samuel Insull. Insull, a Chicago electric and railroad entrepreneur and protégé of Thomas Edison, had invented the concept of the holding company and was the leading practitioner of highly leveraged investing. This was a path to great wealth so long as times stayed good.

But when the economy went sour, Insull's empire collapsed, and the companies under his control had to be reorganized to escape bankruptcy.[27] WTU sold off its natural gas service in 1931 as part of its restructuring.[28] Abilene's streetcar service, another subsidiary of the electric company, also fell victim to the reorganization and was discontinued.[29] But the depression did not affect electrical usage in the WTU system; electricity had become a necessity. All the WTU indicators—generating capacity, employee numbers, capital investment, and gross income—either remained stable or increased, even during the depression.[30]

Waldrop's Furniture held a major sale in early 1933 aimed at reducing inventory. The company explained that it had purchased substantial amounts of goods at what it thought were low prices, in the expectation that things would turn around and it could sell them at a good profit. But that gambit failed, the spokesmen said, so they must reduce inventory, saying "we are compelled to raise immediate cash for current obligations and operating costs." To that end, the store was holding a giant auction, "not as a quit business auction" but as a "cash-raising auction."[31] Other businesses found themselves resorting to similar expedients.

By 1936, things really were looking better. One could see signs of increased construction activity—the ongoing construction of the railroad and its underpasses, the erection of a new wing at the West Texas Baptist Hospital, improvements on the federal building, among others. Building permits for the month of April 1936 were $18,942 compared to $1,944 for the same month of 1935. The two banks reported twenty percent more cash on hand than the year before, more deposits than the year before, fewer bad loans outstanding. The Radford grocery chain announced it was opening its first new enterprise since the depression began, bringing the company's outlets to twenty-six. The new acquisition, in Elk City, Oklahoma, gave the company stores in three states.[32]

The Hendricks—the Hospital and the Home

The West Texas Baptist Sanitarium entered the Great Depression in fair condition, but it did not long stay that way. Patients often were unable to pay their bills on time, if at all. The hospital took in what indigent patients it could, but some expenses could not be pared below a certain level and the balance of income and outflow was not favorable. The traditional sources of gifts also dried up, and the program skated closer and closer to bankruptcy.

By 1936, things were desperate indeed when Mr. and Mrs. T.G. Hendrick came to the rescue. E.M. Collier, the head of the sanitarium, decided to approach Tom Hendrick, a West Texan who had prospered in ranching, oil, banking, and other enterprises and who had retired to Abilene. Hendrick was known to hate solicitations, so this was a risky move, but Collier was desperate. He found Hendrick in a generous mood, prepared to pay off the institution's debt without blinking. His gift of some $40,000 settled the existing debts, including a mortgage. He balked, however, when Collier mentioned that the hospital also needed a new wing. Ten days later, Hendrick walked into Collier's office with the offer to pay for the wing after all.[33] The trustees responded to this unexpected largesse by renaming the institution Hendrick Memorial Hospital.[34]

The depression placed strains on families, sometime beyond the breaking point, Numerous men, for example, embarrassed that they could not care for their families as a man should, got a "poor man's divorce"—they abandoned them. The Hendricks were aware of this problem, which extended into the wartime years and, for that matter, beyond. They originally had willed a large portion of their estate to a home for tuberculars and a home for the elderly. But tuberculosis was on the retreat across the country and the Social Security program offered relief for the elderly, so they changed the will in 1936 to benefit a home for children.[35] To care for displaced children, they established

Hendrick Hospital, with its new wing, ca. 1937. COURTESY OF BETTY LOU GIDDENS

the Hendrick Home for Children on a fifty-two-acre plot in south Abilene. The idea was to give a safe haven for children from two to twelve years of age whose families could not provide adequate care. Completed in 1939, it opened with twelve kids. The residents, in keeping with Hendrick's wishes, attended Abilene schools, helped with chores around the home, kept in touch with their natural families as much as possible, and attended church. The original gift of $300,000 acquired the land and erected a beautiful main building, along with other needed facilities.[36] The home added to Abilene's payroll, purchased needed supplies from local merchants, and boosted public school attendance, so it helped the town as well as the children who resided there.

The Hardins—ACC and Simmons

Abilene Christian College moved into its new campus in 1929, expecting finances and enrollment to continue to climb. But 1930 "brought the cold hand of depression tighter around the purse strings and living habits of the citizens of West Texas."[37] Enrollment dropped and donations began to dry up, despite a massive "$10,000 Club" campaign. In 1931, ACC President Batsell Baxter unexpectedly resigned to become head of David Lipscomb College in Nashville. Dean James Cox replaced him as president, facing a terrible challenge. He initiated a work program on campus that would enable more students to enroll, and that plan succeeded very well. But the underlying problem remained where to find the funds to finance operations and debt.

One step was to cut salaries, and this was done, but it was not enough. The school could pay its faculty only half of the contracted amount. "Every corner that could be cut was cut. Every stitch that could be saved was saved. Every extra that could be sliced, was sliced. But times kept getting harder and harder."[38] One expedient was to get a loan, and an Austin company was on the verge of making one when it backed out. A company in Nashville agreed to fill the need. "This loan afforded only temporary relief."[39] J.M. Radford, the wholesale grocery magnate, always helped Abilene causes, and he gave unstintingly to ACC, though he was a Methodist himself. A stock deal with Radford was in the offing in 1933 when Radford died, and the whole thing fell through. By October, it looked as though ACC would go bankrupt. The school's creditors were demanding that something be done.

Someone suggested Mr. and Mrs. John Hardin of Burkburnett, oil millionaires. The Hardins had been generous donors to Baptist causes over the years, but the first Mrs. Hardin had been a member of the Church of Christ. In late 1933, ACC representatives met with Hardin's people in Wichita Falls. After a lengthy series of negotiations, which included provisions that looked very much like kickbacks, the Hardins agreed to make a major donation in February 1934. On campus, students rang the school's cherished old "bean bell" to celebrate the gift, and the bell cracked! After more negotiations with creditors, and the loan of another $40,000 from Hardin, the school was over the hump, and things began to get better. In gratitude for the gift that saved ACC, the school named its main building the "Hardin Administration Building."[40]

Conditions were no better at Abilene's oldest college, Simmons. The school reduced staff salaries by ten percent in 1931, then thirty percent more the next year, and even those lower salaries could only be paid part of the time. The trustees personally encumbered themselves to the limit, since the school's charter prohibited indebtedness. The school started a "Dollar-A-Month" club to induce its Baptist constituents to help as much as possible. It didn't help much, and Simmons came close to losing its cherished Southern Association accreditation.[41]

John G. Hardin, benefactor of both Abilene Christian and Hardin-Simmons. COURTESY OF HARDIN-SIMMONS UNIVERSITY

Tapping all available resources, the school reached out to wealthy donors and got some substantial aid from H.O. Coleman, a Philadelphia Presbyterian, and from local Baptist Tom Hendrick. In 1934, Simmons heard that John G. Hardin, the Baptist philanthropist of Burkburnett, had given $200,000 to ACC. Was the Church of Christ walking on Baptist grass here? President Sandefer hurried north to see what could be done. After a series of negotiations similar to those of its collegiate neighbor, Simmons secured a grant of $200,000, just what ACC had gotten, and under similar dubious terms. The Hardins, who were already supporting an orphanage, Mary Hardin-Baylor College in Belton, Hardin (Junior) College in Wichita Falls, and, of course, ACC, decided that was enough.

The school was delighted at the grant but disappointed that a potential gift of nearly three-quarters of a million more was being reconsidered and would probably be withheld. To rescue that money, the school adopted a desperate ploy. It would rename itself—"Hardin University" or "Hardin-Simmons" or "Simmons-Hardin," whatever the donors pleased. That move was decisive, and the school became Hardin-Simmons from 1934 on. When the Hardins passed away a couple of years later, the entire corpus came to the college.[42] After the Hardin bailout, the road was clearer for both Hardin-Simmons and Abilene Christian. The Hardins had rescued both schools from dissolution.

McMurry and the Death of Dr. Hunt

The same problems that plagued the other schools also debilitated McMurry. Even before the crash, the school had formed the habit of borrowing at the end of the school year to meet salaries. In the depression, that continued, but even then salaries were not met. Faculty members were forced to accept less than they had contracted for, or be dismissed. Faculty income dropped in some cases to half the contracted amount, with only vague promises of future reimbursement—perhaps. The school closed a dormitory, shrank the college newspaper, suspended the literary magazine, dropped subscription to scholarly journals, shortened the yearbook. The trustees dipped into the endowment to meet current expenses.[43]

Little McMurry had no such angel as the Hardins. Worse yet, the founder and president J.W. Hunt worked himself so hard to keep his school afloat that he died of a heart attack at the age of fifty-nine in March 1934. As a cost-cutting measure, he had assumed the duties of dean as well as president. He was constantly on the road raising money or fighting to save prohibition. Neither enterprise was very successful—the odds were too great against him. His death could have been the last straw, the fatal blow to the college.[44]

After a short interim presidency by the St. Paul pastor, O.P. Clark, McMurry secured the services of another Methodist preacher, Cluster Q. Smith. In seventeen months, he somehow raised enough money to pay off the standing indebtedness, at least temporarily. It is not clear how he managed it; perhaps it was just that times were better, but he managed to do it. He was so successful that he received, and accepted, a call from SMU to be its vice president for development in 1936.[45]

Rev. Tom Brabham, another proven fundraiser, was president of Texas Woman's College in Fort Worth when he agreed to take the McMurry presidency. He served until the fall of 1938. By that time, the severe crisis was over, though the college was by no means on sound footing.[46] In the collegiate atmosphere of the 1930s, just the mere fact of survival was a major accomplishment in itself, and Abilene was fortunate that all of its colleges endured.

Churches under Stress

Abilene always prided itself on its spiritual tone, as seen in the number and quality of its churches. But these were also human institutions, dependent upon the contributions of their members. When the membership suffered the pangs of the depression, so did the church organization. Abilene churches had to tighten belts for the duration of the crisis.

At First Baptist Church in 1931, things got so tight that the employees volunteered to donate back twenty percent of their salaries "to alleviate the present need." The church had to take out a commercial loan to cover its debts in 1932 and had to renegotiate a loan repayment owed to Simmons, defaulting on payments from 1930 to 1934, at precisely the time when the college needed the money most. But there was none to be had, and Simmons could not lean too hard on First Baptist in any case. By 1935, the church could begin to pick itself up financially with a new tithing campaign.[47]

Sacred Heart Catholic Church was the anchor of Catholicism in the Abilene area. Its veteran priest, Father Henry Knufer, was beloved in the city by Catholics and Protestants alike. He belonged to the Abilene Rotary Club and was chosen as one of the club's delegates to the international convention in Belgium in 1927.[48] Knufer began raising funds for a new church building in the late 1920s, and contributions came from all sides, including Protestants. But the timing was poor—the building was just being completed in 1930 when the contributions dried up. Father Knufer and the congregation had to borrow $22,000 just to get the plumbing, wiring, and furnishings in; Knufer put up his life insurance as collateral.[49]

O.P. Clark, pastor of St. Paul Methodist, refused to receive his salary for three months in 1937 because the salary was to be paid in preference to the church's benevolence budget. Eventually, the church managed to pay the salary in arrears.[50] At First Methodist, the congregation had to abandon a projected building program temporarily. Indeed, the depression "made the church debt a burden for nearly a decade." It paid only $3,000 of a promised $4,000 pastor's salary in 1931, $2,212 of a promised $3,000 in 1932, and $2,300 of a projected $2,400 in 1933. But the stewards pledged to pay him $3,000 in 1934 and managed to do it that year and from then on.[51]

Another unfortunately timed building program was that of Highland Church of Christ. When ACC moved from North First and Graham to the hill northeast of town in 1929, the school took the College Church of Christ with it, leaving behind a neighborhood with a high concentration of members. Those who did not choose to attend church several miles away banded together, found an available lot at South Fifth and Highland, and formed Highland Church of Christ. They completed the basement on a projected main building when the depression hit. They met in that basement until 1938, when the superstructure could at last go up. The minister's $200-a-month salary had to be cut to $125 in 1932 just to make ends meet.[52] The College Church of Christ, now located on "the Hill," got off to a good start in 1929. The depression caused minister F.W. McMillan to request a reduction in his salary from $50 per week to $40 in February 1932, then to $30 in June. The 1934 budget allocated a salary of $2,600 a year ($50 a week), a goal which was met.[53]

The Crisis of Agriculture
The Dust Bowl

The meteorological crisis that afflicted the southern plains in the "dirty thirties" did not affect Abilene nearly so much. Plains weather was notoriously extreme, but from 1930 to about 1938, it was *extremely* extreme. The so-called Dust Bowl was hammered by drought, flood, hail, dust storms, blizzards, tornadoes, subzero temperatures—each of these occasionally killing people. The primary visual image of the era is a "roller," a roiling, boiling, twisting wall of dirt looming over a horrified population and landscape. The worst of them all came on "Black Sunday," April 14, 1935, when a vicious cold front swept across the plains, bearing an incredible load of dust. Several people, caught in the open, died in the event. Some motorists found that their cars had lost their ignition systems to the static electricity generated by the dust.[54] It covered the plains of Kansas, Colorado, Oklahoma, New Mexico, and Texas and sent its dusty remains over many other states as well.[55]

Black Sunday was perhaps the worst storm, but it was not the only one in the "dirty thirties." One study by the Soil Conservation Service counted 14 in 1932, 38 in 1933, 22 in 1934, 40 in 1935, 68 in 1936, 72 in 1937, 61 in 1938, then 30, in 1939, and 17 in 1940.[56] Another survey, taken in Goodwell, Oklahoma, the center of the Dust Bowl, recorded 70 in 1933, 22 in 1934, 53 in 1935, 73 in 1936 and 134 in 1937.[57] These show that, however bad Black Sunday may have been, things could get worse, in frequency if not in intensity.

In Abilene, Black Sunday was front-page news but not quite the stuff of banner headlines. Amarillo, the paper reported, was blotted out, and loads of dust hit Alpine, Wichita Falls, Lubbock, and Abilene, but Austin, Dallas, and Paris barely noticed it. "Residents of the southwestern dust bowl marked up another black duster today and wondered how long it would take before another one came along."[58] That is the language of an outside observer, not of someone who was seriously involved. The Dust Bowl drought of the plains affected the Abilene country, but to a much smaller degree than places north and west. After Abilene's wettest year ever in 1932, just less than double the yearly average, the dry spell set in. From 1933 through 1940, the city received an average of twenty-two inches a year, about two inches below normal.[59] That's dry, but not radically so—nothing like the 1950s drought. In the years 1935 and 1938, the city had above-average rainfall.

Nevertheless, the drought had an impact in the region. 1934 was an especially bad year for farmers. Reporting on a drop in bank deposits, the local paper explained that "the decreases sharply reflected the drouth that, in 1934, cut Taylor County cotton production from nearly 40,000 bales to an edge over 18,000 bales."[60] Abilene-area farmers and ranchers qualified for federal drought relief. The Agricultural Adjustment Administration, before it was declared unconstitutional, ran a cattle-buying program in 1934 and even extended it a couple of weeks past its expiration date for the Texas Panhandle, the Big Bend, and West Central Texas, including Taylor County and its neighbors. [61]

The Federal Anti-Depression Programs

Quite apart from the ecological crisis, American agriculture was in trouble. The source of the problem lay a few years in the past. American farmers prospered enormously during World War I, expanding their land holdings and investing in mechanized devices. Many thought the wartime boom would continue indefinitely, but farm prosperity began to flounder by 1920 because the need for war-related products dried up and because European farmers were recovering, reducing still further the demand for American products. Many American farmers were caught overextended. Their solution was to produce more, but that overproduction drove prices down, so they were working harder and harder for less and less return. Texas farmers were well aware of "hard times" two or three years before the rest of the country experienced "depression."

This was particularly true for producers of wheat and cotton, the mainstays of Taylor County agriculture. Wheat prices fell from $2.04 a bushel in 1920 to $0.34 in 1932; cotton went from seventeen cents a pound to six cents.[62] The AAA, with its focus on reducing market glut by paying farmers to leave fields fallow, was a popular agency in Abilene. The AAA also provided some price floors for commodities. This double approach reduced surpluses while providing a reliable return for products. In 1935, the AAA spent $416,600 in Taylor County, mostly for cotton acreage reduction. Further, twenty-nine wheat farmers signed a crop reduction pledge, and the county agent organized eleven community associations to support the program.[63]

After the Supreme Court declared the AAA unconstitutional, the government sought ways to effect the same results with more acceptable laws. One plan called for farmers to cooperate with government planners via "community committeemen to serve for the new agricultural programs provided by the soil conservation and domestic allotment act."[64] In 1936, Taylor County farmers complied by electing their representatives at four precinct meetings at the courthouse in Abilene, at Merkel, at Buffalo Gap, and at Bradshaw.[65]

One farm boy from the shinnery remembered it thus: "President Roosevelt had come up with the idea of paying the ranchers a small price for the cattle and killing them off. I think it was about $14 for grown cows and bulls and about $8 for yearlings. The government hired a feller to kill off all the cattle that weren't good enough to butcher. There was a pen with about 100 head of cows, including ours and our neighbors. He stepped inside the pen and started shooting. After he'd killed all the undesirables, he took a hammer and knocked all the baby calves in the head. When he'd killed the cows, another guy would drag them north of the barn and stack them up."[66]

Modernization and Change

Long-term trends, associated with neither the depression nor the drought, also affected Taylor County agriculture. One was mechanization. A good indicator of animal power was the number of mules in the county. In 1925, there were 6,416 of those draft animals in use, but the number was declining; ten years later, there were only 4,204, and ten years after that (1945), there were only 371.[67] The county boasted 204 tractors in 1930 and 1,877 by the end of the war.[68] One tractor could do the work of several mules.

Farms got larger, from 233 acres on average in 1935 to 338 in 1950 and 660 by 1960. The number of tenant farmers continued to decrease over the period. Tenants accounted for sixty-two percent of Taylor County farm operators in 1925, fifty-seven percent in 1930, and forty-seven percent in 1940.[69] Many of those tenants found jobs in town and moved off the farms.

The problems of staple agriculture led many to shift gears toward ranching. Taylor County had 14,689 cattle and a small number of sheep in 1920. In 1930, those numbers rose to 21,450 cattle and 17,844 sheep and in 1940, 24,708 cattle and 41,392 sheep. Cotton production dropped in the same period. 1920 saw the county gin 43,983 bales, and 1925 had 55,969. By 1930, the count was only 13,799. Through the depression, those number rose slightly, and cotton farmers prospered during World War II, but the bottom fell out after the war. Cotton was no longer king in Taylor County, and the cotton belt moved farther west.[70]

The Fair Once Again

Despite the ominous economic news, the West Texas Fair Association held its signature event in 1930, but a combination of the growing depression and unfortunate weather made it a flop. The deficit was so bad that the association was forced to sell its assets to the city and abandon hope of putting on a 1931 edition. The city agreed that the West Texas Fair could go on, but only if the Fair Association leased the grounds on an annual basis. So the association continued in being, but only as a shadow of its former self until times got better and it could resume the annual event.[71]

It appeared that good times were sufficiently at hand that the association put on what it called "the West Texas Free Fair" in 1937. There were no general admission fees to the grounds, but selected venues (horse races, grandstands, some amusements) charged admission, and the association made some money from parking fees. There was no charge for the many displays of agricultural products and handicrafts, which were always popular draws. An innovation was the introduction of a rodeo to the festivities, and it proved to be quite an attraction. Further, a very popular cotton parade culminated by the selection of a Cotton Queen from among forty-two nominated Duchesses representing area towns.[72]

The 1937 fair did well enough that it was repeated in 1938. The Cotton Parade featured sixty floats, fifteen bands, and numerous marchers. The fair also honored a rising industry in the area—oil. There was a demonstration derrick and an oilman's day.⁷³ While the 1939 fair did not quite make expenses, the 1940 version recouped those losses and then some. In 1941, the fair seemingly well-established again, the central theme was the looming war. Camp Barkeley was now brimming with bored troops, and the fair was a marvelous opportunity to provide entertainment. But by 1942, it was clear that, once again, the fair would have to be suspended because of events far beyond Abilene's control.⁷⁴

Around the World Backwards

The Great Depression hit Abilene restaurant owner Plennie L. Wingo as hard as everybody else. He lost his business and was reduced to working for one of his rivals for $12 a week—and that wasn't enough to support the family. At his daughter's sixteenth birthday party, he was talking with some of her classmates when the conversation turned to all the weird stunts people had come up with in the preceding decade. Everything had been done, they said. Wingo responded, "Not everything! Nobody has ever walked around the world backwards." A few of the boys tried walking backwards, fell over the furniture, laughed, and forgot about it. But not Wingo.

He became obsessed with the notion that he could raise a lot of money if he were to try to circumambulate the globe walking backwards. He sought sponsors for the stunt in Abilene, but to no avail. Fort Worth seemed more promising, but that's all it was—promising. Undaunted, he decided to try it without a sponsor, supporting himself by selling postcards of his journey as he went. After six months of training, and with the very reluctant assent of his wife, he set out in February 1931 from Fort Worth. He was armed with letters from the Abilene Chamber of Commerce, the police chief, and Mayor Tom Hayden, testifying to his good character and asking people to help him if they could. He also was wearing a pair of glasses with mirrors on the sides so he could see where he was going without having to turn around.

After numerous adventures on the road, he reached New York City. There he received a plaintive letter from his wife asking him to come home; he had not been able to do more than support himself, and the family needed help. But the obsession was too great, and he wangled a passage on a steamship to Hamburg, Germany to continue his walk.

Reaching Germany, he persuaded someone to write a sign for his backpack, which of course was preceding, not following, him. The sign said in German, "Backwards around the world." Similar signs in Czech, Hungarian, and Bulgarian got him to Turkey, but there he was arrested on unknown charges. The American consul succeeded in getting him out but absolutely forbade him to try to through or beyond Turkey. The adventure was over!

Well, not quite. He worked his way back to America on a steamer. As the ship was approaching New York, United States Immigration Service officials boarded to check out the passengers. One of them challenged Wingo's bona fides, asking if he was really from Abilene, Texas. The inspector said, "Do you know anyone there by the name of Roach?" Wingo responded that he had some neighbors by that name and proceeded to name the family members. The inspector laughed. The head of the Roach family was his brother, and the children were his nephews and nieces.

After disembarking, Wingo found a ride across the U.S. to San Diego. From there, he resumed his backwards march, headed for his starting place at Fort Worth. He passed down Abilene's South First Street just as Abilene High was letting out and met the same group of teenaged boys who had started the whole thing. After sharing stories with them, he continued on to Fort Worth and the end of his journey. He really accomplished half of what he had started out to do but ended up as broke as when he left.

And he was single. Mrs. Wingo had had enough of non-support and divorced him. What a surprise!

Source: Plennie L. Wingo, *Around the World Backwards* (Austin: Eakin Press, 1982); quote from pp. 132-33.

Chapter Twelve
Possibility 1933-1940

The Great Depression eventually reached bottom, and slowly things began to look up. One element of recovery was simply going to be the passage of time, while old debts were slowly paid off and aging appliances slowly wore out. But a shining ray of hope in the meantime was the inauguration of a new administration in Washington. The New Deal might not have the key to rapid recovery, but it did have the key to national endurance; that key was hope.

Abilene and the New Deal
The New Deal

In the fall of 1932, the United States voted Herbert Hoover out of office and chose in his place the Democrat Franklin D. Roosevelt. Roosevelt came with an eclectic platform of anti-depression legislation that he called "the New Deal." It centered on federal spending to provide jobs and to replace the dried-up private investments. Abilene welcomed the New Deal. Most Abilenians were Democrats by tradition and persuasion, and perhaps partially repented their votes for Hoover in 1928. Though the newspaper was restrained in its criticism of the Hoover administration, most citizens were not happy with the way things were going and placed the blame on the president.

Hoover's continued affirmations that things were about to change were echoed in Abilene by business leaders through 1930, 1931, and 1932, but all that optimism seemed forced, and looked more and more like whistling in the dark. Things did *not* get better; indeed, they kept getting worse, and the statistical and personal indicators of that were everywhere at hand.

So, on the eve of the inauguration, Abilene businessmen sponsored a full-page advertisement in the newspaper. "Hail to the Chief! We're with you, Mr. President."[1] Abilene's one reservation about the new president was his apparent endorsement of the Twenty-first Amendment, repealing the Eighteenth (prohibition) Amendment. Even as FDR prepared to assume the reins of office, the House was debating repeal, while the Senate had under consideration a revision of the Volstead Act that would allow beer sales even before ratification.[2] In February, Congress sent the Twenty-first Amendment to the states for ratification.[3] When Texans had a chance to vote on the issue in August, Taylor County opposed repeal by a five-to-three margin.[4] Repeal went through anyway, but the county was able to continue dry under local option provisions.

Otherwise, Abilene was pleased with the new president and his programs, and continued to be so throughout the decade, tempered only by a few doubts now and again.

The WPA, Lake Fort Phantom Hill, and Other Projects

The Works Progress Administration was an oft-criticized New Deal program begun in 1935 to supplement the existing Civil Works Administration and Public Works Administration. It was led by presidential advisor Harry Hopkins and was intended to provide jobs. Up until its end in 1943, it employed almost nine million people. Critics of the WPA charged that (a) jobs were apportioned politically, (b) the program employed too many Negroes, (c) the projects were unnecessary "boondoggles," and (d) little work was actually done by the employees. In some places, the first charge may have been true, and the second had its basis in the fact that the WPA employed the needy, and no one was more needy than blacks; but the latter two were not appropriate in Abilene. What the WPA did in Abilene was to build Lake Fort Phantom Hill dam, run a pipeline from the lake to town, and improve city streets. As for the charge that no one worked very hard (some said the initials stood for "We Piddle Around"), one Abilenian employed by the agency differed. "Some people used to make fun of the WPA labor force, saying all they did was lean on their shovel, but that sure wasn't true with our job. Getting a job with the WPA was the biggest break I'd had up to then, but it was back-breaking work. There wasn't very much machinery used; all the work was done the hard, manual way to provide jobs for more men."[5] He referred to a 1939 job digging a pipeline from the east side of Abilene to the center of the lake. They dug a line that ran sixteen feet deep under railroad tracks and ten feet deep in open country. Without much machinery, they used bars and sledgehammers to break through the underlying rock and caliche.

Abilene had wanted to develop a more secure water supply, as the town gave signs of outgrowing the lakes it already had. The city planners' eyes fell on the Elm Creek valley north of town, and they began to seek ways of building an impoundment there. To that end, the city began to purchase land at the proposed site. "In the hard years of the depression," Archie Jeffries recalled, "the City of Abilene . . . bought up all the land in Elm Creek bottom to build a big lake. Nearly all the farmers had sold up and moved off the land." Altogether, Abilene paid over $100,000 for the various tracts.

Then along came the WPA. The city leaders began negotiations on the dam early in the depression and felt they had presidential approval. In August 1936, Mayor C.J. Johnson went to San Antonio to negotiate with WPA officials there. They kicked it up to Washington but ran into a technical glitch; the project was approved to benefit Taylor County, but the actual dam was in Jones County.[6] That delayed things awhile, but eventually, in June 1937, the city signed a contract with the WPA for construction of the dam at a projected cost of $230,570. Work began at once on "construction of workmen's camps, the laying of water and sewer lines, building of necessary roads, completion of test soil borings, etc."[7]

The dam was completed in 1938 and began to fill. Completion of the lake assured Abilene of a secure water supply for years to come.

A slow awakening to the needs of black schoolchildren led the city to seek WPA aid in another arena. The poor quality of the building that housed the black school was increasingly glaring. So the city bought eleven acres on the east side and contracted with the WPA to erect a new school building, the first time Abilene's black children had ever been in a *new* school. Completed in 1936, the school so improved the quality of education that it received a "Class A" accreditation in 1938.[8]

Yet another WPA service for the city was street paving. Abilene's residential streets were mostly still unimproved. WPA workers expanded from the paved downtown area by curbing, grading, and gravelling several miles worth of suburban streets. Much of this work began in 1936, even before the dam project was approved.[9]

The PWA and the Railroad Grade

The New Deal program that most affected the downtown Abilene scene was the raising of the railroad grade through town. It was long overdue, for the tracks were a hazard for any enterprise that crossed them. When the old ACC dorm at North First and Graham caught fire soon after the move to the Hill in 1929, firefighting was disrupted when a train came through and cut the fire hoses that were drawing water from the south side. The tracks were of course a problem for stu-

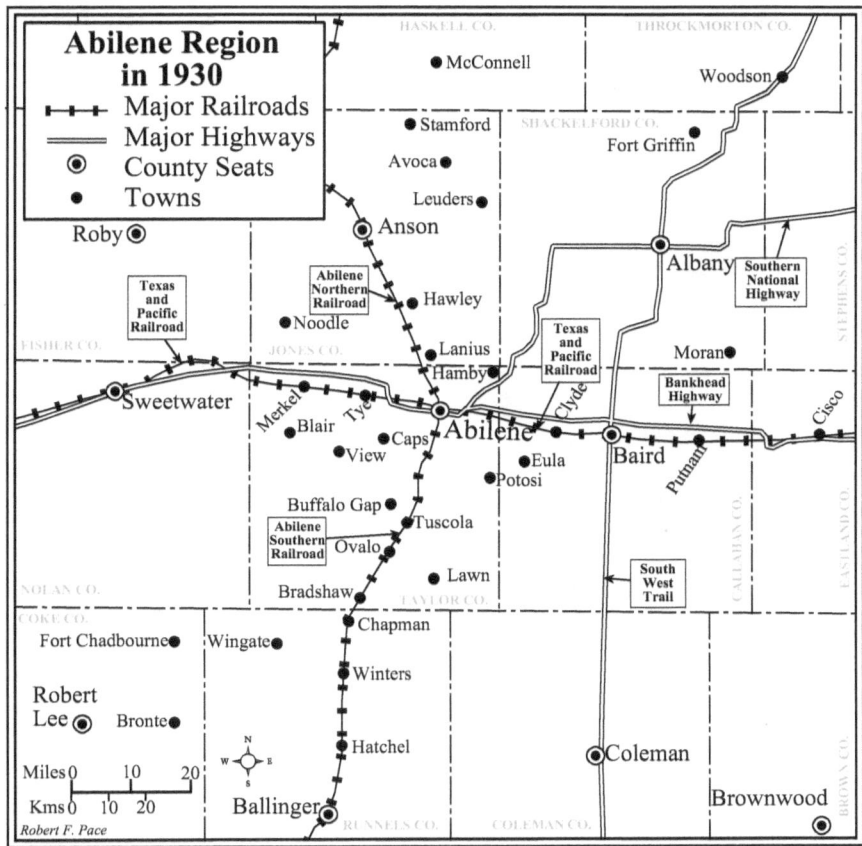

Transportation access grew rapidly over the years, making Abilene a mercantile and business center for the region. This map shows some, but not all, of the new arteries that fed rail and automobile traffic into the city. Note that the numbering of roads was in its infancy in 1930.

dents from the north side attending the high school on South First. The grade crossings were not well marked and not well regulated, a constant danger.

Raising the grade through the downtown meant that passages needed to be built. Though Frank Grimes crusaded for the railroad to be lowered, not raised, the decision was to lift it up.[10] Therefore passage from one side of town to the other had to be facilitated by underpasses in the downtown area.

Editor Frank Grimes.
COURTESY OF HARDIN-SIMMONS UNIVERSITY

The New Deal agency called the Public Works Administration agreed to do the work. Construction began in January 1936 on underpasses at the south ends of Pine and Cedar Streets. The first task was building "temporary passing tracks" around the main line so that the work could go forward. Two draglines were already on the site by January 3, waiting for ballast to arrive for the temporary tracks.[11] By April, the engineer in charge said the work was twenty-seven percent complete, with excavation finished and only the drainage and walling off of the underpasses remaining.[12]

In August, the construction was eighty-two percent complete, the foreman estimated, and he expected traffic to flow through the Pine and Cedar Street underpasses by October 1. The main track crossing the underpasses was ready to use in early September, so work could begin on taking up the temporary bypass track.[13]

The CCC and Abilene State Park

The city of Abilene, desperate for means of providing for the depression-born problems of unemployment, reacted quickly to an early New Deal program called the Civilian Conservation Corps. Owning

The Pine Street underpass after the rebuilding of the railroad through downtown Abilene, ca. 1938. COURTESY OF BETTY LOU GIDDENS

several sections of land around Lake Abilene, the city deeded a tract of 507 acres just below the dam to the Texas State Parks Board for development as a state park in 1933. Things moved swiftly after that.

The movement to create and develop state parks had begun a decade earlier under Governor Pat Neff, initially in an effort to preserve state historical landmarks like the Alamo, Goliad, and San Jacinto battlefields, but had expanded over the years to include scenic areas like Palo Duro Canyon and the Davis Mountains. The emergence of auto touring in the 1920s provided a powerful impetus to develop tourist attractions. When Miriam A. Ferguson took the oath for her second term as governor in January 1933, state relief projects were high on her agenda, and the parks program was a major part of that.

At almost the same time that Ferguson resumed office, President-elect Franklin Roosevelt was huddled with his advisors and new cabinet members to plan for a massive public works program that would provide employment for youths just coming into the labor market and finding no jobs. Less than half were finding full-time work.[14] He delegated to his cabinet nominees in the War Department (the Army), the Interior Department, the Department of Agriculture, and the Department of Labor the task of creating an agency for that purpose. Their proposal became the Civilian Conservation Corps, which would tackle public works programs related to parks, reclamation, and reforestation. The idea was to undertake tasks that would not compete with private enterprise.[15]

The new president and congress acted quickly on this proposal, and the CCC was in place within two weeks of the inauguration. It called for the enrollment of young men, single, physically fit, unemployed, aged seventeen to twenty-eight, to work principally in the nation's forests. Exceptions to the age limitations could be made for veterans of World War I. In return for a forty-hour workweek, they would be paid $30 a month plus food, uniforms, and shelter. Of that sum, $25 would go to their dependents. The term of service was six months, with an additional six-month hitch possible.[16]

No matter how fast the president and congress moved, bureaucratic issues slowed the process, so Abilene received no consideration in the first projects to be approved for the spring and early summer. However, Texas Relief Commission head L.W. Westbrook requested that Abilene receive a CCC company in August 1933.[17] In September, the state board agreed that Abilene would be one of the targeted spots for what was called the "second period of CCC camp assignments," and the Abilene State Park construction received official designation as Project SP-26.[18] The board appointed F.A. Riney, "who had engineered the adjacent city lake years before," to be project superintendent.[19] The first "CCC boys" arrived in the fall of 1933 and set up the camp. This camp, called Company 1823 (V), employed veterans of both races, a daring experiment and one of the first faltering steps of the New Deal toward racial equality.[20] This was official CCC policy, which specifically prohibited discrimination on the basis of race, creed, or color—at least at first.[21]

High on the list of improvements for Lake Abilene State Park was a swimming pool, designed by the state park architectural team in Austin.[22] The designs for the remaining structures—concession building, water tower, a dance terrace, and other facilities—were left to local architects, in this case, David Castle of Abilene.[23] Riney and others supervised the corps members in erecting living and recreation quarters for themselves and doing the construction work for the park.

Mayor C.L. Johnson, 1933-37.
COURTESY OF THE CITY OF ABILENE

After most of the park work was completed, the CCC transferred the racially integrated Company 1823 (V) to work on a park at Lake Sweetwater in October 1934.[24] A bit later, in April 1935, a decision came down from Washington to segregate the CCC; the white members of Company 1823 were shipped off, leaving the company now designated as 1823 (CV).[25] The residents of Sweetwater erupted in protest, petitioning Congressman Tom Blanton of Abilene, the CCC, the commanding general in San Antonio, and anyone else they could think of to get the Negroes out of town. Gov. Jimmy Allred threw his weight behind the Sweetwater protest, demanding that the white men be returned.[26] The following day, Rep. Blanton got word from Washington that the company would be moved, but no orders came that day, and no one knew where the company would go.[27]

Abilene knew where it should go. The mayor and the Chamber of Commerce polled the citizenry about bringing Company 1823 (CV) back to Lake Abilene to complete the park, which still lacked some finishing touches. There was no dissent, and Mayor C.L. Johnson shot off a wire to Washington, saying "Abilene will be delighted to have the Negro CCC camp now located at Lake Sweetwater transferred to Lake Abilene Park to complete the work there. The camp will receive a welcome."[28] Abilene was not necessarily all that much more enlightened than Sweetwater. The work at Sweetwater was close to town and to white housing, while the state park was remote to any concentration of dwellings—plus, Abilene *really* wanted the park completely finished. Still, that line "the camp will receive a welcome" was quite gracious. In June, the company was back at Lake Abilene. This company and another in East Texas were the only ones in the state affected by the resegregation policy. The federal authorities quietly backed away from any further racial experiments. The men remained at Abilene State Park until September 1935, when they moved to work at Kerrville. The black veterans in this camp were all Texas residents, in keeping with a statewide policy.[29]

Sweetwater did not lose the CCC completely. Another company, all white, was recruited in Abilene for work at Lake Sweetwater. Thirty-four Taylor County "selectees" went to Nolan County immediately to finish the job at the lake. At the same time, as many as 160 others from the county were called up to interview for CCC jobs in Arizona.[30]

There was a premature ceremonial opening of Abilene State Park in 1934, but it was not really quite ready for use, so work continued, as noted, through most of 1935.[31] On May 1, 1936, the Lake Abilene facility, like many other state parks, was ready to open, timed to coincide with the Texas Centennial celebrations taking place all over the state.[32] Abilenians wanted the CCC to remain even longer and continue to upgrade the park. Mrs. Dallas Scarborough, an ardent supporter of city and state parks, pushed to keep the CCC "in order that it might continue the development of the state park there."[33] The city officially added its voice, requesting that the CCC extend its enlistments, not only to complete the state park but also to develop a city park of 1,600 acres "now under the city's care." This referred to the land surrounding Lake Abilene, which was handy to the camp at the state park.[34] This initiative fell through, however.

The NYA and Roadside Parks

Fearing that even the CCC was not employing enough young people, First Lady Eleanor Roosevelt prevailed upon her husband to begin another work program called the National Youth Administration to provide jobs both in and out of colleges. Lyndon B. Johnson, a twenty-six-year-old congressional aide in Washington, received appointment in July 1935 as the NYA administrator for Texas, the youngest person in such a role and the one with the most territory to cover. Assembling a team, he set up offices in Austin and began to cast about for ideas to enable him to employ thousands of young people in tasks that (a) provided a useful service; (b) would not be done by any existing entity; (c) employed unskilled young people; and (d) expended more than seventy-five percent of the allocated funds as salaries. In Austin, the Johnson team considered and discarded numerous ideas until one struck a chord—roadside parks. Most Texas highways of the day had no shoulders where a tired driver or a disabled car could pull over. The result was a spate of accidents. But a roadside park would provide a rest stop, could be constructed with few supplies and much labor, could be supervised by the state highway department, could blanket the state, could provide jobs! From this bureaucratic dilemma emerged an idea that spread to the NYA programs in other states and eventually provided a nationwide network of highway rest stops.[35]

Abilene was one of the early beneficiaries of the NYA. It became the seat of a regional NYA headquarters. Pressure from Austin demanded results—that is, lots of people employed . . . and quickly. In January 1936, work began on a roadside park a few miles south of town. The county provided three acres of land for the facility, with sixty-two youths to be put to work at once. Ninety percent of those to be employed came from families on the relief rolls. Six other projects were also lined up for areas near Sweetwater, Snyder, and Ranger.[36]

Hardin-Simmons benefited from the NYA, which aimed at helping students stay in college as well as providing highway work. Jobs on campus, ones not normally done by employees, were available for $15 a month, which sum accrued to the school as the total tuition for the month. The university thus employed some forty-five to sixty students as faculty assistants or other chores under NYA grants. It was good for the students and good for the school.[37]

Another Side of the Depression
A State Football Championship

The coach's name was Dewey Mayhew. The team's name was "Eagles," but the local press dubbed them the "Wild Elephants." They were picked to win the "Oil Belt" district high school football championship in the fall of 1931.[38] That was not an easy task, with tough teams like Breckenridge, Cisco, Eastland, and Brownwood in the district.

By the first of December, it was official—Abilene was the Oil Belt champ. The following Friday, they beat Sweetwater in bi-district and went on to face the Lubbock Westerners. A victory over Lubbock put the "Wild Elephants" into the semifinals against a strong Greenville team. There the winning streak came to an end, when the game ended in a scoreless tie. But Abilene advanced on penetrations, 4-1, and went to the finals to face mighty Beaumont, which had just beaten the state's only undefeated team, Corsicana. The town was brimming with excitement and expectation.

Beaumont and Abilene decided to play the championship game in Fort Worth, and a special train was set up to haul fans to the game for two dollars a head round trip. The game was set for Christmas Day 1931, and no one regretted the inconvenience of spending Christmas morning on a train. It was worth every penny. The teams traded possessions for three quarters, and no one scored. In the fourth quarter, the "Wild Elephants" broke loose for two touchdowns by halfback Linnon Blackmon, and the championship came home to Abilene, 13-0. All-state players included left tackle Wilson Groseclose, center Stanley Smith, and left half Blackmon, with left end Ralph Balfanz and quarterback Glynn Wyatt on the second team and right tackle Pete Barber and fullback Sam Jones on the third team.[39]

Sunday Movies

One of the means of escape from the realities of the depression was the movies. The censorship of the 1920s was largely forgotten, though there were still occasional rumblings from Abilene pulpits about the morals displayed. But Hollywood had heeded some of the public outcry in the 1920s when the studios collaborated to install former postmaster-general Will Hays as the "czar" over movie quality in Hollywood. While the guidelines that Hays developed were voluntary, they were nearly always observed. With the advent of sound, this matter became even more urgent.

The issue for Abilene in 1931 was not the moral content of the films but whether the city would amend its rules to allow screenings on Sunday afternoons, from 1 to 7 P.M. This idea was attractive to a majority of the City Council, and the word got around that it was being considered. There was an immediate outburst from local churches.

Rev. C.A. Powell of University Baptist invited his clergy colleagues to the Carnegie Library on October 15, 1931, to muster public opinion against the proposed action.[40] Next day at a mass meeting attended by over 300 people, President J.W. Hunt of McMurry roundly denounced the proposal.[41] Resisting a tide of voter anger, three city councilmen voted to allow Sunday afternoon movies. Another councilman and Mayor Lee York opposed the measure. After passing through several readings with no change, the mayor finally invoked a seldom-used rule that allowed him to veto the proposal.[42] The issue died for the time being, to be raised again when World War II filled Abilene with bored soldiers on Sunday afternoons.

Other Amusements

A popular entertainment during the depression was professional wrestling. There was a "rassle arena" at North First and Graham that hosted weekly matches, such as "the bald-pated, cruel-hearted Nick Beginis" versus "handsome Danny McShain" in January 1936.[43] Deacon Lauer's weekly wrestling card in October 1931 featured a match won by Jack Gotman, who took two out of three falls from Benny Mathis with his "double Japanese toe hold."[44] One of the main events of 1936 was the match between Walter "Strong Boy" Stratton of Boston and Dale Haddock of Detroit. It was significant because the referee was the former heavyweight boxing champion Jess Willard.[45]

The comic pages included a strip called "Wash Tubbs," about a bespectacled adventurer and his friend, Captain Easy. The nationally syndicated strip was the product of Roy Crane, son of the Nolan County judge. Though he grew up in Sweetwater, the cartoonist was a native of Abilene and attended Simmons briefly.

The newspaper published daily radio programming schedules for three radio networks. Though some radio reception was available in Abilene, there was great rejoicing when the *Reporter* announced the opening of a broadcast station in 1936—KRBC (Reporter Broadcasting Company). The transmitter, a building by a 179-foot tower, stood just east of Treadaway on Ambler. The station built a special penthouse atop the Hilton Hotel to house the studios.[46] In anticipation of its opening on September 15, the station began auditions for musical and vocal talent to fill the broadcasting hours.[47]

Over the years, the station often hired local talent. Archie Jeffries said, "I was sure proud when I won a talent contest at the Queen Theater in 1938. This led to a bigger thrill when the manager of KRBC radio approached me on the street and wanted me to start a weekly solo program. I was billed as the 'Lonesome Cowboy' and my theme song was 'When It's Roundup Time in Texas.' I played and sang cowboy songs—they were about the only western songs back then."[48] Later he formed a duo with a fellow Lone Star Gas employee as "The Blue Sky Boys." They decided to play for dances and needed more performers, so they added several others.[49] In 1947, the band signed on to do a five-day-a-week live radio show on KRBC for Fraley's Butane Company and a one-hour broadcast on Saturday night. They called themselves the "Blue Flame Boys" but were better known as "Fraley's Butane Boys." They were very successful until 1953, when Jeffries decided he'd had enough and they "disbanded."

A New Day Dawning
Autos and Oil

Even before the Second World War turned the twentieth century upside down, signs of a new era were emerging. In April 1936, the state of Texas began to enforce a law requiring driver's licenses for all motor vehicle operators. Upon payment of the fee, a current driver would be issued a three-year license without being required to take either a written test or a field test. The state estimated it would issue three million licenses under that provision. Persons who wished to qualify later would have to undergo testing.[50] Another sign of increasing automobile traffic was the institution of parking time limits. J. Frank Dobie of the University of Texas, Texas's leading folklorist, announced that he would go to jail rather than pay an overtime parking ticket. Frank Grimes rather agreed with him in an editorial. Grimes had heard that some cities were even going to install parking meters, which Grimes called "renting the curb."[51]

For Abilene, another sign of the future came to light in the decade—the oil business. Taylor County was unlucky in the matter of big oil discoveries such as were happening at Ranger, Desdemona, Burkburnett, Breckenridge, and other neighboring sites over the fifteen years preceding the depression. A few oilmen had moved to Abilene as a base for the activities in the vicinity, but Taylor County did not have a significant discovery—until 1929. In that year, the Taylor County Regular Field came in as a commercially viable source.[52]

Over the next few years, the county produced modest amounts, the peak being 47,199 barrels in 1935, providing a source of hope in the weak economy. In 1940, the total jumped to 124,469 barrels.[53] There was enough activity in and around the county to justify the organization of an Abilene Geological Society.[54] By 1940, Abilene thus could claim to have a petroleum community, though nothing like what would happen after the war.

The World Scene

The people of Abilene were not nearly as insular and isolationist as one might expect from an inland community. "America isn't a hermit nation," editor Grimes proclaimed in 1920.[55] Abilenians were aware of the impending world crisis. They watched carefully when Japan invaded Manchuria in 1931. J.M Radford made a business trip to the Far East later that year and returned to give his assessment. The newspaper took note of the rising Nazi Party in Germany and its leader, Adolf

Hitler. He was more than just a bump on the horizon, but nobody knew quite what to make of him. When President von Hindenburg asked the National Socialist Party leader to be Chancellor of Germany, Editor Grimes suggested that maybe von Hindenburg was simply giving the gadfly Hitler enough rope to hang himself. "Hitler may find, after all, that being chancellor isn't all beer and skittles."[56] That assessment was held by many people at the time, but it proved to be a mistake in judgment.

Through the growing number of military rumblings in Asia and Europe, the newspaper kept the locals fully abreast of developments. Editor Grimes was a great advocate for preparedness. In 1933, he called for enlisting up to a million young men in the armed forces for limited periods, explaining it as a solution to the growing unemployment.[57]

Over the years, Grimes (and he probably represented Abilene's consensus in this) argued for preparedness as the best means of staying out of war. In this, he often took a more aggressive stance than the rest of the country. He was no warmonger, for war was evil and destructive of all that mankind aspired to, but the country must be safe, and he came more and more to the point of view that our two great national moats, the Pacific and the Atlantic, were no longer adequate. "We want nothing but peace, but in order to get it we have to go armed like an old-fashioned border marshal, otherwise the desperadoes would have us in the bag by nightfall."[58] In general, his editorials, and therefore the people he influenced, were ahead of the changing American attitudes toward preparedness. President Roosevelt, like Grimes, saw further ahead than did American public opinion. As the president inched the country closer to an open break with the Germans and the Japanese, he had a firm ally at the *Abilene Reporter-News*.[59]

If Grimes sometimes sounded jingoistic, he did not mean it so. His stance was not merely an ivory-tower attitude. When the war erupted in the Pacific on December 7, 1941, his son, Capt. Rudyard Kipling

Grimes, was at his station in the Philippines. The Japanese captured Capt. Grimes, and he survived the Bataan "Death March" only to die a few months later at Cabanatuan POW Camp No. 1.[60]

The march of events proved Grimes to be right. The Italian attack on Ethiopia in 1935, the ongoing Spanish Civil War, the Japanese invasion of China in 1937, and the German invasions of Czechoslovakia and Poland in 1939 guaranteed that the newspapers, the magazines, and the radio reports would be full of war news. It became increasingly obvious that the United States needed to be prepared for war, to train troops, perhaps even to invoke a draft law to fill out the armed forces. With the fall of France in 1940, the United States finally began to awake to the perils that Grimes had been pointing out. We had to get ready. What might be Abilene's role in that?

And what might the war do to Abilene?

Stuck In The Mud

Progress couldn't wait just because there was a depression. Abilene had to get the airport out of the mud if it wished to continue to have regular service. Most airfields of the day featured grass runways, which was more than adequate for most of the light aircraft then flying. But if heavier, multi-engine planes attempted to land on such surfaces, there could be problems.

Abilene's Kinsolving Field had grass runways, which was fine unless it rained. In early October 1931, it rained and then rained some more. On October 12, airport authorities had to tell a westbound American Airways plane, a Fokker tri-motor, that it could not land because of the soggy condition of the field. Accordingly, the plane just flew low over the field and dropped the mail sack. The situation was intolerable, and American Airways representatives met with Mayor Lee York to discuss the runway problem. Kinsolving Field could lose its certification if something was not done.

The following day, with the field dried out some, the airport management decided it was all right. The scheduled airliner, with five passengers and the mail aboard, landed and promptly got stuck. Ground personnel and some trucks pushed and shoved, and the pilots jockeyed the engines, and they finally got the plane to drier ground, dry enough, anyway, to allow a takeoff. That episode got the city council members in high gear. Two days after the incident, they approved expenditures for three hard-surfaced runways. It was a good thing they did, because they got a note from American Airways staff saying their planes would not land in Abilene again until the problem was fixed. By the end of the month, work was under way and the issue was resolved.

Sources: *ADR*, October 12, 1931, p.1; October 13, 1931, p. 1; October 15, 1931, p. 1; October 27, 1931, p. 1.

Abbreviations Used in Reference Notes

ADR—Abilene Daily Reporter

ARN—Abilene Reporter-News

HOTO—Handbook of Texas Online

WTHAYB—West Texas Historical Association Year Book

Notes

Preliminary

[1] Alfred E. Menn, "The Abilene Story." p. 1. Original in the Katharyn Duff Papers in The Woman's Collection at Texas Woman's University. This is a lengthy hand-written document encompassing three main sections. The first section (seven pages not numbered) is an account of the days before the auction, and the second (ten pages not numbered) is a list of the original Taylor County landowners. After the first two sections, the pages of the document are numbered consecutively (pp. 1-135, missing pp. 37-38). The vast majority of entries appear to have been taken verbatim from the *Abilene Reporter* from its inception through 1886. Copies of that paper from 1881 to 1885 apparently no longer exist, so Menn's manuscript is the only running record of that period. It has news items that caught Menn's fancy but omits advertisements, quotations from other newspapers, and local items that Menn found unimportant.

[2] *Abilene Reporter News*, March 15, 1981, p. 10. Hereafter called ARN. (The *Reporter-News* published a centennial series over a span of six weeks in Spring 1981; the six parts of the series were subsequently reprinted and bound as *Abilene Remembered: Our Centennial Treasury Book, 1881-1981*); Vernon G. Spence, *Judge Legett of Abilene* (College Station, TX: Texas A&M Press, 1977), p. 33; Menn, "The Abilene Story," p. 1.

[3] Karen Anderson Turner, "Abilene at the Beginning of the Twentieth Century: An Analysis of the United States Census," master's thesis, Abilene Christian University, 1989.

[4] A.C. Greene, *A Personal Country* (New York: A.A. Knopf, 1969), pp. 321-22.

[5] Spence, *Legett*, pp. 33-4; Hugh Cosby, ed. *The History of Abilene* (Abilene: Hugh E. Cosby Co., 1955), pp. 9-10.

[6] Cosby, *History of Abilene*, p. 9; Spence, *Legett*, pp. 34-5.

Chapter One

[1] Walter Prescott Webb, *The Great Plains* (Boston, New York, Chicago, London: Ginn and Co. 1931).

[2] Lytle Creek was called "Hole Creek" on an 1854 map and "Live Oak Creek" on an 1858 map.

[3] Robert E. Gabler, et al., *Essentials of Physical Geography, Third Ed.* (New York: Holt, Rinehart and Winston, 1987) pp. 204-224.

[4] See A.C. Greene, *A Personal Country*, p. 15. "Rain is scarcer in many parts of the world, but most of the time those places don't depend on it because they know it isn't coming. But West Texas lives right on the edge of its annual precipitation.... One identification of West Texas is simply that it is dry. Dryness creates a way of life more demanding than the facts of heat or height or abnormal wetness."

[5] Mollie Clack and Tommie Clack, *Pioneer Days...Two Views*, Katharyn Duff and Betty Kay Seibt, ed. (Abilene: Reporter Publishing Co, 1979) p. 113.

[6] *Abilene Daily Reporter*, May 5, 1928, p. 20. Hereafter referred to as *ADR*.

[7] *ADR*, May 5, 1928, p. 20. A.C. Greene writes: "Some say the mesquite was brought up from South Texas by the longhorn drives that trailed across West Texas on the way to Kansas. However, I find emphatic references to the prevalent presence of mesquite... in the writings of the earliest explorers." *A Personal Country*, p. 28.

[8] *ADR*, May 5, 1928, p. 20.

[9] *ARN,* July 7, 1977.

[10] Samuel L. Chalk, "Early Experiences in the Abilene Country," in *West Texas Historical Association Year Book,* IV (1928), p. 96. Hereafter referred to as *WTHAYB.*

[11] Clack, *Pioneer Days,* p. 184.

[12] Clack, *Pioneer Days,* p. 123.

[13] Clack, *Pioneer Days,* p. 166.

[14] See, for example, Cyrus N. Ray, "The Facts Concerning the Clear Fork Culture," in *American Antiquity,* Vol. 13, No. 4 (April, 1948) pp. 320-22; Cyrus N. Ray, "Accuracy in Terminology" in *American Antiquity,* Vol. 1, No. 3 (January, 1936), pp. 222-24, plus related articles by J. Charles Kelley, Alex Krieger, Ted Sayles, and perhaps others. A.C. Greene knew Dr. Ray and brought Ray several of his own finds from the Mountain Pass area, which Ray identified as Clear Fork items. Greene, *A Personal Country,* pp. 235-36; See also Duane Hale, "Cyrus N. Ray, The Abilene Man," in *WTHAYB* LV (1979), pp. 17-36. Hale said that Ray's sometimes abrasive personality and his amateur status led professional archeologists to ignore his findings or attribute them to others. The multi-talented Ray was the organizing force behind the Abilene Founder's Lion's Club, which was itself one of the chapters that began Lions International.

[15] www.texasbeyondhistory.net/faq/index.html. September 5, 2007.

[16] Quoted in Donald E. Worcester, ed. *Forked Tongues and Broken Treaties* (Caldwell, ID: Caxton Printers, 1975) p. 168. "Comanche" was the Ute word for "enemy" – p. 172.

[17] Rupert N. Richardson, *The Comanche Barrier to South Plains Settlement,* (Glendale, CA: Arthur E. Clark Co., 1933) pp. 17-18.

[18] Worcester, *Forked Tongues,* p. 169.

Chapter Two

[1] Greene, *Personal Country,* p. 50

[2] Rupert N. Richardson, *The Frontier of Northwest Texas,* 1846-1876 (Glendale, CA: Arthur C. Clark Co, 1963), pp. 95-96.

[3] Clack, *Pioneer Days,* pp. 95-100.

[4] Quoted in Wm. C. Pool, *A Historical Atlas of Texas* (Austin: Encino Press, 1975), p. 111.

[5] The colorful history of the post and the town is celebrated each summer in Albany's "Fandangle" pageant.

[6] The story of the "Red River War" that ended the Comanche threat is told in many places, most notably Rupert Richardson's *The Comanche Barrier to South Plains Settlement* and most recently in *Frontier Texas,* by Robert Pace and Donald Frazier (Abilene: State House Press, 2004).

[7] See David Nevin, *The Expressmen,* Time-Life Old West Series (New York: Time-Life Books, 1974), passim.

[8] A.C. Greene, ed., *900 Miles on the Butterfield Trail* (Denton: University of North Texas Press, 1994), p. 49

[9] Waterman L. Ormsby, *The Butterfield Overland Mail* (San Mateo CA: The Huntington Library, reprint 1955), p. 51.

[10] Greene, *Butterfield Trail,* p. 53.

[11] J. Wright Mooar and James Winford Hunt, *Buffalo Days,* Robert F. Pace, ed. (Abilene: State House Press, 2005).

[12] Wayne Gard, *The Great Buffalo Hunt* (New York: A.A. Knopf, 1959), p. 296.

[13] Ralph A. Smith, "The West Texas Bone Business," in *WTHAYB,* LV (1979), pp. 111-134, esp. pp. 119-120.

[14] Gard, *Great Buffalo Hunt,* pp. 302-03.

[15] Clack, *Pioneer Days,* p. 154.

[16] Benjamin Capps, *The Great Chiefs,* Time-Life Old West Series (New York: Time-Life Books, 1975), p. 114.

[17] Juanita Zachry, *A History of Rural Taylor County* (Burnet, TX: Nortex Press, 1980), pp. 191-93.

[18] Zachry, *Rural Taylor County,* p. 156.

[19] Zachry, *Rural Taylor County,* pp. 115-116.

[20] Cosby, *History of Abilene,* p. 34.

[21] Clack, *Pioneer Days,* p. 103.

[22] Clack, *Pioneer Days,* pp. 100-102.

[23] Hybernia Grace, "The First Trip West on the Butterfield Stage," in *WTHAYB,* VIII (1932), p. 72.

[24] Cosby, *History of Abilene,* p. 35.

[25] Zachry, *Rural Taylor County,* p. 156.

[26] Clack, *Pioneer Days,* p. 106.

[27] Cosby, *History of Abilene,* pp. 34-5, obviously based on legend rather than concrete evidence.

[28] See T.R. Havins, "Sheepmen-Cattlemen Antagonisms on the Texas Frontier" in *WTHAYB,* XVIII (1942), pp. 10-23, for further explanations. Havins detailed the animosity that cattlemen felt for shepherds but distinguished between sheep "drifters" and sheepmen who owned or leased their ranges. The drifters took the brunt of the anger.

[29] U.S. census, Agricultural Census, Taylor County, Precinct 1, 1880.

[30] U.S. census, Population Census, Taylor County, 1880; Agricultural Census, Taylor County, 1880; Taylor County patent map, State of Texas Land Office.

[31] See Daniel J. Boorstin, *The Americans: The National Experience* (New York: Random House, 1965), pp. 51-57.

[32] B.C. Chrisman, *Early Days in Callahan County,* (Abilene: by the author, 1966) p. 89; see Susan D. Navarro, *Eagle City: 1878 Colony on Lytle Creek* (Abilene: by the author, 1981).

[33] S.L. Chalk to R.C. Crane, letter dated April 29, 1928, and printed in *Abilene Reporter-News,* May 20, 1928, p. 18B.

[34] Virginia H. Taylor, "Franco-Texan Land Company," Handbook of Texas Online – http://www.tshasonline.org/. Hereafter referred to as HOTO.

[35] Taylor, "Franco-Texan Land Company," in HOTO.

[36] Gard, *Great Buffalo Hunt,* p. 189.

[37] Tommie Clack, "Buffalo Gap College," in *WTHAYB* XXXV (1959), p. 132.

[38] Zachry, *Rural Taylor County,* p. 83.

[39] Sam Chalk to R.C. Crane, quoted in *WTHAYB* IV(1928), p. 95.

[40] Chalk, *WTHAYB*, IV (1928), p. 96; Tommie Clack, "Buffalo Gap College"; and Katharyn Duff, *Abilene... On Catclaw Creek* (Abilene: Reporter Publishing Co., 1969), pp. 36-38.

[41] Duff, *Abilene*, p. 38; Joan Upton Hall, *Just Visitin' Old Texas Jails* (Abilene: State House Press, 2007), pp. 54-56; Donald S. Frazier, Robert F. Pace, Robert P. Wettemann, *The Texas You Expect: The Story of Buffalo Gap Historic Village* (Abilene: State House Press, 2006), p. 14.

[42] Duff, *Abilene*, p. 39.

[43] U.S. census, Population Census, Taylor County, Precinct 1, 1880.

Chapter Three

[1] See Stephen M. Ambrose, *Nothing Like It in the World* (New York: Simon and Schuster, 2000).

[2] Stanley P. Hirshson, *Grenville M. Dodge: Soldier, Politician, Railroad Pioneer* (Bloomington: University of Indiana Press, 1967), pp. 193-4.

[3] Grenville M. Dodge, *How We Built the Union Pacific Railway and Other Railway Papers and Addresses* (Thousand Oaks, CA: Sage Publications, reprint, 1965), pp. 133-36.

[4] John R. Hutto, "Pioneering the Texas and Pacific," in *WTHAYB*, XII (1936), p. 126.

[5] Quoted in Naomi Kincaid, "The Founding of Abilene, The 'Future Great' of the Texas and Pacific Railway," in *WTHAYB* XXII (1946) p. 16. Kincaid also quoted another early authority that claimed that a survey had already been made through the Gap and up the Elm Creek valley and to the southwest.

[6] R.M. Wagstaff, "Buffalo Gap vs. Taylor City," in *WTHAYB* XLV (1969), pp.105-114.

[7] Greene, *Personal Country*, p. 95.

[8] Naomi Hatton Kincaid, "Simpson, John Nicholas," in HOTO.

[9] H. Allen Anderson, "Amarillo, TX," in HOTO; Naomi Kincaid, "Founding of Abilene," pp. 15-25.

[10] Albert Sidney Johnston, as colonel of the U.S. Second Cavalry, was the officer who set up Camp Cooper on the Clear Fork in 1856, before turning it over to his Lt. Col., Robert E. Lee. Johnston was killed at the Battle of Shiloh in 1862.

[11] That includes the current author. See, among others, Robert W. Sledge, "Boosters, Boasters, and MAGGI," paper delivered at Texas State Historical Association annual meeting, 1965; Greene, *Personal Country*, p. 107; and Katharyn Duff with Betty Kay Seibt, *Catclaw Country*, (Burnet, TX: Eakin Press, 1980), p. 3.

[12] The seminal story of Abilene is newspaper columnist Katharyn Duff's *Abilene... on Catclaw Creek*. While intriguing, the title does not reflect the original town, which was located on Cedar Creek, not Catclaw. Catclaw Creek wanders through an area that was out in the country well to the west of the original town site. In a sequel, *Catclaw Country*, Duff explained that "many areas of the nation have a Cedar Creek, an Elm Creek, other such streams with ordinary names. Hardly anyone has a Catclaw." (p. vi).

[13] See U.S. Geological Service topographic maps for the Abilene area or travel along South Seventh, South First, North First, or parallel thoroughfares. The area from North First and northward had ample demonstration of that tendency in the flood of 2007, and the area south of the tracks saw the same problem in 2002, to mention two recent examples. Likewise, see Gary McLean, "Abilene's Founders and the Power of Entrepreneurial Enterprise," unpublished M.A. thesis, Hardin-Simmons University, 2005, p. 22n. McLean quoted C.E. Gilbert, first publisher of the *Abilene Reporter*, as saying that Stoddard Johnston "induced

NOTES

The Texas and Pacific Railway Company to locate the place where it rests, *on a high rolling healthy site, instead of upon the lowlands two miles westward"* (italics mine –RWS).

[14] The name originated from the Bible (Luke 3:1) and was alleged to mean "grassy plain," a description that fit both American Abilenes.

[15] S.B. McAllister, "Building the Texas and Pacific Railroad West of Fort Worth," in *WTHAYB* IV (1928) p. 52.

[16] *From Ox-Teams to Eagles* (Dallas: The Texas and Pacific Railway Company, ca. 1945), p. 35.

[17] McAllister, "Building the Texas and Pacific Railroad West of Fort Worth," p. 52.

[18] Hutto, "Pioneering the T&P," pp. 126-131.

[19] Martha Ann Rogers, *The Saga of Grandma Rogers*, J.W. Hunt, ed. (no publication data included, ca. 1923), copy in Abilene Public Library, pp. 20-21.

[20] Chrisman, *Callahan County*, p. 166. Several histories say that there were about 300 men working on the line, but that number simply represented one crew. See, for example, Zachry, *Rural Taylor County*, p. 4.

[21] See 1880 Population Census for Callahan and Taylor counties.

[22] Rogers, *Grandma Rogers*, p. 20.

[23] Hutto, "Pioneering the T&P," p. 127; Kincaid, "Founding Abilene," p. 20.

[24] Cosby, *History of Abilene*, p. 9.

[25] Cosby, *History of Abilene*, p. 9.

[26] Cosby, *History of Abilene*, p. 8.

Chapter Four

[1] Boorstin, *The Americans: The National Experience*, p. 80. Boorstin, a distinguished American historian and legal expert, served as Librarian of Congress for several years.

[2] Johnson Hooper, *Some Adventures of Captain Simon Suggs*, (n.p.: 1845).

[3] See David Hackett Fischer, *Albion's Seed: Four British Folkways in America* (New York and Oxford: Oxford University Press, 1989), pp. 605-782, which discusses the roots and character of the "borderer" culture, and pp. 832-834, which shows how that culture spread across the United States, including the Abilene area. See also Robert McCrum, William Cran, and Robert MacNeil, *The Story of English* (New York: Elizabeth Sifton Books - Viking Press, 1986), p. 238, which maps the American speech dialect known as "South Midland." That dialect encompasses most of North and West Texas, but not the Panhandle. Its American origins are in the Appalachians, including all of Kentucky and most of Tennessee.

[4] Clack, *Pioneer Days*, pp. 220-21.

[5] Menn, "The Abilene Story," p. 8

[6] Spence, *Judge Legett*, p. 38

[7] National Register of Historic Places, Continuation Sheet, "The Railroad and Abilene's Development into A Wholesale and Distribution Center in West Texas, 1881-1939," p. E5.

[8] Menn, "The Abilene Story," p. 10.

[9] Menn, "The Abilene Story," pp. 24-25.

[10] Duff, *Abilene*, p. 87.

[11] *Taylor County News*, April 23, 1886; May 14, 1886; May 28, 1886.

[12] Andy Adams, *The Log of A Cowboy* (Boston and New York: Houghton Mifflin Co., 1905, 1931), pp. 102-03.

[13] Karen Turner, "Abilene at the Beginning of the Twentieth Century," pp. 59, 203-06.

[14] Adams, *Log of A Cowboy*, pp. 102-03. One observer noted that "Abilene was full of cowboys . . . and whiskey and fiddles were rampant." Menn, "The Abilene Story," p. 89.

[15] Cosby, *History of Abilene*, pp. 24-5.

[16] Cosby, *History of Abilene*, p. 24.

[17] Duff, *Abilene*, p. 73.

[18] Spence, *Legett*, p. 39.

[19] Spence, *Legett*, p. 39.

[20] Cosby, *History of Abilene*, pp. 23-24.

[21] Isaac M. Cline, *Storms, Floods, and Sunshine* (Gretna, LA: Pelican Publishing Co., 2000), p. 47.

[22] Cosby, *History of Abilene*, pp. 25-26.

[23] Duff, *Abilene*, p. 71, *Abilene Remembered: Our Centennial Treasury Book, 1881* - March 15, 1981, p. 15.

[24] Cosby, *History of Abilene*, pp. 25-26.

[25] R.D. Holt, "The Introduction of Barbed Wire into Texas and the Fence Cutting War," in *WTHAYB* VI (1930) p. 70.

[26] Holt, "Barbed Wire," pp. 72-73.

[27] Holt, "Barbed Wire," p. 76.

[28] Cosby, *History of Abilene*, pp. 20-21.

[29] Menn, "The Abilene Story," p. 77.

[30] Menn, "The Abilene Story," p. 81.

[31] Menn, "The Abilene Story," pp. 72-75.

[32] Cosby, *History of Abilene*, p. 21.

[33] Duff, *Abilene*, pp. 98-99.

[34] Cosby, *History of Abilene*, p. 21.

Chapter Five

[1] Robert W. Sledge, "Taming the T&P Towns," *Permian Basin Historical Annual* XIII (1973), pp. 20-21.

[2] Menn, "The Abilene Story," January 4, 1882, p. 30.

[3] Menn, "The Abilene Story," p. 49.

[4] Menn, "The Abilene Story," p. 65.

[5] Menn, "The Abilene Story," p. 67.

[6] *Abilene Remembered: Our Centennial Treasury Book, 1881-1981*, March 15, 1981, p. 18.

[7] Menn, "The Abilene Story," p. 67, February 5, 1883.

[8] *Abilene Remembered: Our Centennial Treasury Book, 1881-1981*, March 15, 1981, p. 14.

[9] Letter, G.A. Kirkland to "Stribling," November 29, 1878, in Duff Collection at Texas Woman's University, box beginning with *Facts and Sources* book.

NOTES

[10] Paul D. Lack et al., *History of Abilene: Facts and Sources* (Abilene: McMurry College, 1981), p. 39.

[11] *Taylor County News*, April 24, 1885

[12] Lack, *Facts and Sources*, p. 48; *Abilene Remembered: Our Centennial Treasury Book, 1881-1981*, March 15, 1981, p. 15.

[13] Menn, "The Abilene Story," p. 10; Duff, *Abilene*, p. 93.

[14] Cline, *Storms, Floods and Sunshine*, p. 52.

[15] Juanita Zachry, *A Living History: Taylor County and the Big Country* (Abilene: by the author, 1999), p. 54. The Bible was preserved in the Abilene Weather Bureau until it closed, at which time it was rescued from the trash by Darrel Crawford, a retiring weatherman.

[16] Erik Larson, *Isaac's Storm* (New York: Crown Publishers, 1999), pp. 33-66, 257-58; B.W. Aston, "Another Day—Another Time: Abilene in 1885," in *WTHAYB* LIV (1978), p. 36; Cline, *Storms, Floods, and Sunshine*, pp. 57-63.

[17] *Taylor County: An Early History of Pioneer Settlers* (Abilene: Taylor County Old Settlers Association, 1923), pp.16-17.

[18] Duff, *Abilene*, pp. 73-74, 93; Cosby, *History of Abilene*, p. 46; *Abilene Remembered: Our Centennial Treasury Book, 1881-1981*, March 15, 1981, p. 19; Tom Hill's home is now at the Buffalo Gap Historic Village, where his ghost allegedly walks the halls.

[19] Aston, "Abilene in 1885," p. 36.

[20] Cosby, *History of Abilene*, p. 46; *Abilene Remembered: Our Centennial Treasury Book, 1881-1981*, March 15, 1981, p. 19.

[21] *Abilene Remembered: Our Centennial Treasury Book, 1881-1981*, April 12, 1981, p. 15

[22] *Abilene Remembered: Our Centennial Treasury Book, 1881-1981*, March 15, 1981, p. 52.

[23] *Abilene Remembered: Our Centennial Treasury Book, 1881-1981*, April 12, 1981, p. 24.

[24] Duff, *Abilene*, p. 141; *Abilene Remembered: Our Centennial Treasury Book, 1881-1981*, April 12, 1981, p. 24.

[25] Menn, "The Abilene Story," p. 105.

[26] Menn, "The Abilene Story," p. 111.

[27] Menn, "The Abilene Story," pp. 112-13.

[28] Menn, "The Abilene Story," p. 127.

[29] *Abilene Remembered: Our Centennial Treasury Book, 1881-1981*, April 12, 1981, p. 20; Cosby, *History of Abilene*, p. 82; see *Insurance Map of Abilene, Texas* (New York: Sanborn Map Co. 1929, with updates to 1952), Key page. It shows the "lake" and the dam on Lytle Creek, though other sources say it was on Cedar. The Sanborn map is taken as definitive in this case.

[30] Cosby, *History of Abilene*, p. 82; Menn "The Abilene Story," p. 105.

[31] Menn, "The Abilene Story," p. 115, April 3, 1886.

[32] Menn, "The Abilene Story," p. 121.

[33] Menn, "The Abilene Story," p. 126.

[34] Menn, "The Abilene Story," p. 124.

[35] Menn, "The Abilene Story," p. 127.

[36] Cosby, *History of Abilene*, p. 78.

37 Cosby, *History of Abilene*, pp. 78-79; Duff, *Abilene*, p. 170.

38 Menn, "The Abilene Story," p. 131.

39 Cosby, *History of Abilene*, p. 79; Duff, *Abilene*, pp. 170-1.

40 Menn, "The Abilene Story," pp. 106-07.

41 Menn, "The Abilene Story," p. 115, April 3, 1886.

42 Menn, "The Abilene Story," p. 119.

43 Menn, "The Abilene Story," p. 124.

44 Menn, "The Abilene Story," p. 89.

45 Menn, "The Abilene Story," p. 99.

46 Duff, *Abilene*, p. 170.

47 Clack, *Pioneer Days*, p. 205; see more on early education pp. 205-213.

48 *Abilene Remembered: Our Centennial Treasury Book, 1881-1981*, March 15, 1981, p. 18.

49 *Taylor County, An Early History of Pioneer Settlers*, p. 6.

50 Clack, *Pioneer Days*, pp. 207-08, 227-230.

51 Lack, *Facts and Sources*, p. 62; Clack, *Pioneer Days*, pp. 206-07; Cole's papers are in the Center for American History at the University of Texas at Austin.

52 Menn, "The Abilene Story," pp. 58-59.

53 Typescript, "Chronological History of the Abilene Independent School District," p. 1; see also National Register of Historic Places Continuation Sheet for Abilene, Texas – Education, p. 1.

54 Rupert N. Richardson, *Famous Are Thy Halls* (Abilene: Abilene Printing and Stationery Co., 1964), pp. 20-21.

55 Clack, *Pioneer Days*, pp. 214-17.

56 National Register Continuation Sheet – Education – pp. 4-5; Duff, *Abilene*, pp. 152-55.

57 *Abilene Remembered: Our Centennial Treasury Book, 1881-1981*, April 12, 1981, p. 4.

58 *Abilene Remembered: Our Centennial Treasury Book, 1881-1981*, April 12, 1981, p. 5; Jewell Posey, *First United Methodist Mosaic* (Abilene: First United Methodist Church, [1981]), p. 38.

59 *Abilene Remembered: Our Centennial Treasury Book, 1881-1981*, April 12, 1981, p. 6.

60 Menn, "The Abilene Story," p. 71.

61 *Abilene Remembered: Our Centennial Treasury Book, 1881-1981*, April 12, 1981, p. 6.

62 Menn, "The Abilene Story," p. 91; revivals of the era usually came in the late summer, a slack time in the agricultural calendar and a time when the climate was suitable for evening meetings; however, urban revivals could also come in the spring.

63 Menn, "The Abilene Story," p. 78; that is the present site of First Baptist Church.

64 *Abilene Remembered: Our Centennial Treasury Book, 1881-1981*, April 12, 1981, p. 2.

65 See *Abilene Remembered: Our Centennial Treasury Book, 1881-1981*, April 12, 1981, pp. 4 and 7 for differing versions of the founding of these churches in Abilene; Duff, *Abilene*, pp. 84-85.

66 *Abilene Remembered: Our Centennial Treasury Book, 1881-1981*, April 12, 1981, p. 9; Duff, *Abilene*, pp. 82-83.

67 Duff, *Abilene*, pp. 83-84; *Abilene Remembered: Our Centennial Treasury Book, 1881-1981*, April 12, 1981, p. 2; Robert W. Sledge, *God's Field, God's Building* (Abilene: Potosi United

Methodist Church, 1986), pp. 25-27, 96, 97.

[68] Duff, *Abilene*, p. 142; however, a local newspaper article in 1923 conceded priority to a club in Victoria; *ADR*, September 23, 1923, Sec. 2, p. 6.

[69] Duff, *Abilene*, pp. 143-4.

[70] J.C. Furnas, *The Americans* (New York: Capricorn Books, 1969), pp. 890-93.

[71] Menn, "The Abilene Story," p. 79.

[72] Duff, *Abilene*, pp. 141-42.

[73] Duff, *Abilene*, p. 142, Menn, "The Abilene Story," p. 66.

[74] Menn, "The Abilene Story," p. 64; Duff, *Abilene*, pp. 142, 145; *Taylor County, An Early History of Pioneer Settlers*, p. 4.

[75] Menn, "The Abilene Story," p. 64; Clack, *Pioneer Days*, p. 186.

[76] Clack, *Pioneer Days*, p. 215.

[77] Clack, *Pioneer Days*, p. 151.

[78] Menn, "The Abilene Story," p. 97.

[79] Menn, "The Abilene Story," p. 106.

[80] Menn, "The Abilene Story," p. 123.

[81] John Merchant, for one; little Miss Tommie Clack wanted to go, but the area was off limits to women and girls; Clack, *Pioneer Days,* pp. 224-6.

[82] Cosby, *History of Abilene*, p. 54.

[83] It eventually moved to "Fair Park," on the banks of Catclaw Creek between South Seventh and South Ninth.

[84] Cosby, *History of Abilene*, p. 55.

[85] Landers, "From Range Cattle to Blooded Stock Farming in the Abilene Country," *WTHAYB* IX (1933), p. 70.

[86] See early maps of the city; Clack, *Pioneer Days*, pp. 220-21.

[87] Grace, "Butterfield Stage," p. 71.

[88] Cosby, *History of Abilene*, p. 34; Zachry, *Rural Taylor County*, p. 156; Clack, *Pioneer Days*, p. 153.

[89] Grace, "Butterfield Stage," p. 72.

[90] Menn, "The Abilene Story," p. 45.

[91] Grace, "Butterfield Stage," p. 72.

[92] Cosby, *History of Abilene*, p. 56.

[93] Clack, *Pioneer Days*, p. 221.

[94] Menn, "The Abilene Story," pp. 62-63, Dec. 26, 1882.

[95] Menn, "The Abilene Story," p. 97.

[96] Menn, "The Abilene Story," p. 69.

[97] Menn, "The Abilene Story," pp. 69, 81-82.

[98] Menn, "The Abilene Story," pp. 82-83.

[99] Menn, "The Abilene Story," p. 85.

[100] Menn, "The Abilene Story," pp. 93-94.

[101] Menn, "The Abilene Story," p. 35.

[102] Menn, "The Abilene Story," p. 94.

[103] Menn, "The Abilene Story," p. 96.

[104] Menn, "The Abilene Story," p. 135, September 27, 1886.

[105] Lack, *Facts and Sources*, pp. 16-17.

[106] Emmett M. Landers, "From Range Cattle to Blooded Stock Farming in the Abilene Country," pp. 76-77.

[107] C. Richard King, "Black's Muleshoe Ranch," in *WTHAYB* XLI (1965), pp. 13-14.

[108] Duff, *Abilene*, p. 104.

[109] Duff, *Abilene*, p. 104.

[110] Duff, *Abilene*, p. 105.

[111] Quoted in Sledge, *God's Field, God's Building*, p. 10.

[112] Menn, "The Abilene Story," p. 71, in 1883.

[113] R.C. Crane, "Early Days in Sweetwater," in *WTHAYB* VIII (1932), pp. 119-20.

[114] Menn, "The Abilene Story," p. 103, January 10, 1886.

[115] Lack, *Facts and Sources*, pp. 24, 34, 35.

[116] B.W. Aston, "Another Day—Another Time: Abilene in 1885," p. 32.

[117] Menn, "The Abilene Story," p. 34, for example.

[118] Menn, "The Abilene Story," pp. 116-18.

Chapter Six

[1] William Curry Holden, *Alkali Trails* (Dallas: Southwest Press, 1930), pp. 140, 214.

[2] Duff, *Abilene*, pp. 168-9; Turner, "Abilene at the Beginning of the Twentieth Century," p. 30; Shirley Eoff, "Abilene, Texas, 1888 to 1900: A Town Striving for Success," unpublished M.A. thesis, Hardin-Simmons University, 1978, p. 35.

[3] Turner, "Abilene at the Beginning of the Twentieth Century," pp. 30-31.

[4] Quoted in Turner, "Abilene at the Beginning of the Twentieth Century," p. 31.

[5] Eoff, "Abilene, Texas, 1888 to 1900," pp. 35-36; Turner, "Abilene at the Beginning of the Twentieth Century," pp. 30-32.

[6] Turner, "Abilene at the Beginning of the Twentieth Century," pp. 1-6.

[7] Turner, "Abilene at the Beginning of the Twentieth Century," pp. 7-11.

[8] Duff, *Abilene*, p. 169.

[9] *Dallas Morning News*, April 15, 1894, p. 11.

[10] Chandler Davidson, *Race and Class in Texas Politics* (Princeton, NJ: Princeton University Press, 1990), p. xxiv. See elections record book in the Taylor County Elections Office for the results of these races. The elections book does not identify the party affiliations except for presidential electors. The *Abilene Daily Reporter*, unabashedly Democratic, published only Democratic slates and encouraged its readers to vote for them. It mentioned Populism only by quoting negative evaluations from other newspapers. It was not what one would call "fair and balanced."

[11] Davidson, *Race and Class*, p. xxiv.

[12] See Eoff, "Abilene, Texas, 1888 to 1900: A Town Striving for Success," in which the author

NOTES

makes a case for a modest Republican presence. Speaking of the 1894 off-year election, she said "the election demonstrated that the balance of power was gradually shifting toward the Republican Party in Taylor County" (p. 86.) However that might have seemed in 1894, election returns for the next sixty years showed that the Democrats were even stronger than before.

[13] *ADR*, July 8, 1898, p. 2; September. 2, 1898, p. 1.

[14] *ADR*, May 27, 1898 p. 4.

[15] *ADR*, June 3, 1898, p. 3.

[16] *ADR*, September 16, 1898, p. 4; *Abilene Remembered: Our Centennial Treasury Book, 1881-1981*, March 29, 1981, p. 2.

[17] *Abilene Remembered: Our Centennial Treasury Book, 1881-1981*, April 5, 1981, p. 34; Duff, *Abilene*, p. 89; Robert G. Porterfield Jr., "The Early History of Abilene up to 1920," master's thesis, Hardin-Simmons University, 1969, p. 36.

[18] Eoff, "Abilene, Texas, 1888 to 1900," pp. 33-34.

[19] Turner "Abilene at the Beginning of the Twentieth Century," p. 29.

[20] Cosby, History of Abilene, pp. 252-254.

[21] Eoff, "Abilene, Texas, 1888 to 1900," p. 13.

[22] Eoff, "Abilene, Texas, 1888 to 1900," p. 14-15.

[23] Eoff, "Abilene, Texas, 1888 to 1900," p. 32.

[24] Porterfield, "The Early History of Abilene," pp. 49-50; Duff, *Abilene*, p. 171.

[25] Porterfield, "The Early History of Abilene," p. 66.

[26] Porterfield, "The Early History of Abilene," p. 50; Cosby, *History of Abilene*, pp. 292-93.

[27] Cosby, *History of Abilene*, 93.

[28] *Taylor County Yearbook, 1913*, pp. 2, 5.

[29] Cosby, *History of Abilene*, pp. 94-95; Duff, *Abilene*, p. 171.

[30] Lack, *Facts and Sources*, p. 60.

[31] Cosby, *History of Abilene*, p. 90.

[32] Duff, *Abilene*, pp. 171-72; Cosby, *History of Abilene*, p. 59. Though her relation to the hero of San Jacinto did not hurt, it was still quite unusual for a woman to hold such a position of authority.

[33] Margery Taylor, "The Establishment and Early History of the Abilene State School," WTHAYB, XXXVII (1961), pp. 45-54; "Abilene State School History," http://www.dads.state.tx.us/ (Texas Department of Aging and Disability Services), February 8, 2007.

[34] "Abilene State School History," February 8, 2007.

[35] Duff, *Abilene*, pp. 173-4.

[36] Duff, *Abilene*, pp. 172-4; Taylor, "History of the Abilene State School," pp. 45-56; "Abilene State School History," February 8, 2007.

[37] Quoted in Juanita Daniel Zachry, "Pioneering in Range Conservation: The Abilene Agricultural Experiment Station, 1889-1901," WTHAYB XLIV (1968), pp. 145-150.

[38] Zachry, "Pioneering in Range Conservation," pp. 154-6.

[39] Robert Fink, pamphlet "Abilene Public Library Turns 100," p. 1.

[40] *Taylor County Yearbook, 1913*, back cover; Turner, "Abilene at the Beginning of the Twentieth Century," p. 46

[41] *Taylor County Yearbook*, 1913, p. 53.

[42] Cosby, *History of Abilene*, pp. 296-97; Porterfield, "The Early History of Abilene," p. 51.

[43] Cosby, *History of Abilene*, pp. 316-17; Porterfield, "The Early History of Abilene," pp. 51-52.

[44] Vernon Gladden Spence, "Colonel Morgan Jones: Master Builder of Texas Railroads," in *WTHAYB* XLIV (1968), pp.15-25.

[45] Spence, "Colonel Morgan Jones, Master Builder"; Duff, *Abilene*, pp. 192-195; Vernon Gladden Spence, "Jones, Morgan," in HOTO; Carl Kieke, "Col. Morgan Jones helped bring railroad to Abilene" in *ARN*, January 27, 2006.

[46] Eoff, "Abilene, Texas, 1888 to 1900," pp. 23-24.

[47] Eoff, "Abilene, Texas, 1888 to 1900," pp. 30-31.

[48] Eoff, "Abilene, Texas, 1888 to 1900," p. 31.

[49] Porterfield, "The Early History of Abilene," p. 64.

[50] Eoff, "Abilene, Texas, 1888 to 1900," pp. 24-25, 31.

[51] Lack, *Facts and Sources*, p. 2.

[52] William Richard Kohl, "A History of the Fairs of Abilene," unpublished M.A. thesis, Hardin-Simmons University, 1961, pp. 15-18.

[53] Kohl, "A History of the Fairs of Abilene," pp. 22-23.

[54] Lack, *Facts and Sources*, p. 17; Kohl, "A History of the Fairs of Abilene," pp. 26-29.

[55] Kohl, "A History of the Fairs of Abilene," pp. 29-37.

[56] Eoff, "Abilene, Texas, 1888 to 1900," pp. 59-60.

[57] Lack, *Facts and Sources*, F&S, p. 48.

[58] Duff and Seibt, *Catclaw Country*, pp. 97-100.

[59] *ADR*, February 16, 1894, p. 5.

[60] Eoff, "Abilene, Texas, 1888 to 1900," p. 67.

[61] Eoff, "Abilene, Texas, 1888 to 1900," pp. 54-55.

[62] Walter N. Vernon, et al., *The Methodist Excitement in Texas* (Dallas: Texas United Methodist Historical Society, 1984), pp. 178-180.

[63] Eoff, "Abilene, Texas, 1888 to 1900," pp. 65-69.

[64] Eoff, "Abilene, Texas, 1888 to 1900," p. 61.

[65] Turner, "Abilene at the Beginning of the Twentieth Century," pp. 102, 140, 152, 165, 170, 184.

[66] Turner, "Abilene at the Beginning of the Twentieth Century," pp. 102, 140, 152, 165, 170, 184.

[67] Turner, "Abilene at the Beginning of the Twentieth Century," pp. 69-86.

[68] Eoff, "Abilene, Texas, 1888 to 1900," p. 50.

[69] Eoff, "Abilene, Texas, 1888 to 1900," pp. 51-52.

[70] Richardson, *Famous Are Thy Halls*, pp. 22-29.

[71] Richardson, *Famous Are Thy Halls*, p. 30; Cooper High School in Abilene is named in his honor.

[72] Lack, *Facts and Sources*, p. 66.

[73] Richardson, *Famous Are Thy Halls*, pp. 30-39.

[74] See Vernon, *The Methodist Excitement in Texas*, p. 177. Texas Methodists insisted that "the chief design of the Sabbath school is to lead children to Christ, and this part of our work should be made purely evangelical."

[75] Richardson, *Famous Are Thy Halls*, p. 20; see also Vernon, *The Methodist Excitement in Texas*, pp. 247-53, which argues that the Sunday school movement changed around the turn of the century toward a more educational, and less evangelistic, focus.

[76] National Register Continuation Sheet – Education, pp. 4-5.

[77] Guy A. Scruggs, "Abilene Christian College," in *WTHAYB* XXI (1945), pp. 3-4.

[78] Cosby, *History of Abilene*, p. 165.

[79] Cosby, *History of Abilene*, p. 166.

[80] Scruggs, "Abilene Christian College," pp. 5-7.

[81] National Register Continuation Sheet – Education, p. 6; Scruggs, "Abilene Christian College," pp. 7-8.

[82] National Register Continuation Sheet – Education, pp. 1-2; AISD brochure, "A Historical Reflection on Abilene Schools."

Chapter Seven

[1] Lack, *Facts and Sources*, p. 39.

[2] *ADR*, May 8, 1911, p. 7; according to the "Dillon Rule" in American jurisprudence, cities have no inherent powers of their own but instead receive their authority as a grant from the state. Thus, the state sets the ground rules and limits by which municipalities may govern themselves. Both houses of the Legislature passed the "Charter Bill" for Abilene, which Governor Colquitt signed. See *ADR*, March 7, 1911, p. 1.

[3] *Taylor County Year Book*, 1913, p. 32.

[4] For development of the city structure, see Robbie Malone, "Early Abilene: The Quieter Side of the West," in *WTHAYB* LIX (1983), pp. 90-97]

[5] The complete charter took up eight full pages of the *Abilene Daily Reporter* for March 23, 1911 – pp. 13-20.

[6] Davidson, *Race and Class in Texas Politics*, p. xxv.

[7] Davidson, *Race and Class in Texas Politics*, pp. xxv-xxvi; *ADR*, January 31, 1911, p. 2. The list included the usual suspects – K.K. Legett, Henry Sayles Sr., W. A. Minter, F.C. Digby Roberts, Will Stith, George L. Paxton, H.O. Wooten, J.M. Radford, M.H. Compere, among others.

[8] *ADR*, April 9, 1911, p. 3.

[9] *ADR*, April 21, p. 5.

[10] Porterfield, "The Early History of Abilene Up to 1920," pp. 37-38.

[11] Lack, *Facts and Sources*, pp. 42-43.

[12] *Taylor County Yearbook*, 1913, p. 27.

[13] *Abilene Semi-Weekly Reporter*, May 12, 1914.

[14] Richardson, *Famous Are Thy Halls*, p. 79.

[15] Richardson, *Famous Are Thy Halls*, pp. 73-78.

[16] Don H. Morris, *Like Stars Shining Brightly* (Abilene: Abilene Christian College Press, 1953), p. 54.

[17] *Taylor County Year Book*, 1913, p. 4

[18] James A. Roberson, "A History of Education in Taylor County, Texas, 1878-1950," master's thesis, University of Texas, 1951, p. 92n.

[19] Duff, *Abilene*, p. 160; Cosby, *History of Abilene*, pp. 167-170; *Abilene Remembered: Our Centennial Treasury Book, 1881-1981*, April 5, 1981, p. 29; Morris, *Like Stars Burning Brightly*, pp. 57-111.

[20] See Roberson, "A History of Education in Taylor County, Texas," pp. 30, 37; Zachry, *Taylor County*, pp. 126, 238; *Texas Almanac* (Dallas: A.H. Belo Corporation, 1927), p. 112; pamphlet "Chronological History of AISD"; *ADR*, May 8, 1911, p. 1.

[21] *ADR*, February 14, 1909, p. 1.

[22] *ADR*, February 14, 1909, p. 1.

[23] *ADR*, February 14, 1909, p. 7.

[24] *ADR*, February 14, 1909, p. 1.

[25] Robert Fink, pamphlet "Abilene Public Library Turns 100," p. 3.

[26] Juanita D. Zachry, *A Living History: Taylor County and the Big Country* (Abilene: Quality Printing, 1999), pp. 53-54; *Abilene Historical Landmarks* (Abilene: City of Abilene, 1987) No. 31.

[27] *Taylor County Year Book*, 1913, p. 46.

[28] *Taylor County Yearbook*, 1913, p. 27.

[29] *ADR*, March 31, 1913, p. 4.

[30] *ADR*, March 24, 1913, p. 4.

[31] *ADR*, March 31, 1913, p. 4.

[32] *ADR*, July 16, 1913, p. 4.

[33] *Taylor County Yearbook*, 1913, p. 46.

[34] *Taylor County Yearbook*, 1913, pp. 38-39.

[35] *Abilene Semi-Weekly Reporter*, July 15, 1913, p. 4.

[36] Brochure "History of the Abilene Parks and Recreation System" (Abilene Parks Department, ca. 1984), pp. 1-2.

[37] *ADR*, August 1, 1919, p. 4.

[38] Chris Cravens, "Abilene and Southern Railway," in HOTO; Duff, *Abilene*, p. 196; Vernon Gladden Spence, *Colonel Morgan Jones, Grand Old Man of Texas Railroading* (Norman: University of Oklahoma Press, 1971), pp. 173 ff.

[39] Spence, *Colonel Morgan Jones*, pp. 173-182.

[40] Spence, *Colonel Morgan Jones*, pp. 184-190.

[41] Spence, *Colonel Morgan Jones*, pp. 191-197.

[42] Peggy W. Sledge, *The Littlest Smuggler* (Abilene: privately published, 1988), pp. xii-xiii; interviews with the author.

[43] *ADR*, September 9, 1923, p. 7.

[44] Kohl, "A History of the Fairs of Abilene," pp. 38-49.

[45] *Abilene Remembered: Our Centennial Treasury Book, 1881-1981*, March 22, 1981, p. 4.

[46] *Abilene Remembered: Our Centennial Treasury Book, 1881-1981*, March 22, 1981, p. 10.

[47] *ADR*, November 17, 1918, Section 3, p. 1.
[48] *ADR*, January 9, 1917, p. 4; *ADR*, January 11, 1917, p. 1.
[49] *ADR*, July 11, 1917, p. 1.
[50] *ADR*, September 23, 1918, p. 4.
[51] *ADR*, November 17, 1918, Section 3, p. 1.

Chapter Eight

[1] *ADR*, August 1, 1911, pp. 1, 5.
[2] *ADR*, August 2, 1911, p. 1.
[3] *Taylor County Yearbook*, 1913, p. 38.
[4] *ADR*, November 24, 1913, p. 1.
[5] *ADR*, November 24, 1913, p. 1.
[6] *ADR*, November 25, 1913, p. 1.
[7] *ADR*, April 20, 1919, p. 1.
[8] *ADR*, April 22, 1919, p. 1.
[9] *ADR*, April 20, 1919, pp. 1, 2.
[10] *ADR*, April 20, 1919, p. 4.
[11] *ADR*, April 20, 1919, p. 2.
[12] Lack, *Facts and Sources*, pp. 16-17.
[13] *ADR*, January 14, 1917, p. 2.
[14] *Abilene Remembered: Our Centennial Treasury Book, 1881-1981*, March 15, 1981, p. 17.
[15] *ADR*, March 21, 1917, p. 1.
[16] *ADR*, September 3, 1918, p. 1.
[17] O.F. Sensabaugh, typescript, "Recollections" in Hunt Collection, section titled Abilene District, first page.
[18] *ADR*, September 17, 1918, p. 6.
[19] *ADR*, September 24, 1918, p. 4.
[20] Essay dated 1981 titled "The First Abilenians," p. 11, in the Duff Collection, Texas Woman's University. No author indicated.
[21] *ADR*, June 29, 1917, p. 1.
[22] *ADR*, July 1, 1917, p. 1.
[23] *ADR*, July 1, 1917, p. 1.
[24] *ADR*, July 5, 1917, p. 1.
[25] *ADR*, July 17, 1917, p. 1.
[26] *ADR*, June 29, 1917, p. 1.
[27] *ADR*, June 29, 1917, p. 1; *ADR*, July 1, 1917, p. 1.
[28] *ADR*, July 3, 1917, p. 1.
[29] *ADR*, July 1, 1917, p. 2; *ADR*, July 4, 1917, p. 4; *ADR*, July 8, 1917, p. 6.
[30] *ADR*, July 9, 1917, p. 1.

[31] *ADR*, July 8, 1917, p. 1.

[32] Lawrence L. Graves, "Texas Tech University," in HOTO; "The West Texas Agricultural and Mechanical College Movement and the Founding of Texas Technological College," an article by one of the participants, Judge R.C. Crane of Sweetwater, giving the whole story in great detail, but not from the Abilene point of view - *WTHAYB* VII (1931), pp. 3-34.

[33] See, for example, *ADR*, November 20, 1918, and November 6, 1918.

[34] *ADR*, September 6, 1918.

[35] Richardson, *Famous Are Thy Halls*, p. 92; Don Morris, *Like Stars Shining Brightly*, p. 107.

[36] Richardson, *Famous Are Thy Halls*, pp. 93-4.

[37] *ADR*, November 6, 1918, p. 6.

[38] *ADR*, November 6, 1918, p. 2.

[39] Joan Drusedow Griggs, "Old Glory, Texas," in HOTO.

[40] *ADR*, October 8, 1918, p. 1

[41] *ADR*, September 23, 1918, pp. 1-2.

[42] *ADR*, April 13, 1917, p. 1.

[43] *ADR*, September 1, 1918, p. 1.

[44] *ADR*, September 22, 1918, p. 1.

[45] *ADR*, September 1, 1918, p. 1.

[46] Interview with Vivian (Mrs. J. Riley) Miller, Potosi, 1978.

[47] *ADR*, September 10, 1918, p. 1.

[48] *ADR*, October 4, 1918, p. 1.

[49] *ADR*, October 6, 1918, p. 3.

[50] *ADR*, October 2, 1918, p. 1.

[51] *ADR*, November 7, 1918, p. 1.

[52] *ADR*, November 15, p. 1.

[53] *ADR*, October 20, p. 1.

[54] *ADR*, November 10, 1918, p. 2.

[55] O.F. Sensabaugh, "Recollections," section titled Abilene District, first page.

[56] O.F. Sensabaugh, "Recollections," section titled Abilene District, first page.

[57] *ADR*, August 14, 1919, p. 1.

[58] *ADR*, August 2, 1919, p. 1.

[59] *ADR*, August 15, 1919, p. 4.

[60] *ADR*, August 17, 1919, p. 7.

[61] *Taylor County Yearbook*, 1913, p. 5.

[62] *Taylor County Yearbook*, 1913, p. 51.

[63] *ADR*, August 21, 1919, p. 1.

[64] Lack, *Facts and Sources*, p. 12.

NOTES

Chapter Nine

[1] Bruce Barton, *The Man Nobody Knows* (New York: Bobbs-Merrill, 1924).

[2] Lack, *Facts and Sources*, p. 2.

[3] *ADR*, September 23, 1923, Section 2, p. 8.

[4] Lack, *Facts and Sources*, p. 60.

[5] Lack, *Facts and Sources*, p. 59.

[6] Lack, *Facts and Sources*, p. 66.

[7] Sanborn Insurance map, City of Abilene, 1929-1950, p. 402.

[8] Abilene Independent School District, pamphlet, "A Historical Reflection on Abilene Schools," 1995.

[9] *Abilene Historic Landmarks*, No. 74; Curtis Tate, "Abilene's Golden Era: The Emergence of a West Texas City during the 1920s," unpublished M.A. thesis, Hardin-Simmons University, 1991, pp. 25-26; the building was subsequently renamed the Windsor.

[10] Tate, "Abilene's Golden Era," pp. 28-9.

[11] Tate, "Abilene's Golden Era," p. 24.

[12] Tate, "Abilene's Golden Era," pp. 22-23.

[13] Tate, "Abilene's Golden Era," p. 25.

[14] *Abilene Historic Landmarks* Nos. 6, 14, 15, 58; Tate, "Abilene's Golden Era," pp. 27-28.

[15] *ADR*, Sept 9, 1923, pp. 7-8.

[16] *ADR*, September 23, 1923, Home Ed. p. 2.

[17] Tate, "Abilene's Golden Era," p. 68.

[18] *Abilene Historic Landmarks*, No. 17.

[19] http://www.ehendrick.org/ (Hendrick Medical Center); *Abilene Remembered: Our Centennial Treasury Book, 1881-1981*, April 12, 1981, p. 47.

[20] *ADR*, September 23, 1923, p. 8.

[21] *Abilene Historic Landmarks* No. 53; *Abilene Remembered: Our Centennial Treasury Book, 1881-1981*, April 12, 1981, p. 9.

[22] *Abilene Historic Landmarks*, p. 11.

[23] Typescript, "History of the Abilene Public Parks and Recreation System, p. 3; Tate, "Abilene's Golden Era," 39.

[24] *ADR*, January 23, 1921, Section 3, p. 1.

[25] *Abilene Remembered: Our Centennial Treasury Book, 1881-1981*, April 12, 1981, p. 20.

[26] Lack, *Facts and Sources*, pp. 18-19; *Abilene Remembered: Our Centennial Treasury Book, 1881-1981*, April 12, 1981, p. 20.

[27] *ADR*, January 30, 1921, p. 3.

[28] *ADR*, March 13, 1921, Section 3, p. 5; "Cedar Gap Pike" was another name for Peach Street, and "Buffalo Gap Pike" was an alternate name for Vine Street. The city did not extend as far south as the present-day Buffalo Gap Road at that time.

[29] *Abilene Historic Landmarks*, #20.

[30] See, for example, *Abilene Historic Landmarks* Nos. 1, 2, 4, 5,12, 28, 29, 36, 49, 54, 57, 59, and 63.

[31] Tate, "Abilene's Golden Era," pp. 19-22.

[32] Lack, *Facts and Sources*, p. 2.

[33] Lack, *Facts and Sources*, p. 57.

[34] Lack, *Facts and Sources*, pp. 16-19.

[35] Richard Schroeder, *Texas Signs On* (College Station: TAMU Press, 1998), p. 13.

[36] *ADR*, April 30, 1923, p. 1.

[37] *Abilene Remembered: Our Centennial Treasury Book, 1881-1981*, April 19, 1981, p. 55.

[38] By this time, the U.S. had standardized its call letter system, so that all stations west of the Mississippi would begin with K while those east of the river would begin with W. The RBC in the call sign stood for Reporter Broadcasting Company.

[39] *ADR*, January 6, 1929, p. 8.

[40] *ADR*, January 21, 1921, p. 3.

[41] *ADR*, January 30, 1921, p. 8.

[42] *ADR*, March 6, 1921, Section 3, p. 5.

[43] *ADR*, March 6, 1921, Section 3, p. 6.

[44] Tate, "Abilene's Golden Era," pp. 14-15.

[45] Tate, "Abilene's Golden Era," pp. 12-14.

[46] Tate, "Abilene's Golden Era," pp. 16-17.

[47] Tate, "Abilene's Golden Era," p. 14.

[48] *ADR*, March 20, 1921, Section 3, p. 8.

[49] Tate, "Abilene's Golden Era," p. 17.

[50] See *ADR*, January 1929, passim.

[51] *ADR*, April 17, 1923, Section 2, p. 3; April 18, 1923, p. 6.

[52] Duff, *Abilene*, p. 202.

[53] Tate, "Abilene's Golden Era," pp. 50-51.

[54] Duff, *Abilene*, pp. 203-04; Tate, "Abilene's Golden Era," pp. 53-54.

[55] Duff, *Abilene*, pp. 203-04; Tate, "Abilene's Golden Era," pp. 53-54.

[56] *ADR*, March 20, 1921 Section 3, p. 2; *Abilene Historical Landmarks*, No.18.

[57] Tate, "Abilene's Golden Era," pp. 15-16.

[58] *ADR*, January 4, 1929, p. 4.

[59] *ADR*, January 22, 29, p. 3.

[60] *ADR*, January 24, 1929, p. 5.

[61] *ADR*, January 27, 1929, p. 11.

[62] Heat from the interior of the icebox was absorbed by the ice, causing it to melt. The melting process was the cooling agent.

[63] *ADR*, January 20, 1929, Section 2, p. 14.

[64] Lawrence L. Graves, "Texas Tech University," in HOTO; Duff, *Abilene*, pp. 217-18.

[65] *Flashlight*, 1927, p. 81.

[66] *Flashlight*, 1928, p. 82.

NOTES

[67] *Flashlight*, 1948, n.p.

[68] Lack, *Facts and Sources*, p. 64.

[69] The twelfth grade of high school was added to public school education in Texas just before World War II. Kindergarten classes and preschool work were additions of an even later period.

[70] U.S. Dept. of Interior, National Register of Historic Places Continuation Sheet, Section E, p. 3.

[71] U.S. Dept. of Interior, National Register of Historic Places Continuation Sheet, Section E, pp. 2-3.

[72] *Abilene Remembered: Our Centennial Treasury Book, 1881-1981*, April 12, 1981, p.35. Females did not hold administrative positions. Female elementary school principals were virtually unheard of in Abilene, unlike in other towns, even into the 1960s.

Chapter Ten

[1] Lack, *Facts and Sources*, p. 2.

[2] Tate, "Abilene's Golden Era," pp. 99-102.

[3] Tate, "Abilene's Golden Era," pp. 107-109.

[4] Tate, "Abilene's Golden Era," pp. 105-107.

[5] *ADR*, April 30, 1923, Section 2, p. 8.

[6] Tate, "Abilene's Golden Era," p. 116. The present author's impression is at odds with that of A.C. Greene, who said, "The KKK died quickly in Abilene in its 1920's revival, killed by the courage of Editor Frank Grimes." - *A Personal Country*, p. 319.

[7] Tate, "Abilene's Golden Era," p. 114; Paul D. Lack and Gerald McDaniel, "Did The Jazz Age Come to Abilene?" DVD of 1981 presentation at Abilene Public Library.

[8] Lack, *Facts and Sources*, p. 42.

[9] Lack, *Facts and Sources*, p. 47; Mildred Paxton Moody, wife of the Democratic candidate for governor, was an Abilenian.

[10] Lack, *Facts and Sources*, pp. 8-9.

[11] Tate, "Abilene's Golden Era," pp. 103-04.

[12] Tate, "Abilene's Golden Era," pp. 112-13.

[13] Tate, "Abilene's Golden Era," p. 115.

[14] Tate, "Abilene's Golden Era," pp. 115-16; this from an editor who was vigorously anti-Darwinist. Grimes was and is widely regarded as a fine journalist, but his comments here illustrate that the best of people in every age can have serious moral blind spots and that even great editors can be logically inconsistent.

[15] Jewell G. Pritchett, *The Black Community in Abilene* (Abilene: Pritchett Publications, 1984), p. 46.

[16] "A Chronological History of the Abilene Independent School District" (2004); Pritchett, The Black Community", pp. 10-11. One source suggested that fifteen black students were enrolled in the mainstream of Abilene schools in 1885 and were not segregated until 1890. – U.S. Dept. of Interior, National Register of Historic Places Continuation Sheet, Section E, p. 4; Tommie Clack reported that she had a black schoolmate at Colony Hill School before the founding of Abilene. Clack, *Pioneer Days*, p. 179.

[17] *ADR*, January 17, 1918, p. 1; the contraband alcohol supposedly came from that den of iniquity, San Angelo.

[18] *ADR*, January 14, 1917 p. 4.

[19] *ADR* February 25, 1921; quoted in Tate, "Abilene's Golden Era," p. 104.

[20] "A Chronological History of the AISD"; Lack, *Facts and Sources*, p. 9.

[21] *ADR*, March 28, 1911, p. 1; an ad for the Vendome Theater said it had just hired a new pianist from New York City.

[22] *ADR*, January 12, 1921, p. 5.

[23] *ADR*, January 9, 1921, Section 2, p. 8.

[24] *ADR*, January 14, 1921, pp. 7, 8; January 13, 1921, p. 2.

[25] Tate, "Abilene's Golden Era," p. 82.

[26] Tate, "Abilene's Golden Era," pp. 83-85.

[27] *ADR*, September 9, 1923, p. 10.

[28] The term "vamp" came into common usage after the Theda Bara film "A Fool There Was" in which she played a sexually predatory woman called "The Vamp" (for "vampire"). Vamping came to mean excessive flirtatiousness, possibly promising more than was actually being offered.

[29] *ADR*, April 24, 1921, p. 1.

[30] *ADR*, January 17, 1921, p. 1.

[31] *ADR*, January 17, 1921, p. 1.

[32] http://www.minorleague baseball.com/milb/history/top100.jsp?idx=94, February 7, 2007.

[33] *Flashlight*, 1923 (the yearbook for Abilene High School); Estes was grandfather to the professional golfer of the same name.

[34] The first public use of the name as applied to Abilene High came in late November 1923. See *ADR*, November 23, 1923, p. 8.

[35] *Flashlight*, 1924.

[36] *ADR*, December 23, 1923, p. 2. All-state mention was reserved for players on the playoff teams.

[37] *ADR*, December 30, 1923, p. 3.

[38] *Flashlight*, 1928.

[39] Al Pickett, *Team of the Century* (Abilene: State House Press, 2004), p. 20.

Chapter Eleven

[1] Interview with Mary Helen Girdner, Abilene, May 7, 2008.

[2] Tate, "Abilene's Golden Era," pp. 19-22.

[3] Lack, *Facts and Sources*, p. 52; *ADR*, January 4, 1936, p. 11.

[4] *ADR*, January 4, 1936, p. 1.

[5] *ADR* January 4, 1936, p. 11.

[6] *ADR*, January 4, 1936, p. 11.

[7] John Henry Hatcher, "A History of Dyess Air Force Base in Its First Decade," unpublished M.A. thesis, Hardin-Simmons University, 1963, p. 464.

NOTES

[8] Lack, *Facts and Sources*, p. 62; *ADR*, January 6, 1936, p. 1.

[9] Lack, *Facts and Sources*, pp. 66-67.

[10] *Abilene Remembered: Our Centennial Treasury Book, 1881-1981*, March 15, 1981, p. 34.

[11] *ADR*, January 1, 1935, p. 6.

[12] *Abilene Remembered: Our Centennial Treasury Book, 1881-1981*, March 15, 1981, p. 34.

[13] Oscar K. Bowen, *Mr. Hendrick* (Abilene: Hendrick Home for Children, 1962), pp. 91-92.

[14] *Abilene Remembered: Our Centennial Treasury Book, 1881-1981*, March 15, 1981, p. 34.

[15] Interview with Mary Helen Girdner, May 8, 2008.

[16] In her book, *Abilene... On Catclaw Creek*, Kathryn Duff told the story of Lawrence Welk, a rising young bandleader who had no further engagements and so "stayed around Abilene for a long time, hanging on until his luck could change." According to the story, the small band played at the Hilton for room and board (p. 216). Welk did not remember his Abilene ties quite that way. If he was ever "stranded" in Abilene, he didn't say so. In one autobiography, he mentioned "Abilene, where I played lunch and dinner music for a man named Earl Guitar" (Lawrence Welk with Bernice McGeehan *Ah-One, Ah-Two* [Englewood Cliffs, NJ: Prentice-Hall, 1974] p. 58). The Guitars were among the partners in the Hilton Hotel. In another account, Welk recalled traveling around West Texas for the Hilton Hotel chain—Lubbock, Dallas, Fort Worth and Abilene, among others, "but we had nothing steady" until he accepted a standing engagement at the Broadmoor Country Club in Denver in 1932. His memories of traveling West Texas in the late 1920s and early 1930s read like a B-grade western movie—cactus, rattlesnakes, guns and holsters, shootouts at dances—the whole Wild West works. He told of arranging the piano at one dance hall so that the band could take refuge behind it when the shooting started, as it invariably did. One wonders whether he might not have been in Hollywood a little too long. (Lawrence Welk with Bernice McGeehan, *Wunnerful, Wunnerful* [Englewood Cliffs, NJ: Prentice-Hall, 1971], pp. 67-71, 112, 116).

[17] Interview with Mary Helen Girdner, May 8, 2008.

[18] *ADR*, October 16, 1931.

[19] *ADR*, October 1, 1931, p. 9.

[20] *ADR*, March 7, 1933, p. 1.

[21] *ADR*, March 7, 1933, p. 1.

[22] *ADR*, March 3, 1933, p. 1.

[23] *ADR*, March 6, 1933, p. 4.

[24] *ADR*, March 7, 1933, p. 1.

[25] *Abilene Remembered: Our Centennial Treasury Book, 1881-1981*, March 15, 1981, p. 34.

[26] *Abilene Remembered: Our Centennial Treasury Book, 1881-1981*, April 5, 1981, p. 35.

[27] *Abilene Remembered: Our Centennial Treasury Book, 1881-1981*, March 15, 1981, p. 34.

[28] *Abilene Remembered: Our Centennial Treasury Book, 1881-1981*, March 15, 1981, p. 4.

[29] *Abilene Remembered: Our Centennial Treasury Book, 1881-1981*, April 5, 1981, p. 23.

[30] *Abilene Remembered: Our Centennial Treasury Book, 1881-1981*, April 5, 1981, p. 24.

[31] *ADR*, Jan. 2, 1933, p. 8.

[32] *ADR*, April 1, 1936, pp. 1, 11.

[33] Oscar K. Bowen, *Mr. Hendrick*, pp. 87-88.

[34] Winston T. Beard, "Hendrick Medical Center," in HOTO.

[35] Oscar K. Bowen, *Mr. Hendrick*, pp. 93-98.

[36] Lynda Taylor, "Hendrick Home for Children," in HOTO.

[37] Morris, *Like Stars Shining Brightly*, p. 159.

[38] Morris, *Like Stars Shining Brightly*, pp. 170-71.

[39] Morris, *Like Stars Shining Brightly*, p. 173.

[40] Morris, *Like Stars Shining Brightly*, pp. 178-192.

[41] Richardson, *Famous Are Thy Halls*, pp. 140-45.

[42] Richardson, *Famous Are Thy Halls*, pp. 144-56.

[43] Whisenhunt, "Years of Crisis," in Fane Downs and Robert W. Sledge, eds., *Pride of Our Western Prairies* (Abilene: McMurry College, 1989), pp. 33-40, 46-47.

[44] Whisenhunt, "Years of Crisis," pp. 47-8.

[45] Whisenhunt, "Surviving the Depression" in Downs and Sledge, *Pride of Our Western Prairies* (Abilene: McMurry College, 1989), pp 49-52.

[46] Donald Whisenhunt, "Surviving the Depression," pp. 53-4.

[47] J. Edward Gray, "The History of the First Baptist Church of Abilene, Texas," unpublished M.A. thesis, Hardin-Simmons University, 1957, pp. 116-118, 126.

[48] Edward J.M. Schroeder, "Sacred Heart and the Catholic Church in Abilene," unpublished M.A. thesis, Hardin-Simmons University, 1973, p. 31.

[49] Schroeder, "Sacred Heart and the Catholic Church in Abilene," pp. 47-48.

[50] Darris L. Egger, *A Church Named St. Paul* (Abilene: St. Paul United Methodist Church, 1995), p. 40.

[51] Jewell Posey, *Methodist Mosaic* (Abilene: First United Methodist Church, 1981), p. 62.

[52] Andrew B. Fanelli, *From Roots to Wings: A History of Highland Church of Christ* (Abilene: Classic Printing Consultants, 1988), pp. 10-12.

[53] Walter H. Adams, *Serving Abilene and the World for 80 Years* (Abilene: n.p., 1981), pp. 14-15.

[54] *ADR*, April 15, 1935, p. 1; Donald Worster, *Dust Bowl: The Southern Plains in the 1930s* (New York, Oxford: Oxford University Press, 1979), p. 19.

[55] Worster, *Dust Bowl*, p. 18.

[56] Worster, *Dust Bowl*, p. 15.

[57] Paul Bonnifield, *The Dust Bowl: Men, Dirt, and Depression* (Albuquerque: University of New Mexico Press, 1979), p. 71.

[58] *ADR*, April 15, 1935, p. 1.

[59] Lack, *Facts and Sources*, p. 19.

[60] *ADR*, January 3, 1935, p. 1,

[61] *ADR*, January 1, 1935, p. 8.

[62] Henry C. Dethloff and Garry L. Nall, "Agriculture," in HOTO.

[63] *ADR*, January 2, 1936, p. 1.

[64] *ADR*, April 3, 1936, p. 12.

[65] *ADR*, April 3, 1936, p. 12.

[66] Archie Jeffries, *A West Texas Life* (Canberra, Australia: Bettye Pearce, 1996), p. 27.

NOTES

[67] Lack, *Facts and Sources*, p. 56
[68] Lack, *Facts and Sources*, p. 58.
[69] Lack, *Facts and Sources*, p. 56.
[70] Lack, *Facts and Sources*, pp. 56-57.
[71] Kohl, "A History of the Fairs of Abilene," pp. 70-74.
[72] Kohl, "A History of the Fairs of Abilene," pp. 75-77.
[73] Kohl, "A History of the Fairs of Abilene," pp. 78-79.
[74] Kohl, "A History of the Fairs of Abilene," pp. 79-88.

Chapter Twelve

[1] *ADR*, March 4, 1933, p. 12.
[2] *ADR*, January 2, 1933, p. 1; January 3, 1933, p. 3.
[3] *ADR*, February 20, 1933, p. 1.
[4] Lack, *Facts and Sources*, p. 48.
[5] Jeffries, *A West Texas Life*, p. 38.
[6] *ADR*, August 12, 1936, p. 1.
[7] *ADR*, August 12, 1936, p. 1.
[8] Steven K. Galloway, "A History of the Desegregation of the Public Schools in Abilene, Texas during the Wells Administration, 1954 to 1970," Ph.D. dissertation, Texas Tech University, 1994, p. 61.
[9] See *ADR*, April 5, 1936, p. 12 for a long list of street improvements under way or projected.
[10] Duff, *Abilene*, p. 222.
[11] *ADR*, January 3, 1936, p. 1.
[12] *ADR*, April 5, 1936, p. 12.
[13] *ADR*, September 1, 1936, p. 6.
[14] James Wright Steely, *Parks for Texas: Enduring Landscapes of the New Deal* (Austin: University of Texas Press, 1999), p. 17.
[15] Steely, *Parks for Texas*, pp. 5-18.
[16] Ned H. Dearborn, *Once in a Lifetime: A Guide to the CCC* (New York, Chicago: Charles E. Merrill Co, 1936), pp. 5-7.
[17] Steely, *Parks for Texas*, p. 46.
[18] Steely, *Parks for Texas*, p. 214.
[19] Steely, *Parks for Texas*, p. 60.
[20] Steely, *Parks for Texas*, p. 214.
[21] Dearborn, *Once in a Lifetime*, pp. 7-8.
[22] Steely, *Parks for Texas*, p. 65.
[23] Steely, *Parks for Texas*, pp. 76, 214.
[24] Steely, *Parks for Texas*, p. 80.
[25] Colored Veteran

[26] *ADR*, April 16, 1935.

[27] *ADR*, April 17, 1935.

[28] *ADR*, April 19, 1935, p.1.

[29] Steely, *Parks for Texas*, pp. 88- 89, 96.

[30] *ADR*, April 19, 1935, p. 1.

[31] Steely, *Parks for Texas*, pp. 77, 79.

[32] Steely, *Parks for Texas*, p. 104.

[33] *ADR*, January 7, 1936, p. 1.

[34] *ADR*, January 10, 1936, p. 1.

[35] Robert Caro, *The Path to Power* (New York: A.A. Knopf, 1986), pp. 343-48.

[36] *ADR*, January 9, 1936, p. 14.

[37] Richardson, *Famous Are Thy Halls*, pp. 139-40.

[38] *ADR*, October 13, 1931, p. 2; October 18, 1931, Section 1, p. 4.

[39] *ADR*, December 6, 1931, p. 5; December 13, 1931, p. 4; December 20, 1931, p. 1; December 21, 1931, p. 1; December 22, 1931, p. 1; and December 27, 1931, p. 3; 1932 *Flashlight*.

[40] *ADR*, October 15, 1931, p. 1.

[41] *ADR*, October 16, 1931, p. 1.

[42] *ADR*, October 18, 1931, p. 2; October 27, 1931, p. 1.

[43] *ADR*, January 3, 1936, p. 2.

[44] *ADR*, October 13, 1931, p. 2.

[45] *ADR*, April 3, 1936, p. 3.

[46] *ADR*, August 16, 1936, p. 1.

[47] *ADR*, September 6, 1936, p. 1.

[48] Jeffries, *A West Texas Life*, p. 44.

[49] Jeffries, *A West Texas Life*, p. 45.

[50] *ADR*, April 2, 1936, p. 7.

[51] *ADR*, April 3, 1936, p. 4.

[52] Cosby, *History of Abilene*, p. 115.

[53] Lack, *Facts and Sources*, p. 53.

[54] *Abilene Remembered: Our Centennial Treasury Book, 1881-1981,* March 22, 1981, p. 42.

[55] Quoted in Charles Herbert Marler, "A Historical Study of Military Preparedness and National Defense from the Editorials of Frank Grimes in the Abilene Reporter-News, 1918-1960," master's thesis, Abilene Christian College, 1968, p. 74.

[56] *ADR*, January 31, 1933, p. 1.

[57] *ADR*, January 2, 1933, p. 4.

[58] Quoted in Marler, "A Historical Study of Military Preparedness," p. 80.

[59] Quoted in Marler, "A Historical Study of Military Preparedness," p. 94.

[60] Marler, "A Historical Study of Military Preparedness," p. 114.

Select Bibliography

BOOKS

Abilene Historical Landmarks. Abilene: City of Abilene, 1987.

Adams, Andy. *The Log of A Cowboy.* Boston and New York: Houghton Mifflin Co., 1905, reprint 1931.

Adams, Walter H. *Serving Abilene and the World for 80 Years.* Abilene: n.p., 1981.

Ambrose, Stephen M. *Nothing Like It in the World.* New York: Simon and Schuster, 2000.

Barton, Bruce. *The Man Nobody Knows.* New York: Bobbs-Merrill, 1924.

Boaz, Hiram A. *Eighty-four Golden Years.* Nashville: Parthenon Press, 1951.

Bonnifield, Paul. *The Dust Bowl: Men, Dirt, and Depression.* Albuquerque: University of New Mexico Press, 1979.

Bowen, Oscar K. *Mr. Hendrick.* Abilene: Hendrick Home for Children, 1962.

Capps, Benjamin. *The Great Chiefs.* New York: Time-Life Books, 1975.

Caro, Robert. *The Path to Power.* New York: A.A. Knopf, 1986.

Chrisman, B.C. *Early Days in Callahan County.* Abilene: by the author, 1966.

Clack, Mollie, and Tommie Clack. Edited by Katharyn Duff and Betty Kay Seibt. *Pioneer Days...Two Views.* Abilene: Reporter Publishing Co, 1979.

Cline, Isaac M. *Storms, Floods, and Sunshine.* Gretna, LA: Pelican Publishing Co., 2000.

Cosby, Hugh, ed. *The History of Abilene.* Abilene: Hugh E. Cosby Co., 1955.

Davidson, Chandler. *Race and Class in Texas Politics.* Princeton, NJ: Princeton University Press, 1990.

Dearborn, Ned H. *Once in a Lifetime: A Guide to the CCC.* New York, Chicago: Charles E. Merrill Co, 1936.

Dodge, Grenville M. *How We Built the Union Pacific Railway and Other Railway Papers and Addresses.* Thousand Oaks, CA: Sage Publications, reprint, 1965.

Downs, Fane, and Robert W. Sledge, ed. *Pride of Our Western Prairies.* Abilene: McMurry College, 1989.

Duff, Katharyn. *Abilene... On Catclaw Creek.* Abilene: Reporter Publishing Co., 1969.

Duff, Katharyn with Betty Kay Seibt. *Catclaw Country.* Burnet, TX: Eakin Press, 1980.

Egger, Darris L. *A Church Named St. Paul.* Abilene: St. Paul United Methodist

Church, 1995.

Fanelli, Andrew B. *From Roots to Wings: A History of Highland Church of Christ.* Abilene: Classic Printing Consultants, 1988.

Fischer, David Hackett. *Albion's Seed: Four British Folkways in America.* New York and Oxford: Oxford University Press, 1989.

Frazier, Donald S., Robert F. Pace, Steve Butman. *Abilene Landmarks: An Illustrated Tour.* Abilene: State House Press, 2008.

Frazier, Donald S., Robert F. Pace, Robert P. Wettemann. *The Texas You Expect: The Story of Buffalo Gap Historic Village.* Abilene: State House Press, 2006.

From Ox-Teams to Eagles. Dallas: The Texas and Pacific Railway Company, ca. 1945.

Furnas, J.C. *The Americans.* New York: Capricorn Books, 1969.

Gabler, Robert E., et al. *Essentials of Physical Geography, Third Ed.* New York: Holt, Rinehart and Winston, 1987.

Gard, Wayne. *The Great Buffalo Hunt.* New York: A.A. Knopf, 1959.

Greene, A.C., ed. *900 Miles on the Butterfield Trail.* Denton: University of North Texas Press, 1994.

Greene, A.C. *A Personal Country.* New York: A.A. Knopf, 1969.

Hall, Joan Upton. *Just Visitin' Old Texas Jails.* Abilene: State House Press, 2007.

Holden, William Curry. *Alkali Trails.* Dallas: Southwest Press, 1930.

Hirshson, Stanley P. *Grenville M. Dodge: Soldier, Politician, Railroad Pioneer.* Bloomington: University of Indiana Press, 1967.

Hooper, Johnson. *Some Adventures of Captain Simon Suggs.* N.p., 1845.

Jeffries, Archie. *A West Texas Life.* Canberra, Australia: Bettye Pearce, 1996.

Larson, Erik. *Isaac's Storm.* New York: Crown Publishers, 1999.

McCrum, Robert, William Cran, and Robert MacNeil. *The Story of English.* New York: Elizabeth Sifton Books - Viking Press, 1986.

Mooar, J. Wright, and James Winford Hunt. Edited by Robert F. Pace. *Buffalo Days.* Abilene: State House Press, 2005.

Morris, Don H. *Like Stars Shining Brightly.* Abilene: Abilene Christian College Press, 1953.

Navarro, Susan D. *Eagle City: 1878 Colony on Lytle Creek.* Abilene: by the author, 1981.

Nevin, David *The Expressmen.* New York: Time-Life Books, 1974.

Pace, Robert, and Donald Frazier. *Frontier Texas.* Abilene: State House Press, 2004.

Ormsby, Waterman L. *The Butterfield Overland Mail.* San Mateo, CA: The Huntington Library, reprint 1955.

Pickett, Al. *Team of the Century.* Abilene: State House Press, 2004.

Pool, William. C. *A Historical Atlas of Texas.* Austin: Encino Press, 1975.

Posey, Jewell. *Methodist Mosaic*. Abilene: First United Methodist Church, 1981.

Pritchett, Jewell G. *The Black Community in Abilene*. Abilene: Pritchett Publications, 1984.

Richardson, Rupert N. *Famous Are Thy Halls*. Abilene: Abilene Printing and Stationery Co., 1964.

Richardson, Rupert N. *The Comanche Barrier to South Plains Settlement*. Glendale, CA: Arthur E. Clark Co., 1933.

Richardson, Rupert N. *The Frontier of Northwest Texas, 1846-1876*. Glendale, CA: Arthur C. Clark Co., 1963.

Rickenbacker, Edward V. *Rickenbacker*. Englewood Cliffs, NJ: Prentice-Hall, 1967.

Rogers, Martha Ann. Edited by James W. Hunt. *The Saga of Grandma Rogers*. N. p., ca. 1923.

Sledge, Peggy W. *The Littlest Smuggler*. Abilene: privately published, 1988.

Sledge, Robert W. *God's Field, God's Building*. Abilene: Potosi United Methodist Church, 1986.

Spence, Vernon Gladden. *Colonel Morgan Jones, Grand Old Man of Texas Railroading*. Norman: University of Oklahoma Press, 1971.

Spence, Vernon Gladden. *Judge Legett of Abilene*. College Station, TX: Texas A&M Press, 1977.

Steely, James Wright. *Parks for Texas: Enduring Landscapes of the New Deal*. Austin: University of Texas Press, 1999.

Taylor County: An Early History of Pioneer Settlers. Abilene: Taylor County Old Settlers Association, 1923.

Texas Almanac. Dallas: A.H. Belo Corporation, 1927.

Vernon, Walter N., et al., *The Methodist Excitement in Texas*. Dallas: Texas United Methodist Historical Society, 1984.

Webb, Walter Prescott. *The Great Plains*. Boston, New York, Chicago, London: Ginn and Co., 1931.

Welk, Lawrence, with Bernice McGeehan *Ah-One, Ah-Two*. Englewood Cliffs, NJ: Prentice-Hall, 1974.

Welk, Lawrence, with Bernice McGeehan, *Wunnerful, Wunnerful*. Englewood Cliffs, NJ: Prentice-Hall, 1971.

Wingo, Plennie L. *Around the World Backwards*. Austin: Eakin Press, 1982.

Worcester, Donald E. *Forked Tongues and Broken Treaties*. Caldwell, ID: Caxton Printers, 1975.

Worster, Donald. *Dust Bowl: The Southern Plains in the 1930s*. New York, Oxford: Oxford University Press, 1979.

Zachry, Juanita D. *A History of Rural Taylor County*. Burnet, TX: Nortex Press, 1980.

Zachry, Juanita D. *A Living History: Taylor County and the Big Country.* Abilene: Quality Printing, 1999.

ARTICLES

Aston, B.W. "Another Day – Another Time: Abilene in 1885" in *West Texas Historical Association Year Book*, LIV (1978). Hereafter *WTHAYB*.

Chalk, Samuel L. "Early Experiences in the Abilene Country," *WTHAYB*, IV (1928).

Chalk, Sam to R.C. Crane, quoted in *WTHAYB*, IV1928).

Clack, Tommie. "Buffalo Gap College," *WTHAYB*, XXXV (1959).

Crane, R.C. "Early Days in Sweetwater," *WTHAYB*, VIII (1932).

Crane, R.C. "The West Texas Agricultural and Mechanical College Movement and the Founding of Texas Technological College," *WTHAYB*, VII (1931).

Crane, R.C. "When West Texas Was in the Making," *WTHAYB*, XXIII (1947).

Grace, Hybernia. "The First Trip West on the Butterfield Stage," *WTHAYB*, VIII (1932).

Hale, Duane. "Cyrus N. Ray, The Abilene Man," in *WTHAYB*, LV (1979).

Havins, T.R. "Sheepmen-Cattlemen Antagonisms on the Texas Frontier," *WTHAYB*, XVIII (1942).

Holt, R.D. "The Introduction of Barbed Wire into Texas and the Fence Cutting War," *WTHAYB*, VI (1930).

Hutto, John R. "Pioneering the Texas and Pacific," *WTHAYB*, XII (1936).

Kincaid, Naomi. "The Founding of Abilene, The 'Future Great' of the Texas and Pacific Railway," *WTHAYB*, XXII (1948).

Kincaid, Naomi. "The Founding of Abilene," *WTHAYB*, XXII (1946).

King, C. Richard. "Black's Muleshoe Ranch," *WTHAYB*, XLI (1965).

Landers, Emmett M. "From Range Cattle to Blooded Stock Farming in the Abilene Country," *WTHAYB*, IX (1933).

Malone, Robbie. "Early Abilene: The Quieter Side of the West," *WTHAYB*, LIX (1983).

McAllister, S.B. "Building the Texas and Pacific Railroad West of Fort Worth," *WTHAYB*, IV (1928).

Ray, Cyrus N. "The Facts Concerning the Clear Fork Culture," *American Antiquity*, Vol. 13, No. 4 (April, 1948).

Ray, Cyrus N. "Accuracy in Terminology," *American Antiquity*, Vol. 1, No. 3 (January, 1936).

Sledge, Robert W. "Taming the T&P Towns," *Permian Basin Historical Annual*, XIII (1973).

Smith, Ralph A. "The West Texas Bone Business," *WTHAYB*, LV (1979).

Taylor, Margery. "The Establishment and Early History of the Abilene State School," *WTHAYB*, XXXVII (1961).

Wagstaff, R.M. "Buffalo Gap vs. Taylor City," *WTHAYB*, XLV (1969).

Wagstaff, R.M. "Coronado's Road to Quivira: 'The Greater Weight of the Credible Evidence,'" *WTHAYB*, XLII (1966).

Williams, J.W. "Coronado: From the Rio Grande to the Concho," *WTHAYB*, XXXV (1959).

Zachry, Juanita Daniel. "Pioneering in Range Conservation: The Abilene Agricultural Experiment Station, 1989-1901," *WTHAYB*, XLIV (1968).

INTERVIEWS

Interview with Mary Helen Girdner, Abilene, May 7, 2008.

Interview with Vivian (Mrs. J. Riley) Miller, Potosi, 1978.

THESES AND DISSERTATIONS

Eoff, Shirley. "Abilene, Texas, 1888 to 1900: A Town Striving for Success," master's thesis, Hardin-Simmons University, 1978.

Galloway, Steven K. "A History of the Desegregation of the Public Schools in Abilene, Texas during the Wells Administration, 1954 to 1970," Ph.D. dissertation, Texas Tech University, 1994.

Gray, J. Edward. "The History of the First Baptist Church of Abilene, Texas," master's thesis, Hardin-Simmons University, 1957.

Hatcher, John Henry. "A History of Dyess Air Force Base in Its First Decade," master's thesis, Hardin-Simmons University, 1963.

Kohl, William Richard. "A History of the Fairs of Abilene," master's thesis, Hardin-Simmons University, 1961.

Marler, Charles Herbert. "A Historical Study of Military Preparedness and National Defense from the Editorials of Frank Grimes in the Abilene Reporter-News, 1918-1960," master's thesis, Abilene Christian College, 1968.

McLean, Gary. "Abilene's Founders and the Power of Entrepreneurial Enterprise," master's thesis, Hardin-Simmons University, 2005.

Porterfield, Robert G. Jr., "The Early History of Abilene up to 1920," master's thesis, Hardin-Simmons University, 1969.

Roberson, James A. "A History of Education in Taylor County, Texas, 1878-1950," master's thesis, University of Texas, 1951.

Schroeder, Edward J.M. "Sacred Heart and the Catholic Church in Abilene," master's thesis, Hardin-Simmons University, 1973.

Tate, Curtis. "Abilene's Golden Era: The Emergence of a West Texas City during the 1920s," master's thesis, Hardin-Simmons University, 1991.

Turner, Karen Anderson. "Abilene at the Beginning of the Twentieth Century: An Analysis of the United States Census," master's thesis, Abilene Christian University, 1989.

ONLINE SOURCES

http://www.dads.state.tx.us/ (Texas Department of Aging and Disability).

http://www.ehendrick.org/ (Hendrick Medical Center).

http://www.minorleague baseball.com/milb/history/top100.jsp?idx=94. (Minor League Baseball Top 100 Seasons).

http://www.texasbeyondhistory.net/faq/index.html. (U.T. Austin College of Liberal Arts).

http://www.tshaonline.org/ (Handbook of Texas Online).

PAMPHLETS

Abilene Independent School District. "A Historical Reflection on Abilene Schools," 1995.

Fink, Robert. "Abilene Public Library Turns 100,"

PUBLIC RECORDS

National Register of Historic Places. Continuation Sheet for Abilene, Texas, "Education."

National Register of Historic Places. Continuation Sheet for Abilene, Texas, "The Railroad and Abilene's Development into a Wholesale and Distribution Center in West Texas, 1881-1939."

Texas General Land Office. Taylor County Patent Map.

U.S. Census. Agricultural Census, Taylor County, Precinct 1, 1880.

U.S. Census. 1880 Population Census for Callahan and Taylor Counties.

OTHER

Abilene Daily Reporter.

Abilene Reporter-News.

Abilene Semi-Weekly Reporter.

Dallas Morning News.

Flashlight (Abilene High School).

Insurance Map of Abilene, Texas. New York: Sanborn Map Co., 1929, with updates to 1952.

Kirkland, G.A. to "Stribling," November 29, 1878, in Kathryn Duff Papers, Texas Woman's University.

SELECT BIBLIOGRAPHY

Lack, Paul D., and Gerald McDaniel, "Did The Jazz Age Come to Abilene?" DVD of 1981 presentation at Abilene Public Library.

Menn, Alfred F. "The Abilene Story," in Katharyn Duff Papers, Texas Woman's University.

Taylor County News.

Sensabaugh, O.F. Typescript, "Recollections" in Hunt Collection, McMurry University.

Sledge, Robert W. "Boosters, Boasters, and MAGGI," paper delivered at Texas State Historical Association annual meeting, 1965.

Abilene Independent School District. Typescript, "Chronological History of the Abilene Independent School District."

City of Abilene. Typescript, "History of the Abilene Public Parks and Recreation System."

Appendixes

ABILENE MAYORS

Dan B. Corley	1883-85	Morgan Weaver	1905-07
G.A. Kirkland	1885-86	E.N. Kirby	1907-19
D.W. Wriston	1886-91	Dallas Scarborough	1919-23
H.A. Porter	1891-93	Charles E. Coombs	1923-27
D.W. Wriston	1893-97	Thomas E. Hayden	1927-31
A.M. Robertson	1897-99	Lee R. York	1931-33
John Bowyer	1899-01	C.L. Johnson	1933-35
F.C. Digby Roberts	1901-04	W.W. Hair	1937-47
R.W. Ellis	1904-05		

VOTER REGISTRATION IN TAYLOR COUNTY

YEAR	VOTERS	YEAR	VOTERS
1908	3,374	1928	9,163
1909	3,140	1930	8,194
1922	6,348	1932	6,671
1924	7,600	1944	10,143
1926	8,114		

POPULATION
Big Country Population Trends, 1880-1940

	1880	1890	1900	1910	1920	1930	1940
Abilene County		3,194	3,411	9,204	10,274	23,175	26,612
Callahan	3,453	5,457	8,768	12,973	11,844	12,785	11,568
Coke		2,059	3,430	6,412	4,557	5,253	4,590
Coleman	3,603	6,112	10,077	22,618	18,805	23,669	20,571
Fisher	136	2,996	3,708	12,596	11,009	13,563	12,932
Jones	546	3,797	7,053	24,299	22,323	24,233	23,378
Nolan	640	1,573	2,611	11,999	10,868	19,323	17,309
Runnels	980	3,193	5,379	20,853	17,074	21,821	17,309
Shackelford	2,037	2,012	2,461	4,201	4,960	6,695	6,211
Taylor		6,957	10,499	26,293	24,081	41,023	44,147
Taylor (Without Abilene)	1,736	3,763	7,088	15,089	13,707	17,848	17,335
Texas (x 1000)	1,592	2,236	3,049	3,897	4,663	5,825	6,415

APPENDIXES

POPULAR VOTE FOR PRESIDENT
TAYLOR COUNTY

Year	Dem	Repub.	Dem.	v.	Repub.
1880	n/a	n/a	Hancock	v.	Garfield
1884	n/a	n/a	Cleveland	v.	Blaine
1888	376	78	Cleveland	v.	B. Harrison
1892	575	113	Cleveland	v.	B. Harrison
1896	1,019	245	Bryan	v.	McKinley
1900	1,253	440	Bryan	v.	McKinley
1904	1,056	120	Parker	v.	T. Roosevelt
1908	1,706	177	Bryan	v.	Taft
1912	735	24	Wilson	v.	Taft etc
1916	2,134	121	Wilson	v.	Hughes
1920	1,560	244	Cox	v.	Harding
1924	3,693	441	Davis	v.	Coolidge
1928	1,891	4,050	Smith	v.	Hoover
1932	5,235	639	F.D. Roosevelt	v.	Hoover
1936	5,853	666	F.D. Roosevelt	v.	Landon
1940	7,830	982	F.D. Roosevelt	v.	Willkie
1944	7,975	602	F.D. Roosevelt	v.	Dewey

SUPERINTENDENTS OF ABILENE INDEPENDENT SCHOOL DISTRICT

Professor Barnes	?-1882	C.E. Evans	1906-1908
Professor F.W. James	1882-1885	John H. Burnett	1908-1915
Colonel J.R. Cole	1885-1889	J.L. Brooks	1915-1917
G.W. Roach	1889-1897	R.D. Green	1917-1937
F.W. Chatfield	1897-1906	L.E. Dudley	1937-1947

UNIVERSITY PRESIDENTS

ACU Presidents	Years Served	McM Presidents	Years Served
Allen Booker Barret	1906-1908	James Winford Hunt	1923-1934
H.C. Darden	1908-1909	O.P. Clark	1934
Robertson Lafayette Whiteside	1909-1922	Cluster Q. Smith	1934-1935
James F. Cox	1911-1912	Thomas W. Brabham	1935-1938
Jesse Parker Sewell	1912-1924	Frank L. Turner	1938-1942
Batsell Baxter	1924-1932	Harold G. Cooke	1942-1958
James F. Cox	1932-1940		
Don H. Morris	1940-1969		

HSU Presidents	Years Served
W.C. Friley	1892-1894
George O. Thatcher	1894-1898
O.C. Pope	1898-1901
C.R. Hairfield	1901-1902
Oscar H. Cooper	1902-1909
Jefferson Davis Sandefer	1909-1940
Lucian Q. Campbell, acting president	1940
William R. White	1940-1943
Rupert N. Richardson	1943-1953

RAINFALL

Year	Annual Rainfall (in.)	Year	Annual Rainfall (in.)	Year	Annual Rainfall (in.)
1885	—	1904	17.80	1923	32.77
1886	19.14	1905	33.06	1924	20.23
1887	24.64	1906	29.05	1925	24.14
1888	30.58	1907	18.33	1926	31.50
1889	25.28	1908	34.97	1927	19.40
1890	28.50	1909	14.97	1928	29.68
1891	17.57	1910	15.93	1929	19.11
1892	28.48	1911	25.83	1930	26.86
1893	16.27	1912	15.43	1931	28.26
1894	24.39	1913	27.81	1932	46.43
1895	35.30	1914	41.60	1933	17.72
1896	20.74	1915	23.40	1934	13.41
1897	23.30	1916	18.28	1935	29.42
1898	22.13	1917	10.85	1936	22.85
1899	23.41	1918	19.84	1937	19.86
1900	32.11	1919	28.67	1938	32.18
1901	15.71	1920	35.47	1939	21.36
1902	27.5	1921	15.61	1940	19.87
1903	26.53	1922	24.78		

REPRESENTATIVES OF ABILENE IN THE TEXAS LEGISLATURE

Legislature	Chamber	Member	Address
1881-2	Senate	Davenport, J.H.	Hamilton
	House	Stribling, C.K.	Fort Griffin
1883-4	Senate	Fleming, J. R.	Cisco
	House	Browning, J.N.	Clarendon
1885-6	Senate	Calhoun, James H.	Eastland
	House	Browning, J.N.	Mobeetie
1887-8	Senate	Calhoun, James H.	Eastland
	House	Browning, J.N.	Mobeetie
1889-90	Senate	Sims, H.T.	Coleman
	House	Tolar, Alfred H.H.	Abilene
1891-2	Senate	Sims, H.T.	Coleman
	House	Browning, J.N.	Clarendon
1893-4	Senate	Baldwin, J.C.	Haskell
	House	Cunningham, Jr., J.R.	Anson
1895-6	Senate	Gage, R.D.	Barstow
	House	Gilliland	Baird
1897-8	Senate	Tillett, H.A.	Abilene
	House	Tucker, John H.	Merkel
1899-1900	Senate	Sebastian, W.P.	Breckenridge
	House	Tucker, John H.	Merkel
1901-2	Senate	Sebastian, W.P.	Breckenridge
	House	Bryan, W.J.	Abilene
1903-04	Senate	Sebastian, W.P.	Breckenridge
	House	Bryan, W.J.	Abilene
1905-6	Senate	Hawkins, A.S.	Abilene
	House	Bryan, W.J.	Abilene
1807-8	Senate	Hawkins, A.S.	Abilene
	Senate	Cunningham, W.J.	Abilene
	House	Bryan, W.J.	Abilene
1909-10	Senate	Bryan, W.J.	Abilene
	House	Barrett, T. J.	Anson
1911-2	Senate	Bryan, W.J.	Abilene
	House	Barrett, T. J.	Anson
1913-4	Senate	Brelsford, H.P.	Eastland
	House	Wagstaff, J.M.	Abilene
1915-6	Senate	Brelsford, H.P.	Eastland
	House	Wagstaff, J.M.	Abilene
1917-8	Senate	Buchanan, C.R.	Snyder
	House	DeBogory, Eugene	Abilene
1919-20	Senate	Buchanan, C.R.	Snyder
	House	Cox, Ben L.	Abilene
1921-2	Senate	Russell, J.A.	Eastland
	Senate	Burkett, Joe	Eastland
	House	Cox, Ben L.	Abilene
1923-4	Senate	Burkett, Joe	Eastland
	House	Green, W.P.	Abilene

(continued)

Legislature	Chamber	Member	Address
1925-6	Senate	Smith, Jesse R.	Breckenridge
	House	Cummings, E.S.	Merkel
1927-8	Senate	Smith, Jesse R.	Breckenridge
	House	Cummings, E.S.	Merkel
1929-30	Senate	Cunningham, Oliver	Abilene
	House	Speck, C.D.	Abilene
1931-2	Senate	Cunningham, Oliver	Abilene
	House	Wagstaff, R.M.	Abilene
1933-4	Senate	Collie, Wilbourne B.	Eastland
	House	Wagstaff, R.M.	Abilene
1935-6	Senate	Collie, Wilbourne B.	Eastland
	House	Bradbury, Bryan	Abilene
1937-8	Senate	Collie, Wilbourne B.	Eastland
	House	Bradbury, Bryan	Abilene
1939-40	Senate	Collie, Wilbourne B.	Eastland
	House	Bradbury, Bryan	Abilene
1941-2	Senate	Bullock, Pat	Snyder
	House	Humphrey, Joe C.	Abilene

Index

Abercrombie, Lt. Col. John J. 37
Abercrombie Peak 40
Abilene 25,000 Club 115, 116, 130, 184
Abilene and Central Railroad 157
Abilene and Northern Railroad 130-31, 155, 156, 157
Abilene and Southern Railroad 153, 155-156, 157
Abilene Aviation Co. 197
Abilene Baptist College 95, 119
Abilene Board of Trade 100, 113-115
Abilene Building and Loan 187
Abilene Christian University 21, 140-141, 150-151, 176, 178, 184, 185, 191-192, 207, 213, 227, 235-237, 238, 240-241, 252
Abilene Christian College (see Abilene Christian University)
Abilene City Commission 145-147, 197, 200, 218, 219, 223, 267
Abilene City Council 14
Abilene, City of 146, 147, 257
Abilene Colored School 217
Abilene Country Club 191, 207
Abilene Courts 187, 195
Abilene Eagles (high school teams) 221-223
Abilene Eagles (professional baseball team) 221
Abilene Electric Light and Power Co. 92, 120
Abilene geography 9, 14, 17-24, 63-64
Abilene Geological Society 264
Abilene High School 94-95, 141-142, 152, 186, 203-205, 207, 231, 246-247, 252-253, 260-261
Abilene, Kansas 44, 64, 72
Abilene Light and Water Co. 122
Abilene Magnetic Quill 78, 82
Abilene National Bank 105
Abilene Progressive Committee 114
Abilene Reporter 78, 82, 89, 100, 147, 152, 154, 172, 178, 180, 181, 187-188, 189-190, 193, 194, 195, 212, 213, 217, 219, 221, 226, 228, 231-232, 250, 262-263
Abilene Reporter News 11, 265
Abilene Sanitarium 188
Abilene Savings 128
Abilene State Bank 187, 231, 232
Abilene State Park 254-259
Abilene State School 124-126, 165
Abilene Street Railway System 143, 168
Abilene Telephone Co. 123
Abilene Traction Co. 188
Abilene, Wichita Falls, and Kansas City Railroad 110
Abrigg, Larry 11, 12
Adams, Andy 73, 75
Add-Ran College 140
African-Americans 70, 137, 152, 215-217, 251, 252, 256-258
Agricultural Adjustment Administration 228, 242, 243-244
Alamo battleground 255
Albany, Texas 21, 45
Alexander, Dr. J.M. 187
Alexander Building 187
Alexander Sanitarium 153, 188
Alliance movement 115-116
Allred, Jimmy 257
Alpine, Texas 128, 242
Alta Vista School 186, 207
Amarillo, Texas 61, 171, 173
American Airways 267
American National Bank 121, 122
American Public Service Co. 199-200
American Theater 188
Americanization School 186, 217
Anson, Texas 109, 123, 161, 181
Anti-German sentiment 176-177
Apache (Lipan) Indians 31, 72
Aston, B.W. 12
Atl-atl 28
Auction 10-11, 13-15
Austin, Texas 232, 242, 259-260

Baird, Texas 45, 47, 60, 63, 64, 67, 72-73, 74, 87, 89, 170, 214, 231
Balfanz, Ralph 261
Ballinger, Texas 128, 141, 156, 169, 171, 173
Bankhead Highway 57, 163, 187, 194, 196, 230
Barber, Pete 261
Barnes, P.M. 94

305

Barret, A.B. 140-141
Barrett, Thomas J. 181
Barton, Ann McGuffin 12
Barton, Bruce 183
Barton, Clara 108
Bataan Death March 266
Bateman, Mr. 33
Battery, The 205
Baxter, Batsell 236
Beaumont, Texas 159, 261
Bechtol, John 221
Beckham, W.L. 153
"Beer and ice Seminary" 94
Beginis, Nick 262
Bell, Alexander Graham 93
Belle Plain, Texas 45, 50, 95
Belton, Texas 238
Bennett, John H. 152
Berry, J.M. 92
Berry, John T. 15, 61, 63, 70
Berryhill, Carisse 12
Big Country 11
Big Spring, Texas 37, 66, 67, 73, 83, 105, 128, 161, 169
Bison (see Buffalo)
Bizzell, W.B. 172
Black Sunday 241
Blackmon, Linnon 261
Blacks (see African-Americans)
Blanton, Tom 257-258
Blue Flame Boys 263
Bones, buffalo 43-44, 101, 103
Boone, E.H. 146
Boorstin, Daniel 69
Boren, Jody 57
Boren, Joe 57
Boren, Margaret 57
Bounds, Herring 222
Brabham, Tom 239
Bradshaw. Texas 162, 244
Brady, Texas 45
Brandenburg, Texas 176
Breckenridge, Texas 160, 188, 193, 260, 264
Brickley, Fr. H.D. 98
Bronte, Texas 157
Brookreson, Mr. 59
Brooks, J.L. 152
Brooks Dry Goods Co. 187
Brownwood, Texas 42, 78-79, 110, 119, 178, 181, 260
Bryan, Dick 222

Bryan, William Jennings (of Nebraska) 117, 148, 164
Bryan, William J. (of Texas) 125, 181
Bryner, Ben 12
"Buckle of the Bible Belt" 135
Buell, Allen 118-119
Buffalo 25, 27-30, 39, 41-44, 50, 72
Buffalo Gap, Texas 9, 10, 17, 18, 24, 25, 29-30, 37, 44, 47, 50-52, 58-60, 63, 73, 74-75, 79-82, 84, 87, 95, 110, 128, 130, 148, 154, 161, 162, 170, 190, 244
Buffalo Gap College 96
Buffalo Gap Historic Village 28, 37
Burchard farm 173
Burger, Don 223
Burkburnett, Texas 159, 236, 264
Burleson, R.C. 95
Burlington, Mr. and Mrs. 40
Butman, Sam 45, 46
Butterfield Stage Line 38, 39-41, 45, 109
Buttonwillow Creek 20, 21
Bynum, Raymond T. 203

Cal Young Park 90
Caldwell, J.M. 188
Callahan City, Texas 45
Callahan Divide 10, 18, 20, 21, 24, 40, 45, 46, 47, 50
Cameron, William 15, 10
Camp Barkeley, Texas 228, 246
Camp Bowie, Texas 175
Camp Breckinridge, Texas 38
Camp Clinton, Texas 170
Camp Cooper, Texas 38, 39
Camp Pecan, Texas 38
Camp Salmon, Texas 38
Camp Travis, Texas 175, 178
Campbell, William 90
Capital of West Texas 11
Caps, Texas 162
Carnegie Library 127, 153, 262
Carpenter, Dan 12
Carter, J.W. 50, 51
Castle, David 191, 207, 257
Catclaw Creek 20, 21, 184
Cattle 44-47, 101-102, 108, 132, 244-245
Cedar Creek 20, 21, 60-61, 63, 64, 74, 86, 90, 101, 120, 133, 136, 148, 155, 184, 190, 191, 192, 199

INDEX

Cedar Gap 20, 110, 159, 162
Celerity wagons 40
Censorship 219, 261-262
Census, U.S. 35-36, 41
Center Line Trail 56-57, 60
Central Ward School 152
Chalk, Samuel L. 24, 33, 49, 61, 63
Childers Classical Institute (See Abilene Christian University)
Childers, J.W. 140, 151
Chinese 66, 70, 111
Chisholm Trail 44
Church organizations 96-99
Cisco (Red Gap), Texas 60, 74, 128, 260
Citizens National Bank 122, 186, 232
City charter 85
Civilian Conservation Corps 228, 254-259
Clack, Bobbie 103, 111
Clack, John 44
Clack, Mollie 11, 25, 33
Clack, M. M. 46, 51
Clack, Tommie 11, 44, 103-104, 111
Clark, Bell 93
Clark, O.P. 239, 240
Clayton, C.L. 154
Clayton, George W. 108
Clear Fork culture 29
Clear Fork of the Brazos 9, 18, 21, 37, 38, 39, 45, 63, 73, 131
Clear Fork, Post on the (see Fort Phantom Hill)
Clifton, AZ 119
Cline, Isaac 76-77, 85-86
Cline, Cora Bellew 86
Clinton Building 187
Clinton, John J. 87, 90, 180, 187, 219
Clovis culture 27, 32
Clyde, Texas 21, 62, 74
Cobb, H.H. 155

Cockfighting 100
Cockrell, Fred 119-120, 125
Cockrell, Joseph E. 94
Cockrell, J.V. 124
Coffey, David 12
Coffman, D.E. 46
Coldwater, Charles 48-49
Cole, Col. J.H. 94
Coleman, H.O. 237
Coleman, Texas 45, 73, 109, 110, 130, 232
College Church of Christ 240-241
College Heights addition 139, 152, 191
College Heights School 186, 216-217
Collier, E.M. 234
Collins, Frank 76, 84
Collins, Walter 76, 87
Colorado City, Texas 73, 83, 128
Colorado River 21, 25
Colquitt, Oscar 181
Columbian exchange 30
Comanche Indians 31-32, 38, 40, 41, 45, 50
Comanche, Texas 42
Compromise of 1877 58
Compton Building 187
Continental Oil and Cotton Co. 168
Cook, Jack 118
Coolidge, Calvin 183
Coombs, Charles 200
Cooper, Oscar H. 138-139, 172
Cooper High School 15
Corley, Dan B. 51, 84
Coronado, Francisco Vázquez de 36, 53
Corsicana, Texas 261
Cosby, Hugh 11
Cotton 101, 104, 132, 157, 158, 192, 242, 243-245
Covington, Morgan 175
Cox, B.A. 218

Cox colony 72
Cox, James 236
Crane, Roy 262
Crime 76-77
Cross Plains, Texas 231
Cross, Thomas 106
Cross Timbers 20
Cunningham, J.M. 203, 213
Cunningham, John V. 88-89
Cunningham, W.F. 172
Cunningham, W.J. 181

Dallas, Texas 56, 67, 82, 129, 167, 168, 170, 173, 242
Daly, Mrs. Joseph 178
Dancing 135, 172, 220
Darden, H.C. 141
Daugherty, J. M. 105
Davis, Mr. 50
Davis, Fred 173, 174
Davis Mountains scenic area 255
Deaton, Judy 12
Debs, Eugene 148
Deer 26
Dempsey, Jack 221
Denver, CO 130
Depression, Great 183, 225-247, 249-267
Derryberry, L.E. 199
Desdemona, Texas 160, 264
Dillard, Richard 12
Doan's Crossing 45
Dobie, J. Frank 264
Dodge City, Kansas 45, 88
Dodge, Gen. Grenville M. 55-58, 129, 130, 156
Doughty, W.F. 173
Downs, Fane 11
Dromgoole, Glenn 12
Drought 23, 46, 78, 90, 106-109, 159, 169-171, 190, 241-242

Drury, John W. 51, 80-81
Dublin, Texas 222
Dudley, R.R. 96
Dudley, Texas 45
Duff, Katharyn 11
Dust Bowl 24, 241-242
Dyess Air Force Base, Texas 228

Eagle Colony 48-49, 120
Eastland, Texas 50, 66-67, 260
Eddleman, W.H. 122
Ederle, Gertrude 221
Edison, Thomas 232
Edwards Plateau 21
Electra, Texas 159
Electricity 92-93
Elk City, OK 233
Elks Lodge 100, 165
Elm Creek 18, 21, 24, 37, 53, 60, 63, 64, 73, 148, 170, 184, 190, 251
"Elm Hotel" 24
Elmdale, Texas 63, 64, 161
Elmwood addition 184, 192
El Paso, Texas 56, 65, 119, 161, 163
Ely family 186
Ely, Walter R. 215-216
Emporium Millinery 123
Epileptic Colony (see Abilene State School)
Epworth League 135
Estes, Bob 222
Etheridge, W.M. 221
Evans, J.W. Grocery 123
Everett, Grover C. 215
Everman Park 155

Fair Park 155, 190, 212-13
Fair Park City Auditorium 190
Fair Park School 186
Fairs 100-101, 114, 133-134, 155, 157-159, 245-246

INDEX

Farmers and Merchants Bank 232
Farmer's Journal 147
Farming 47-48, 132-133, 242, 243-246
Faust, Otto 176
Fencing (see Wire, barbed)
Ferguson, J.N. 146
Ferguson, Miriam A. 231, 255
Ferguson, James E. 171-174
Ferrier, Frank 180
Ferris, Sylvia 12
Fire 89-90, 128, 168-169, 189, 252
First Baptist Church 95, 97, 188, 219, 220, 239-240
First Methodist Church 97, 189, 240
First Mondays 103-104
First National Bank 232
First Presbyterian Church 96
Flashlight, The 205
Fletcher, J.F. 45, 46
Foley, Dan 90
Folsom culture 27
Fort Belknap, Texas 37, 40
Fort Chadbourne, Texas 41
Fort Concho, Texas 106
Fort Griffin, Texas 39, 41, 42, 45, 67
Fort Phantom Hill, Texas 37-38, 39, 40, 57, 60, 73
Fort Stockton, Texas 222
Fort Worth, Texas 48, 50, 55, 58, 67, 129-30, 175, 239, 246-247, 261
Fort Worth and Denver Railroad 130, 131
Fort Worth-El Paso Highway Association 161
Fox, Frank 159, 160
Franco-Texas Land Co. 49
Fraley's Butane Co. 263
Frazier, Donald S. 12
Free Milk Fund 228
Free Sisters 193
Fredericksburg, Texas 21

Friendly Frontier 11
Friley, W.C. 137-138
Frontier hypothesis (F.J. Turner) 35-36
"Frontier Texas!" 101
Fuller, F.O. 173
Fulwiler Building 187
Fulwiler family 186
Future Great 9, 10, 11, 13, 65, 67, 74

"Galloping Goose" 143
Galveston, Texas 86, 145
Garcia, A.C. 93
George, W.A. 87
Georgeston, C.C. 126
Gerhart, Willis 229
Gibbs, W.E. 82, 98
Giddens, Betty Lou 40, 127, 235, 255
Gilbert, C.E. 82, 97
Gill, C.W. 128
Girard, W.D. 118
Girl With the Jazz Heart, The 218
Glover, L. D. 217
Goedeke, Theo 137
Goliad battlefield 255
Goodwell, OK 241
"Goo-goo eyes" 223
Gordon, Texas 74
Gotman, Jack 262
Gould, Jay 58
Grace Hotel 131, 153, 154, 187, 193
Grace Museum 76, 79, 116, 121, 125, 156, 191
Graham, Texas 37, 40, 81, 124
Grange, Red 221
Grangers 115
Grant, J.H. 59
Great Plains 17-18, 27, 42
Green, Roland D. 179, 205-206
Greenbackers 115
Greene, A.C. 11, 15
Greenville, Texas 260

Grimes, Frank 189, 212, 213, 215-216, 253-254, 264-266
Grimes, Rudyard Kipling 265-266
Groseclose, Wilson 261
Grosscup and Keith Co. 90-91
Grosscup, E.W. 93
Grounds, Doc 46, 50
Guion, Texas 162
Guion, John J. 173
Guitar, Earl 222
Guitar family 186

Haddock, Dale 262
Hall Music Co. 194
Hamby, Texas 161
Hamblen, Stuart 193
Hamlin, Texas 157
Hancock, George W. 63
Hanks, M.B. 191
Hanks family 186
Hanna, Pete 222
Hardin College 238
Hardin, John 236-238
Hardin-Simmons University 21, 26, 91, 95-96, 103, 137-139, 143, 149-150, 155, 161,162, 166, 172, 175-176, 179, 184, 185, 188, 189, 191, 199, 205, 207, 212-213, 227, 237-238, 240, 254, 260, 262
Hardwick, S.P. 120
Hardwicke, A.S. 118
Hare, Gen. 176
Harvey, Mr. 216
Hasack, Capt. J.H. 14
Hash Knife Ranch 49, 60-62, 63
Haskell, Texas 109, 171, 173
Hatton, Naomi Kincaid 11
"Hawley Him" 25
Hayden, Tom 246
Hayes, Rutherford B. 10, 57-58
Hays, Will 261
Heavenly Rest, Church of the 98, 229

Heller, William 59
Hembree, "Tubby" 222
Hemphill, Zeno 76
Henderson, H. 106
Hendrick Home for Children 229, 234-235
Hendrick Hospital 188, 233, 234, 235
Hendrick, Tom 229, 234-235, 237
Heyck, Adolph 92
Heyck, Theo 14, 119, 137, 176
Heyck, Victoria 137
Hicks, Joshua L. 117-118, 147
Highland Church of Christ 240-241
Hill, John Thomas 84, 86-87, 88
Hilton, Conrad 187
Hilton Hotel 263
Hindenburg, Paul von 265
Hispanics (see Mexican-Americans)
Hitler, Adolf 264-265
Hobby, William 173, 174
Hoboes 229-230
Hoover, Dixie 12
Hoover, Herbert 214, 249-250
Hord, H.C. 173
Horn, James R. 231
Horse racing 100
Houston, Sam 86, 124
Houston School 186
Hughes, Charles Evans 148
Hughes, Ed S. 122, 128, 155, 203
Humid subtropical climate 22
Hunch Oil and Gas Co. 160
Hunt, James Winford 72, 179, 202-203, 238-239, 262
Hunter, Abe 50
Huntingdon, Collis P. 65
Hurd, Marshall F. 56, 60

Incorporation 83-84
Indians 27-32, 41-44, 59, 203
Influenza 177-179

INDEX

Insull, Samuel 232-233
Ireland, John 81
Irish 66

Jacksboro, Texas 42
Jackson, "Hog" 50
Jacobs, Kenneth 12
James, F.W. 120
Jazz Age 209, 218-221
Jenkens, Millard 188, 218-219, 220
Jeffries, Archie 251, 263
Johnson, C.L. 251, 257, 258
Johnson, Lyndon B. 259-260
Johnson-Gorsuch Building 187
Johnston, J. Stoddard 63, 64, 70, 85, 93, 97, 113
Jones, Kenneth 12
Jones, M. H. 97
Jones, Col. Morgan 121-122, 129-131, 155-157
Jones, Mrs. Morgan Sr. 228
Jones, Percy 131
Jones, Bobby 221
Jones, Sam 261
Junction, Texas 21

KFYO 193-194
KRBC 194, 263
Kahl, Carly 12
Kaltwasser, Karl (see Coldwater, Charles)
Kentucky 69-70
Kerrville, Texas 21, 172, 173, 258
Key City 11
King, Harry Tom 213
Kinsolving Field 198, 267
Kiowa Indians 41
Kirby, E.N. 115, 145-148, 157, 159, 168, 170, 179, 190
Kirby Lake (see Lake Kirby)
Kirkland, G.A. 15, 51, 84

Knight, S.L. 97
Knights of Honor lodge 99
Knights of Pythias lodge 99
Knufer, Fr. Henry 240
Krause, Karl 138
Ku Klux Klan 209, 211-214, 215

Lack, Paul D. 12
Lake Abilene 148, 170, 190, 255-258
Lake Cameron 90, 168
Lake Fort Phantom Hill 251-252
Lake Kirby 148
Lake Lytle (see Lytle Lake)
Lake Sweetwater 257-258
Lambshead brothers 41, 45
Landers, Emmett 11
Lauer, Deacon 262
Lawn, Texas 162
Leavell, S.H. 89
Legett, Kade K. 15, 51, 95, 203
Lincoln Middle School 95, 186, 207
Lindbergh, Charles A. 198-199, 209
Lindsey, Gary 12
Lion Harness Co. 180
Little Elm Creek 20
Locking, E.A. 197
Locust School 186
Lowden, James G. 118-122, 125
Lubbock, Texas 21-22, 128, 171, 174, 179, 194, 202, 242, 260
Lueders, Texas 177-178
Lyceum Theatre 135
Lytle Cove 45
Lytle Creek 20, 21, 48, 90, 97, 120, 148, 166-168
Lytle Gap 20, 108, 110
Lytle Ice Co. 122
Lytle Lake 120, 125, 133, 165, 166-168, 190
Lytle Water Co. 120
Lytle, John T. 44

Magnetic Quill (see Abilene Magnetic Quill)
Majestic Theater 188
Mall of Abilene 26
Malone, Charles 115
Maltbie Opera House 135
Man Nobody Knows, The 183
Marcy, Randolph B. 36-37
Marshall, Texas 55, 56, 63
Mary Hardin-Baylor College 238
Mashing 220, 223
Mason, Texas 21
Masonic Lodge 96, 99
Massie, J.P. 120
Mayfield, W.D. 200
Mayhew, Dewey 223, 260-261
McDaniel, Gerald 12
McDavid, Alan 175
McKinley, William 117
McMillan, F.W. 241
McMurry College (see McMurry University)
McMurry University 30, 72, 143, 184, 185, 191, 202-203, 204, 207, 222, 227, 238-239, 262
McMurry, William F. 203
McQuistian, Rev. 49
McShain, "Handsome Danny" 262
Mead Bakery 188
Medaris, John 84
Menn, Alfred 11
Merchant, Claiborne 61, 63, 64, 68, 80, 95, 126
Merchant, John D. 45, 61, 63, 68
Merkel, Texas 64, 73, 95, 119, 123, 16, 197, 244
Mesquites 18, 24, 41
Mexia Creek 60
Mexican-Americans 70, 80, 93, 137, 217-218
Miculka, Philip 12
Middleton, Ben 43

Midland, Texas 105
Milepost 407 63, 64, 68
Miller, B. 231
Miller, F.A. 106
Mims Building 187
Mingus, Texas 73
Minter Building 207
Minter, G.L. 191
Minter, W.A. 118
Minter, W.A. Jr. 123, 172
Minter family 186
Monahans, Texas 73
Mooar brothers 42
Moody, Dan 198
Moody, Mildred Paxton 198
Moran, Texas 159
Moro, Texas 109
Morrow, Mary Houston 86, 124
Motz, Charles 191
Mount Zion Baptist Church 216
Mountain Pass 20, 40
Mulberry Canyon 25, 45
Mulberry Creek 64

National Business College 187
National Youth Administration 228, 259-260
Native Americans (see Indians)
Nativism 210-215
Neff, Pat 255
Negro Day Nursery 228
Negroes (see African-Americans)
New Braunfels, Texas 177
New Deal 231, 249-
New Year's Eve 88
North, Jack 61, 87, 167, 214, 216
North Park School 152
North Ward School (Lamar) 141, 152, 216
Northington, Kinch 81
Northington, M.W. 84

INDEX

Northrup, Ed 180
Northwestern Telephone Co. 123

Oak Street Water Trough 195
Oasis Theater 188
O'Daniel, W. Lee 193
Odd Fellows lodge 99
Old Glory, Texas 177
Olsen, Julius 139
Ovalo, Texas 162
Overshiner, E.M. 213

Pace, Robert F. 12, 19, 62, 185, 253
Paint Rock, Texas 163
Palace Theater 188
Palo Duro Canyon park 255
Parachute jump 133
Paramount Theater 129, 188, 207
Paris, Texas 242
Park Office Building 187, 207
Parker, Cynthia Ann
Parker, Quanah 32
Parramore, James H. 95, 97, 119
Patterson, Christine 12
Paxton, George L. 121, 160, 186, 232
Pecan Bayou 37
Penn, W.E. 97
Pershing, John J. 174, 177
Peta Nocona 32
Pfaff, Henry 93
Phantom Hill (see Fort Phantom Hill)
Philadelphia Plan 6
Pioneer Field 198
Pioneer Mills 132
Ponca Motel 187
Pool, A.E. 231
Pope, Owen C. 97, 138
Populism 115-118
Port Arthur, Texas 223
Porter, H.A. 85, 108

Potosi, Texas 47, 161, 191
Powell, C.A. 262
Prairie dogs 33, 126
Preston, John 125
Pritchett, Jewel 11
Prohibition 85, 88, 134, 209, 211, 220-221, 250
Public Works Administration 228, 252-254

Queen City of the West 11

Radford Building 195
Radford, J.M. 105, 128, 155, 166, 187, 196-197, 207, 233, 236, 264
Rainy Creek 20
Ramsey, M.T. 198
Ranger, Texas 73, 128, 160, 260, 264
Rangers, Texas 38, 81
Rath City, Texas 42
Rathmell, Bill, 222
Ray, Dr. Cyrus 29
Redwine, Sam 193
Remington, Frederick 88
Rex Theater 188
Richardson, Rupert N. 11, 149-150, 175-176
Rickenbacker, Edward 164
Riley, G.W. 97
Riney, F.A. 256-257
Roach Family 247
Roberts, C.W. 93, 123
Robertson, A.M. 170
Rodgers, Jimmy 193
Rogers, Martha Ann "Grandma" 66-67
Rolling Plains 18
Roosevelt, Franklin D. 226, 232, 249-250, 255, 265
Roosevelt, Eleanor 259
Roscoe, Texas 74
Rosenbohm, Henry 12

Roswell, NM 128
Round Rock, Texas 50
Ruth, George H. "Babe" 221

SSS Motor Co. 195
Sacred Heart Catholic Church 98, 189, 240
St. Louis, MO 128-129
St. Paul Methodist Church 203, 213-214, 239, 240
Salkeld, Dan 223
Saloons 75-77, 88, 89, 134
San Angelo, Texas 109, 140, 156, 171, 173, 181, 213
San Antonio, Texas 21, 118-119, 173, 251, 257
San Jacinto battlefield 255
Sandefer, Jefferson Davis 149, 175, 179, 188, 212-213, 237
Santa Fe railroad 105, 110, 130, 155, 156
Sayers, Joseph 125
Sayles Boulevard district 192
Sayles, Edwin B. "Ted" 29
Sayles, Henry 85, 95, 192, 203
Sayles, Gen. John 85, 96
Scarborough, Dallas 147, 148, 170, 190, 211-212, 219
Scarborough, Jewel (Mrs. Dallas) 259
Schmidt, Mrs. Benno 228
Schools, public 93-95, 141-142, 152, 179, 185-86, 203-206, 216-217, 221-223, 252
Seay, R.A. 106
Sellers, Isaac 114
Sellers, Nannie Mae 114-115
Sensabaugh, Oscar F. 170-171, 179
Sewell, Jesse P. 150, 213
Seymour, Texas 130
Shackelford, W.O. 146
Sheep 45-48, 102, 105-106, 108, 132, 244-245
"Sheep Republicans" 46

Shenandoah 198
Sheridan, Gen. Philip 44
Shilcutt, Tracy 12
Shinnery 25
"Shotgun refunding" 228
Shotwell, Prince E. "Pete" 221-222
Sierra Blanca, Texas 65
Simmons College (see Hardin-Simmons University)
Simmons, James B. 95, 96, 139
Simmons, S.C. 47, 59
Simpson, John 46-47, 49, 61, 63, 78
Smith, Alfred E. 211, 214
Smith, Amy 12
Smith, Aultman 223
Smith, Cluster Q. 239
Smith, George W. 95, 97
Smith, Stanley 261
Snyder, Texas 171, 260
Socialism 147, 148
Soil Conservation Service 241-242
Sonora, Texas 156
South Ward School (Travis) 141, 152, 186
Spanish-American War 118-119
Specht, Alice 12
Specht, Joe 12
Spence, Vernon Gladden 11
Stamford College 202-203
Stamford, Texas 128, 130, 169
Stark, Dennis 108
Stratton, Walter "Strong Boy" 262
Steffens, Otto 84, 95, 119-122, 137
Steppe climate 22
Stepping stones 71
Stevens, Roy 222
Stewart, Robert S. 98
Stirman, V.I. 98.
Strawn, Texas 73
Streetcars (see Trolley system)
Stuckey, Lewis 213-214

INDEX

Sweetwater, Texas 13, 21, 62, 73, 83, 128, 130, 154, 169, 171, 173, 181, 257-258, 260, 262
Swenson, Willie Gray 121, 122, 131, 143
Swenson family 186
Snyder, Texas 21, 169

Taft, William Howard 148
Tarpley, Maude 111
Taylor County 10
Taylor County Courthouse 37, 51, 79, 80
Taylor County Jail 51, 80, 82
Taylor County News 82, 92
Taylor County Regular Field 264
Telephone 93, 122-123
Temple, Texas 155
Templeton, John 81
Test, Janice 12
Texarkana, Texas 162
Texas and Pacific Railway (T&P) 10, 55-68, 73-74, 85, 90, 104, 109, 110, 120, 129, 130, 136, 155, 159, 167, 186, 233, 252
Texas Midwest 11
Texas Relief Commission 256
Texas Woman's College 239
Texas Sentinel 118
Texas Technological College 174, 202
Thatcher, George 138
Thompson, W.J. 121
Throckmorton, James W. 101
Tilden, Bill 221
Tilden, Samuel J. 57
Tillett, Henry A. 94, 124
Tourist Hotel 187
Trent, John 45
Trent, Texas 73, 163
Trolley system 91, 121, 139, 143, 162, 169, 189, 191, 233

Turner, Eric Bryan 5
Turner, Frederick Jackson 35-36
Turner, Grant 193
Turner, Karen 136
Turner, Robert Ryan 5
Tuscola, Texas 162
Tye (Tebo), Texas 63, 64
Tyler, Texas 128

Underpasses, 253-254, 255
Union Pacific Railroad 55, 56, 129
University Baptist Church 262

Valley Creek 41
Valley View School 186, 207
Vamping 219-220
Vernon, Texas 194
View, Texas 162
Villa, Pancho 174
Volstead Act 250

Waco, Texas 222, 223
WQAQ 193
Wagstaff, John M. 12, 140-141, 213-214
Wagstaff, R.M. 53, 175
Waldrop's Furniture 188, 233
Walter, Esco 223
War Finance Commission 171
Washington, George 85
Water 90-91, 120, 124, 126, 190
Watson, J.T. 222
Weather 22-24, 133-134, 165-166, 193
Weather Bureau, U.S. 106, 153, 166
Weatherford, Texas 42
Weaver, James B. 116
Weaver, Morgan 128
Webb, Walter Prescott 17-18, 69
West Central Texas 11
Wells, Chili 222
West Texas A&M 171-174

West Texas Baptist Sanitarium (see Hendrick Hospital)
West Texas Utilities 200, 201, 207, 232-233
Westbrook, L.W. 256
Westbrook, Texas 73
Western Cattle Trail 45, 72-73
Wheeler, Judge T.B. 81
Whittle, W.A. 97
Wichita Falls, Texas 110, 130, 163, 236, 238, 242
Wichita Indians 31
Wichita Valley Railway 130
Wiggins, George H. 98
"Wild Elephants" 260-261
Willard, Jess 262
Williams, C.C. 84
Williams, J.S. 95
Wilson, Claudia 12
Wilson, Woodrow 148, 174-175
Wind City 11, 113
Windsor hotel 207
Wingo, Plennie 246-247
Winters, Texas 156
Winters Freeway 21
Wire, barbed 46, 77-79
Wise, Louis 75, 76, 114
Withers, Horace C. 61
Women's clubs 99, 127, 135, 136-137
Woodmen of the World lodge 100
Wooten, Dub 222
Wooten, Horace O. 104, 128-129, 187, 188, 191
Wooten, J.P. 146
Wooten Hotel 129, 187, 188, 207
Wooten family 186
World War I 174-177, 181, 198, 217, 243, 256
Works Progress Administration 226, 228, 250-252
Wriston, D.W. 84-85
Wyatt, Glynn 261

Wylie, Col. R.K. 45
Wylie, Mr. 50

York, Lee 262, 267
Young, Terry 12
Young Will, 95

Zachry, Juanita 11

www.ingramcontent.com/pod-product-compliance
Lightning Source LLC
Chambersburg PA
CBHW030305080526
44584CB00012B/444